MEN OF SUBSTANCE

MEN OF SUBSTANCE

A Study of the Thought of Two English Revolutionaries

Henry Parker and Henry Robinson

by

W. K. JORDAN

1967

OCTAGON BOOKS, INC.

New York

Reprinted 1967

by special arrangement with Wilbur K. Jordan

OCTAGON BOOKS, INC.
175 FIFTH AVENUE
NEW YORK, N. Y. 10010

LIBRARY OF CONGRESS CATALOG CARD NUMBER: 67-18770

Printed in U.S.A. by
NOBLE OFFSET PRINTERS, INC.
NEW YORK 3, N. Y.

To the memory of

T. J.

An Englishman of moral substance

ACKNOWLEDGMENTS

THE writer is indebted to Messrs. George Allen and Unwin, London, and to the Harvard University Press for their generous permission to draw upon certain materials from the fourth volume of his earlier *Development of Religious Toleration in England.*

The Social Science Research Committee of the University of Chicago has been at once generous and patient in its support of this study. The Committee has extended invaluable assistance at all the stages that lie between the first search for materials and the checking of the final manuscript draft.

A number of distinguished scholars in the field have placed the author in their debt by helpful and penetrating criticisms of the manuscript. Among these friends and colleagues, Messrs. Dumas Malone, John T. McNeill, Perry Miller, Jacob Viner, and Edward A. Whitney have been particularly frank and searching in their advice on the manuscript. Finally, the list of the author's debts could not be closed without acknowledging the generous and thoughtful assistance of the staff of the University of Chicago Press.

W. K. J.

CHICAGO, ILLINOIS
April 16, 1942

CONTENTS

I

INTRODUCTION

WE ARE considering men gripped with the vision of a nobler world. We are considering men who together were to make a monumental contribution to the ferment of thought which was to dissolve the ancient structure of the English constitution, to destroy forever the theory and practice of a catholic religious society supported by the arm of persecution, and to fashion the design of a new economic and social order. These men were in the vanguard of thought in an age characterized by genius of achievement and notable for the formulation of the ideas which were to become the sturdy sinews of a liberal society destined to dominate the western world for more than two centuries. They were sprung of ancient stock; were endowed with the solid sanctions of status; and they were animated by an almost passionate sense of political and social responsibility. Henry Parker and Henry Robinson were men of substance.

Henry Parker was a member of a prominent Sussex family which had owned extensive landed properties for at least three centuries and which for six generations before his birth had fulfilled with dignity and competence the requirements imposed upon the landed gentry by an astute central government. Henry Robinson, the son of a rich merchant, was descended from a long line of prosperous and irascible merchants, one of whom had in a moment of shrewd investment likewise founded a landed branch. His family had maintained and expanded a considerable fortune during a century and a half in which talent and boldness were the only guaranties against commercial ruin. Parker was a member of the ancient aristocracy of land, the son of a father who had served the great yet heady queen faithfully and importantly during a busy lifetime; Robinson was a scion of one of the oldest of the great merchant families, an almost perfect representative of a class which had grown steadily and rapidly in wealth, knowledge, and power but which still suffered from certain of the inhibitions imposed by insecurity of status.

Both Robinson and Parker enjoyed the personal advantages normally associated with their class. Both men were educated at Oxford, where they may well have known each other. Parker, having taken his degree at the university, was trained for the law in London, though there is no evidence that he ever undertook the practice of his profession. Robinson, after leaving the university, traveled and lived abroad for some years as his father's commercial representative. While on the Continent he acquired facility in several languages, an intimate knowledge of European political and religious conditions, and a cosmopolitan temper rare for his age. Parker, the younger son of a father ambitious for the social advancement of his eldest son, was apparently left, on his father's death, with only a modest portion, which proved insufficient for his needs. Though he was to gain rather lucrative employment during his mature years, there is some evidence that his family was left meagerly endowed at the time of his death. Robinson, on the other hand, was almost certainly a rich man who was never obliged to pursue his business seriously, though his enthusiastic and occasionally quixotic support of extraordinarily diverse undertakings seems to have considerably lessened his inherited fortune.

Parker and Robinson were likewise substantial men of affairs, closely connected with the development of administration and of policy, throughout the revolutionary era. We shall observe that Parker actively supported Parliament during the critical days preceding the outbreak of the war and that he was successively to serve Essex, Parliament, and Cromwell as secretary. Moreover, on several occasions he undertook important commissions for Parliament for which he was later rewarded by a portion of the revenues of the lucrative registry of the Prerogative Office. The indefatigable Robinson was to have an even more distinguished career in public affairs. His services in the post office, in the customs, on numerous parliamentary commissions, and as economic adviser to the government mark him as one of the ablest of a remarkable group of semiofficial advisers who lent valuable support to the Commonwealth and Protectorate.

It should be remarked that both men were among the earliest of those who realized that a true revolution was in progress which could have no successful issue unless the ancient constitution were overthrown and bold experimentation in politics, religion, and economics were embraced. They are not to be confused, therefore, with the time-servers and party hacks who swarmed around the Protectorate directly it was evident that a revolutionary sovereignty had been imposed upon the nation. Both men were throughout their lives in the vanguard of thought, both remained sharply critical of parliamentary policy, and both were able to retain a complete integrity rare indeed during this age.

Despite the originality and boldness of their thought, both Parker and Robinson set very precise limits to the scope of the revolutionary movement. As men of substance, they were alarmed lest the currents of irresponsibility and social radicalism loosed by the revolutionary tempest should destroy the structure of English life and institutions. They were, indeed, essentially aristocratic in their philosophy. As aristocrats they deplored the violence of democratic radicalism, attacked the irresponsibility of the incendiary sects, and steadily taught that the reforms which had been gained must not be endangered by the deterioration of the sovereign functions of government. Fundamentally, both men believed that the English Revolution had swept away an outworn monarchical system which had failed because it had ignored the political maturity, the aspirations, and the capabilities of the landed gentry and the mercantile aristocracy. Their system of politics and their conception of the new English order were, then, framed in terms of a government founded squarely upon an enlarged and deepened definition of the dominant groups in English life. Government, they persistently maintained, must be intelligent, efficient, and, above all else, responsible. They desired to enlarge the sphere of personal liberty, they lent noble defense to the integrity of the individual conscience, and they hoped vastly to expand the scope of individual opportunity; but neither Parker nor Robinson was animated by the democratic persuasion that government should proceed from, or be responsible to, the mass of men. They were both, it should be repeated, men of aristocratic temper.

The historian, unable completely to divest himself of modern preoccupations and preconceptions, is perplexed by the essentially conservative nature of the English Revolution. He is, for that reason, too much inclined to lend his attention and extend his admiration to fragments of thought on the periphery of English ideas during this period. Surely, it need no longer be pointed out that the groups which prosecuted, won, and exploited the revolt against the Caroline interpretation of the constitution were not inspired by democratic idealism. Rather, those groups, including the thinkers under consideration, were quite as profoundly shocked and frightened by the rapidly developing political radicalism of an incendiary like Lilburne as they were by the antisocial conduct and exhibitionistic tendencies of the early Quaker enthusiasts. In periods of political and cultural confusion, when the normal weight of divers types of restraint is relaxed, the ferment and the cultural anarchy which ever smolder beneath the firm topsoil of an ordered society tend to flame through at scattered points in the polity. But history cannot be reconstituted, past ages cannot be understood, in terms of the atypical or by following out the faint threads of thought which a particular age condemned as irresponsible or lunatic.

English revolutionary thought, of which Parker and Robinson are characteristic, though advanced, representatives, was, then, essentially conservative and aspired to limited objectives which did not include the attainment of democratic institutions. Rather it may be said that Parker and Robinson were important architects engaged in the Herculean task of framing the edifice of a liberal society of which the democratic society is a peculiar derivative but with which it is in no sense identical. Parker and Robinson were in complete sympathy with, and were perhaps the most notable theoretical exponents of, the institutional structure which the dominant groups, in Parliament and in the New Model, came slowly to recognize as the goal of the revolutionary dynamic.

Perhaps the most important of the cements which lent cohesion to the revolutionary movement was the vague aspiration, mounting finally into a highly articulate and overwhelming demand, for legal guaranties of religious toleration for those protestant communions which could be regarded as politically trustworthy. The early debates in the Long Parliament, as well as a vast body of pamphlet literature, attest the high importance of opposition to the rigorous courses and the dangerous aspirations of the Laudian system as a cause for the Civil War. The Anglican Establishment, as defined by Laud and Charles, not only laid claims to an exclusive definition of faith which were in point of fact politically insupportable but aroused the fiercest resentment within and without the Church of England. Puritanism rapidly hardened into Presbyterianism under the Laudian pressure and was destined, it seemed during the early months of the struggle, to supply both the impetus and the idealism which are essential to any revolutionary movement. But Presbyterianism was guilty of three fatal errors. It leaned too heavily upon its Scottish allies, who had almost no political interest in the English Civil War; it gravely overestimated its strength in England, since all opposition to episcopal severity and intolerance was mistakenly regarded as support for Presbyterian aspirations; and it was guilty of the grievous error of seeking, with shrill and obstinate insistence, to impose a rigid and intolerant ecclesiastical establishment upon an England which was even then waging a civil war to destroy another exclusive ecclesiastical system.

The consequence was, and it is here that Robinson and Parker lent decisive support, that the revolutionary movement had, in order to preserve intact the loose coalition which was waging the war, to espouse the doctrine of religious toleration as a fundamental tenet of revolutionary faith. The remarkable rise of Independency was due, not so much to the fact that many Englishmen were Congregationalists, as to the fact that it afforded a broad basis for the formation of a loosely knit but extraordinarily effective coalition dedicated to the principles of religious freedom. The espousal of the doctrine of religious toleration was of decisive importance in winning the Civil War and in undergirding the Protectorate with a philosophy and a program which soon won at least the tacit approval and support of the mass of the English people. The triumph of religious toleration was, then, a conservative secular victory, opposed most violently, it should be remarked, by the incendiary sects of the age.

Moreover, it is important to observe, the political aspirations of the leaders of the English Revolution were conservative, were restrained, indeed, by a kind of constitutional nostalgia. In its political aspect the English Civil War was provoked by a suspicion, mounting gradually into a conviction, that the Stuarts were inept in policy and irresponsible in administration. There is no reason to believe that the powerful gentry in and out of the House of Commons in 1640 wanted more than the correction of grievances—though their definition of a political grievance had undergone steady and remarkable expansion during the past forty years—and legal guaranties against the further enlargement of the prerogative. The Civil War was precipitated by conservative men of substance really differentiated from their confreres who moved to the royal standard only by a slightly lesser respect for the person of the king and by a considerably lesser devotion to the integrity of the Anglican system. No civil war has ever been waged with more apologies, with a more stubborn refusal to recognize the fact that levying war on the legally constituted sovereign is after all a revolution. Parker was perhaps the first Englishman to understand what was occurring and to realize that a powerful force had been loosed which must in the end bring about a transfer of sovereignty, in all the implications of that term, to the groups which had embraced revolt.

Hence the revolutionary political settlement, despite dramatic and symbolic incidents like the execution of the king, was extraordinarily conservative in its political philosophy. The frame of English institutions—the law, the courts, the social composition of Parliament, and local administration—was disturbed for a season but was not transformed. The class which had dominated the House of Commons in 1640 dominated the Council, the Parliament, and the courts in 1650. Power had passed solidly into its hands, and the landed gentry, supported by the commercial aristocracy, sought during the Interregnum to define and consolidate an executive which would be circumscribed by the ancient legality and traditions of the crown but which would be responsible, in the last analysis, to the property, the ambitions, and the conservatism of a powerful and intelligent class which embodied the English genius and which was destined to frame the liberal polity of the eighteenth and nineteenth centuries.

Thus it may be said that the English Civil War was waged and a revolutionary settlement effected by men of substance who placed precise and rigid frontiers at which the flood of change must be halted. Parker and Robinson embody the genius and the aspirations of this dominant group, to which by birth they belonged, and are remarkable only for their prescience, for the clarity and the breadth of their vision, and for the boldness with which they pushed out into the rough and tangled terrain which must be traversed by every revolutionary movement.

When viewed as a whole, the thought of Parker and Robinson forms an entity of remarkable scope and depth. It is perhaps not too much to say that their thought dealt more astutely and critically with the manifold problems which harassed England than did any other contribution in the domain of ideas before the age of Locke. Together they explored the complex and explosive problem of religion more thoroughly than did any other thinker of their age, and the solution which they so earnestly recommended was that adopted by England a generation later. Robinson, in particular, was to make a monumental contribution to the development of the theory of religious toleration. Both men were intensely secular in their thought; both approached the tangled problem of religion and of ecclesiastical institutions with a temperate rationalism rare during the era of the Civil War. Parker was of especial importance because of his cold and critical examination of political institutions and the almost ruthless logic which he brought to bear on political theory. In many ways his contribution in this field of thought is quite as significant as that of that intellectual monadnock, Hobbes, whose mature thought apparently owes much to the earlier writer. And, finally, it may be suggested that no thinker of the century rivals Robinson in the breadth, the soundness, and the originality with which he treats the economic and social problems of the age. The two men are perfectly complementary in their thought and interests; their thought in its totality is an impressive contribution to the history of ideas and to the historical development of the age and nation which they loved so well.

Moreover, in mind and temper Parker and Robinson possessed many common characteristics. Both men were inspired by a deep sense of responsibility to England and her institutions. They summoned the aristocracy, the merchants, and the men of property and breeding to the task of framing new and better institutions and demanded that they should shoulder the responsibilities which government must impose upon those who have assumed the mantle of sovereignty. They were deeply persuaded that these classes of men were possessed of the maturity, the traditions, and the intelligence requisite for the foundation and administration of a liberal society. Their thought was likewise distinguished by an amazing boldness, a genius of originality, a sureness of historical instinct, and a most impressive objectivity. The coldness of Parker's thought is relieved by the warmth of Robinson's style, but the two thinkers reared the edifice of their contribution to the history of thought upon the same intellectual and spiritual foundations.

Finally, both Robinson and Parker were animated by an absorbing and passionate love for England. They were inspired by a pervasive patriotism because they believed the Civil War could create in England a nobler habitation for men. They desired to enlarge the ambit of personal liberty, to emancipate the spirit, and to assure to all men opportunities denied them in the medieval society which they believed had been finally shattered by the impact of civil war. Their view of human nature was high; their estimate of the dignity and integrity of the individual man was to constitute a basic assumption in the liberal philosophy of which they were early and worthy exponents. Parker and Robinson made important contributions to the slow development of human freedom and to the fabrication of the institutions within which it was to be nurtured and sustained during a full two centuries.

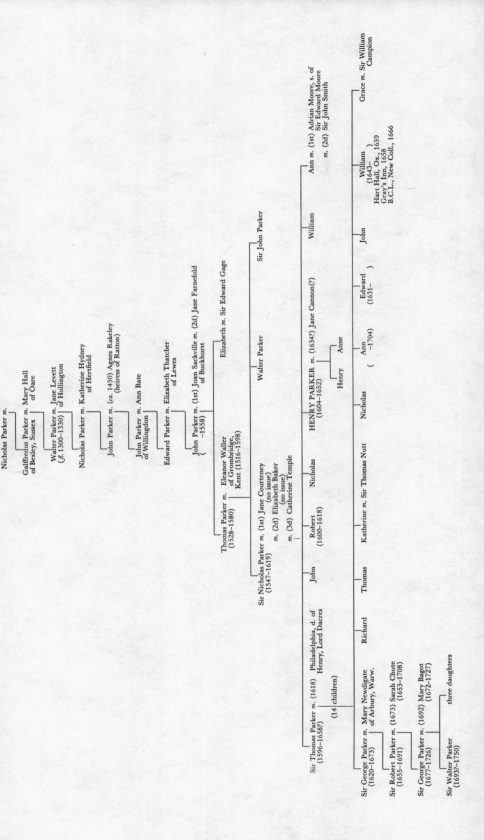

Nicholas Parker *m.*

Galffredus Parker *m.* Mary Hall
of Bexley, Sussex — of Oare

Walter Parker *m.* Jane Levett
(*fl.* 1300–1330) — of Hollington

Nicholas Parker *m.* Katherine Hydney
of Hertfield

John Parker *m.* (*ca.* 1450) Agnes Rakeley
(heiress of Ratton)

John Parker *m.* Ann Bate
of Willingdon

Edward Parker *m.* Elizabeth Thatcher
of Lewes

John Parker *m.* (1st) Joan Sackville *m.* (2d) Jane Farnefold
(–1558) — of Buckhurst

Thomas Parker *m.* Eleanor Waller
(1528–1580) — of Grombridge, Kent (1516–1598)

Elizabeth *m.* Sir Edward Gage

Sir Nicholas Parker *m.* (1st) Jane Courteney
(1547–1619) — (no issue)
m. (2d) Elizabeth Baker
(no issue)
m. (3d) Catherine Temple

Walter Parker

Sir John Parker

Sir Thomas Parker *m.* (1618) Philadelphia, d. of
(1596–1658?) — Henry, Lord Dacres
(14 children)

John

Robert
(1600–1618)

Nicholas

HENRY PARKER *m.* (1634?) Jane Cannon(?)
(1604–1652)

Henry — Anne

William

Ann *m.* (1st) Adrian Moore, s. of
Sir Edward Moore
m. (2d) Sir John Smith

Sir George Parker *m.* Mary Newdigate
(1620–1673) — of Arbury, Warw.

Richard

Thomas

Katherine *m.* Sir Thomas Nutt

Nicholas

Ann
(–1704)

Edward
(1631–)

John

William
(1643–)
Hart Hall, Ox., 1659
Gray's Inn, 1658
B.C.L., New Coll., 1666

Grace *m.* Sir William Campion

Sir Robert Parker *m.* (1673) Sarah Chute
(1655–1691) — (1653–1708)

Sir George Parker *m.* (1692) Mary Bagot
(1677–1726) — (1672–1727)

Sir Walter Parker
(1693?–1750)

three daughters

II

HENRY PARKER (1604–1652): ANTECEDENTS AND LIFE

HENRY PARKER, who was born shortly after the beginning of the troubled Stuart period, was a member of an ancient and prominent Sussex family which had possessed land in Bexhill,[1] Sussex, since the early thirteenth century. In the early decades of the century following, during the lifetime of Walter Parker, it would seem to have considerably bettered its status. This Walter Parker not only held lands in Bexhill, where his seal was found in 1910,[2] but in 1296 he paid an assessment for lands in the near-by township of Ninfield.[3] He stood as a witness to a feoffment executed in 1300, and was guarantor for the appearance of a man before the bailiff of Battle thirty years later.[4]

These foundations of the family fortune were very considerably enlarged and strengthened somewhat more than a century later when John Parker, who was probably the grandson of Walter Parker, married Agnes Rakle (or Rakeley), of Ratton (Willingdon), the surviving member and heiress of an old and wealthy line.[5] The manor of Ratton had for at least two centuries possessed a feudal identity separate from the larger manor and hundred of Willingdon, which since the reign of Henry III had been within the bestowal of the crown. The manor, consisting of about thirty-five hundred acres of gently rolling land of no great fertility, had at a very early date come into the possession of Walter de Rackele (Rakle), who had married the surviving heiress of the

[1] *Sussex Archaeological Society Collections* (London, 1848——), XVIII, 40.

[2] The center of this leaden seal is filled with a conventional fleur-de-lis and is banded with a plain circle.

[3] *Sussex Record Society Publications* (Lewes, 1902——), X, 6.

[4] *Sussex Arch. Soc. Collects.*, LIV, 270.

[5] The marriage occurred about 1450 (*ibid.*, XVIII, 40).

former owners.[6] John Parker likewise acquired, possibly by his fortunate marriage, lands in the Pevensey Marsh in 1455, which were to remain in the possession of the family for at least two centuries and which were to be a constant source of annoyance and expense because of the necessity of maintaining a sea wall.[7] The manor house, one would gather from fragmentary references, was a large and elaborate fifteenth-century structure situated on a site commanding an arresting view of the surrounding countryside. It served the Parker family during their three centuries of ownership, but was demolished in the late years of the eighteenth century.[8]

John Parker's tenure of Ratton, it would appear, was threatened very shortly after his marriage by the political disturbances attending the close of the Hundred Years' War. Sussex and Kent were the centers of the revolutionary movement supported by many men of property which finally flared up into Cade's Rebellion in 1450. Parker was one of numerous gentlemen in Sussex who were pardoned by the crown for their participation in this unsuccessful rising.[9]

During the two generations that followed John Parker of Ratton, the family, though now members of the gentry and holders of extensive properties, seems to have lived quietly and to have taken little part in the troubled public life of the closing decades of the fifteenth century. John Parker's son, who bore the same name, married one Ann Bate, whose family enjoyed no conspicuous place in the affairs of the county. His grandson, Edward Parker, married Elizabeth Thatcher of Lewes, the daughter of a prosperous merchant, and thereby came into possession of certain properties in that town. Indeed, from this time forward the fam-

[6] M. A. Lower, *A Compendious History of Sussex, etc.* (Lewes, 1870), II, 247.

[7] The Pevensey Marsh adjoins the hundred of Willingdon (*Sussex Arch. Soc. Collects.*, LIII, 52–54).

[8] Horsfield, writing in 1834, says that in that year nothing remained of Ratton save the gatehouse, though within the memory of some old men, "it was perfect and entire," the hall being hung with bows and other military mementoes (T. W. Horsfield, *The History, Antiquities, and Topography of the County of Sussex* [Lewes, 1835], I, 288).

[9] *Sussex Arch. Soc. Collects.*, XVIII, 28, 40.

ily began to assume a much more active role in the life of the county town, which lay about twelve miles distant from its seat at Ratton.

Like so many families of their class, well-established and substantial lesser gentry, the Parkers began under the Tudor dynasty to undertake a heavier responsibility for local administration. The great-grandson of the first proprietor of Ratton, John Parker, who was born shortly after the accession of Henry VII to the throne of England, was the first member of the family to be vested with considerable administrative trust, and was by his marriages and his activities to raise his family into the upper ranks of the county gentry. Though there is no evidence that Parker acquired any of the monastic spoils, he none the less considerably increased his estates and the prosperity of his house.

John Parker first married Joan, the daughter of Sir Richard Sackville, a member of a family which was already one of the most distinguished in the county. Thomas Parker, the heir, was born of this marriage, as was Elizabeth Parker, who married Sir Edward Gage, a Knight of the Bath and sheriff for the counties of Sussex and Surrey under Mary Tudor.[10] After the death of his first wife, Joan, Parker married Jane Farnefold, from whom a second line of some eminence stems through a son, Thomas Parker, Junior. As a result of this marriage the manor of Eastbourne, one of four bearing that somewhat generic name, came into the possession of the Parker family, where it was to remain until Sir Walter Parker, the last of the line, bequeathed it in 1750 to Edward Trayton of Lewes.[11]

During the second decade of the sixteenth century, John Parker acquired a number of scattered plots in Willingdon, apparently in an effort to consolidate his holdings, and at about the same time considerably enlarged his lands in the Pevensey Marsh.[12] Parker in 1534 was appointed deputy to the ill-fated Lord Rochford, brother to Anne Boleyn, the Warden of the Cinque Ports,

[10] *Ibid.*, LXXX, 138–39, *ibid.*, LXXVII, 181.

[11] *Ibid.*, XIV, 122.

[12] The original holding there was slightly more than one acre. In 1527 Parker's lands in the Marsh amounted to fifty acres (*ibid.*, XLV, 163, 170).

and in the same year was named one of the Commissioners of Sewers for the Lewes Level.[13] The fall of Rochford in 1536 did not prejudice Parker's position, since he was listed on several occasions a few years later amongst the gentry under consideration at court for appointment as sheriff of Sussex.[14] He was made a justice of the peace in 1544, was again appointed to the Commission of Sewers, and was designated one of the commissioners named to collect the unpopular benevolence of 1544–45.[15] In 1546 Parker was vested with responsibility for setting out beacons and for taking local defensive precautions,[16] a charge which was confirmed under the new ruler by his reappointment as a justice of peace.[17]

It would seem that Parker lay under disfavor during the Marian regime, whether for religious or other reasons is not clear. His appointment as a justice was not renewed and his name was dropped from the long list of Commissioners for the Sewers for the county of Sussex.[18] In 1555 certain of his holdings in Sextrylandes, Sussex, were conveyed to the Earl of Arundel at a nominal rental, and, after the Earl's death in 1557, were placed in the tenure of Parker's kinsman, Thomas Sackville.[19]

John Parker died in the year of Elizabeth's accession, his arms and status having been confirmed in the year of his death.[20] The lands in Willingdon and his other real property were bequeathed to his elder son, Thomas, with survival rights vested in his grandson, Nicholas. The remainder of his estate was bestowed upon his daughter and the younger children by his second marriage.[21]

The family estates passed in 1580 to the grandson, Nicholas Parker (1547–1619), on the death of his undistinguished father,

[13] *Ibid.*, X, 96.

[14] For the list for 1540, *vide Letters and Papers*, *Henry VIII*, xvi, 305; for 1541, *ibid.*, xvi, 1391; for 1542, *ibid.*, xvii, 1154.

[15] *Ibid.*, xx (pt. 1), 622, 623, (pt. 2), 974.

[16] *Sussex Notes and Queries* (Lewes, 1926——), I, 82.

[17] *Calendar of Patent Rolls . . . . Edward VI, 1547–1553* (London, 1924–26), I, 90.

[18] *Calendar of Patent Rolls . . . . Mary, 1553–1558* (London, 1937–39), I, 24.

[19] Harl. MSS (B.M.), 892, f. 10B.

[20] *Sussex Arch. Soc. Collects.*, LXX, 141.

[21] *Sussex Record Society Publications*, XIV, 177.

Thomas Parker.[22] Nicholas Parker, the father of the subject of this essay, was destined during a long and vigorous life to raise the family to the first rank amongst the gentry of the county, considerably to enlarge its properties, and to take a devoted, if somewhat ineffective, interest in the military and administrative affairs of a great reign. Parker seems first to have married Jane (or Joan), daughter of Sir William Courteney of Devonshire, who died shortly without issue.[23] Shortly afterward, he married Elizabeth Baker, daughter of John Baker, Esq., who likewise died without surviving issue. His third marriage was contracted with Catherine, daughter of John Temple, of Stowe, Buckinghamshire.[24] The marriage seems to have been eminently desired by the contracting parties, since an informant, writing to John Temple in April, 1593, said he had induced Sir Nicholas to accept the match and the "days of payment" of the dowry, since

[22] Very little is known concerning the career of Thomas Parker. He married Eleanor Waller, a member of one of the leading families in southern England, and died in 1580. His widow survived until 1598, dying at the age of eighty-two.

[23] Horsfield, *History of Sussex*, I, 288–89; *Sussex Arch. Soc. Collects.*, LXXV, 183; *The Visitations of the County of Sussex*, ed. W. B. Bannerman ("Publications of the Harleian Society" [London, 1905]), p. 22.

[24] Professor Edwin F. Gay, after a careful examination of the Temple papers in the Huntington Library, has given us a valuable study of the rise to wealth and respectability of a vigorous and able family. Peter Temple, the founder of the family fortunes, was a younger son of a younger branch of an old Leicestershire family ("The Rise of an English Country Family: Peter and John Temple to 1603," *Huntington Library Quarterly*, I, 369). He made his fortune in sheep grazing on leased properties at Burton Dassett in Warwickshire. He was actively and successfully engaged in land speculation and in the prosecution of litigation in which he appears to have had strong backing at Court. By 1577 he was able to append "Esquire" to his name (*ibid.*, p. 382), and in the same decade he acquired a long lease on the manor of Stowe, Buckinghamshire, which became the family seat.

John Temple, the eldest son and heir of Peter, succeeded to the properties in 1578. He completed the consolidation of the estates at Stowe and Burton Dassett, in 1589 transforming the lease at Stowe into permanent ownership (*ibid.*, p. 384). He enlarged his holdings in the next decade by the purchase of extensive additional properties in Burton Dassett. John Temple, the father of Catherine Parker, was a shrewd businessman, a careful proprietor of his lands, and a man of influence in his county. His son, Thomas (1567–1637), who was educated at Lincoln's Inn, was a member of Parliament in 1588–89. He married the famous Hester Sandys, a daughter of Miles Sandys, in about 1590. Thomas Temple was created a baronet in 1611.

Parker "liketh well of the gentlewoman and she of him." Indeed, Sir Nicholas preferred the match despite the fact that he was sacrificing £1,000 which he could have had elsewhere.[25] John Temple, who died in 1603, left to Sir Nicholas Parker the sum of £100 by will.[26] Seven children were born to this union. In late life, after the death of Catherine Parker, Sir Nicholas seems to have married a widow, Avis Erisey, whose son, James Erisey, was a well-known commander under Drake in 1588.[27]

Parker seems to have been occupied during the early years of the reign with the management of his estates and with purely local affairs. He had, some years prior to 1566, acquired additional lands in Sussex in the hundred of Lackford,[28] and there is evidence that his successive marriages were in part at least responsible for the rather sharp rise in the family fortunes. His first military experience was gained in 1582, when he served as commander of the foot soldiers in one of the vessels in Fenton's voyage to the East.[29] During the next five years, however, he was residing at Ratton, where he began to take a more active part in the administration of his county. Thus we observe that he was designated in 1584 by the Exchequer one of a commission empowered to enquire into the titles of certain properties unlawfully held in Sussex,[30] while in the next year he served as a member of a commission instructed to examine titles at Friars Minor, Winchelsey.[31] He apparently acquired additional properties during this period, since a survey made in 1587 reveals that he had come into the possession of holdings in the manor of Radmeld-Beverington, from which he derived rents to the value of 24*s*. 8*d*. per annum.[32]

[25] Gay, "The Temples of Stowe and Their Debts: Sir Thomas Temple and Sir Peter Temple, 1603–1653," *Huntington Library Quarterly*, II, 404.

[26] Gay, "The Rise of an English Country Family: Peter and John Temple to 1603," *Huntington Library Quarterly*, I, 390.

[27] *Sussex Arch. Soc. Collects.*, LXXV, 183.

[28] *East Anglian, etc.* (Lowestoft [N.S.], 1885——), III, 242.

[29] This voyage to the East Indies sailed in May, 1582. Prominent members of the government had subscribed to the venture, which was in every sense a disappointment (Conyers Read, *Mr. Secretary Walsingham and the Policy of Queen Elizabeth* [Oxford, 1925], III, 397–98).

[30] *Sussex Record Soc. Pub.*, XXVI, 165.

[31] *Ibid.*, XXVI, 172.

[32] *Ibid.*, XXXIV, 110.

In 1587 Nicholas Parker joined Leicester's expeditionary force in the Netherlands as captain of a company of horse. Though now almost forty years of age, he entered into military life with alacrity and quickly acquired a reputation for gallantry in the field and effectiveness in administration. From this time forward until a few years before his death, indeed, Parker was almost steadily in military service, to the detriment, there is ample evidence, of his estates and personal fortunes. Parker's troop was first engaged on December 22, 1587, when it was ambushed with a loss of ten men.[33] His contingent was stationed at Middleburgh during the early months of 1588,[34] but was active during the closing months of the year in the defense of Bergen-op-Zoom.[35] After this action, Parker's troop was dispatched to Amerongen, where it was apparently joined with Dutch and Scottish units being consolidated in that area.[36]

Meanwhile, however, Lord Willoughby, who had recently replaced Leicester as governor in the Netherlands, was called to England to discuss an expeditionary force which was to be dispatched to France to lend assistance to England's hard-pressed ally, Henry IV. Elizabeth lent the new monarch £20,000 to relieve his more pressing financial requirements and in September, 1589 commissioned Willoughby to lend him military assistance with a force of four thousand men. Willoughby entertained a high regard for Parker, who was appointed master of ordnance for the forces, and designated head of the commissariat, while being permitted to retain the command of his own troop of horse.[37] Parker served with the expeditionary force during most of the next year,[38] but, for reasons which are not entirely clear, returned to England in 1591. On the occasion of the Queen's visit to Sussex in that year, his services were rewarded by knighthood,[39] and

[33] *Historical Manuscripts Commission, Report on the Manuscripts of the Earl of Ancaster, etc.* (London, 1907), pp. 71–72.

[34] *Ibid.*, p. 81. [35] *Ibid.*, pp. 201, 205, 213. [36] *Ibid.*, p. 224.

[37] *S.P. Dom., Elizabeth (Addenda)*, xxx, 115, xxxi, 48, xxxi, 63; Cotton MSS (B.M.), Galba, E. VI, 413–16.

[38] *S.P. Dom., Eliz.*, ccxxx, 72, ccxxvi, 43.

[39] *Sussex Arch. Soc. Collects.*, V, 187; *Visitations of Sussex*, p. 22.

at about the same time he was summoned before the Council in order to discuss the problem of strengthening the castle at Pendennis against the invasion which was then expected.[40]

Parker was without a command in 1592 when the campaign in the Netherlands was resumed with feeble vigor by the wholly reluctant Queen. In April of that year he was finally paid for his services abroad and was considered by the Queen for a command in the forces being raised for the relief of the harassed English contingent then serving in Brittany.[41]

Parker regained his command in 1593 when the Queen at last decided to strengthen her forces in the Netherlands.[42] The conversion of Henry IV to Catholicism in the summer of this year resulted in the withdrawal of numerous English units which had been assisting him in France to Ostend, where they were reassembled under the command of that seasoned soldier, Sir Edward Brooke, and the gallant Sir Francis Vere. Parker's troop fought in the bloody campaign of 1594 in which Vere lent Count Maurice invaluable assistance in the capture of Groningen. Parker was mentioned in several dispatches to Essex, including one from Lord Vere, commending his conduct in a small action in August, 1595, near Wesell. Parker, as commander of the English horse, was described as having behaved "himself very well in this service,"[43] and as having displayed conspicuous gallantry. His command had lost heavily in a number of small but violent actions, however, and in December of the same year he expressed his gratitude for the rehabilitation of his somewhat tattered company.[44] Shortly after this reinforcement, Parker was withdrawn with most of the English forces from the Netherlands. He retired to Ratton, where in 1596, his eldest son, Thomas, was born.

The English government, having withdrawn most of its army from the Continent, was gravely disturbed in April, 1596, when the Spanish occupied the Risbank fort, dominating the defenses of Calais, and laid siege to the town. The quixotic Essex immediate-

[40] *S.P. Dom., Eliz.*, ccxl, 113.

[41] *Ibid.*, ccxli, 126, ccxlii, 117, ccxliii, 101.

[42] *Historical Manuscripts Commission, Calendar of the Manuscripts of . . . . the Marquess of Salisbury, etc.* (London, 1883——), IV, 293.

[43] *Ibid.*, V, 344, 351, 352.

[44] *Ibid.*, V, 483.

ly proposed that an expedition be dispatched for the relief of the garrison, including Parker in his memorandum as a captain with one hundred men from Sussex.[45] Parker, he wrote later in the same year, "hath . . . . been many years captain, and hath done valiantly in all encounters." The force collected for the relief of Calais never proceeded beyond its mobilization point at Dover, however, as the city fell after a short and dispirited defense.

Though now almost fifty years of age, Parker had become enamored with life in the camps and was once more vigorously seeking active service. In September, 1596, having heard that troops were badly needed in the Low Countries, he wrote to Burleigh to remind the secretary that he had "given long and faithful service in the wars, and had great losses." He therefore requested a command "as a comfort for my latter days," in the event additional reinforcements should be dispatched abroad.[46]

Shortly afterward Parker was sent to the Continent on his last tour of duty. During the autumn of 1596 both the English and the Spanish were preoccupied with preparations occasioned by the intended Spanish invasion of England, which was to be frustrated by the wrecking of the Spanish fleet in a heavy storm off Cape Finisterre. There was little military activity in the Netherlands during these critical months, but the English commanders were gravely concerned because of the weakness of their contingents and the rumors of disagreement in the Council on war policy. The aged Burleigh, alarmed because of the expectation that France would soon conclude a separate peace with Spain and persuaded that there was only slight danger of another attempt at a Spanish invasion, was lending the enormous weight of his prestige to the cause of peace. The rash and flighty Essex, on the other hand, was, with every appearance of enjoying the Queen's favor, becoming more and more vociferous in his demand that the war against Spain be prosecuted with redoubled vigor.

Parker, already high in the esteem of Essex, was ordered to return to England in late February, 1597, apparently to lay the case of the military before Essex and the Council. Sir Francis Vere, in a letter to Essex, spoke in flattering terms of Parker, who

[45] *Ibid.*, VI, 205–6, 570.

[46] *S.P. Dom.*, *Eliz.*, cclx, 1.

"deserved exceeding well in this late service," though "for a man of his worth none has received so small encouragement."[47] At about the same time, Sir Robert Sidney asked Essex to lend every consideration to Parker's requirements.[48] Moreover, Maurice wrote to the Council of State, warmly commending Parker's gallantry in the field and supporting his petition for the reinforcement of the English army then serving in the Netherlands.[49] Parker, who was in London during the next two months, was wholly unsuccessful in his representations.[50] In May, 1597, after France had concluded a separate peace, Burleigh and Essex almost came to blows in a stormy session of the Council on the question of war policy, but the cautious inclinations of the secretary were to prevail.

Though wholly unsuccessful in his mission, Parker was able to secure the payment of large arrears in salary which, if we may take his petitions seriously, must have relieved him of considerable personal embarrassment. In April, 1597, he was paid upward of £500 for the services of his seventy-five lancers,[51] and in the next month arrears for a slightly lesser amount were liquidated.[52] In early 1598 the considerable balance due to Sir Nicholas was finally met by a Council warrant.[53]

Nicholas Parker had now attained a leading position in his county. For some years he had been a justice of the peace, he had married well on successive occasions, he was certainly the most prominent soldier of his county in an age of exuberant patriotism, and his properties, despite his constant "official" pleas of poverty, were extensive, if poorly managed. Parker was elected to Parliament in 1597, as a county member for Sussex.[54] For five consecutive generations after him the eldest member of his family was to serve in one or more parliaments as a member either for the county or for the boroughs of Hastings and Seaford within the

[47] *H.M.C., Salisbury Papers,* VII, 84.

[48] *Ibid.,* VII, 119.

[49] *Ibid.,* VII, 85.

[50] *Ibid.,* VII, 180.

[51] *Ibid.,* VII, 178.

[52] *Acts of the Privy Council of England, New Series, 1542–1604* (London, 1890–1907), 1597, p. 143.

[53] *S.P. Dom., Eliz.,* cclxvi, 10.

[54] *Sussex Arch. Soc. Collects.,* XXXIII, 75.

county. The family, after the long tuition so typical of the lesser Tudor gentry, had at last attained status, substance, and responsibility.

England was in a constant state of apprehension during the closing years of the great queen's reign. The war with Spain dragged on its weary course, a fresh invasion attempt was expected every summer, and with the outbreak of a general Irish rebellion in 1598 there was, indeed, serious danger of a Spanish incursion upon the southern coasts of England. The Council therefore determined to put the coastal counties in an adequate state of defense, and Parker, who enjoyed without much justification in fact a considerable reputation as an ordnance and fortification specialist, was given a leading role in this defense effort. In May, 1597, he was sent to his native county to call out the musters in order to select three companies of trained troops for emergency duty. He querulously reported that Sussex was in a poor state of preparation, the musters were inadequately trained, and local co-operation was by no means enthusiastic.[55]

During the autumn England was thrown into a panic when news reached London that a formidable Spanish fleet was on the high seas. Desperate efforts were immediately if belatedly begun to place the antiquated coastal defenses in a state of repair. Parker was dispatched to Cornwall by Essex with general instructions to organize the defenses of that strategic coast.[56] In late October, Parker reported that the region was inadequately supplied with ordnance and that the musters had not been completed, and informed the Council that he was without any information concerning the whereabouts of the expected invasion force.[57] A few weeks later he was ordered to Falmouth with two hundred men under instructions to place that important district in a state of immediate defense.[58] The Council evidently entertained a high opinion of Parker's abilities and was persuaded of his complete loyalty, for both factions seemed to have joined in January, 1598, in advancing him to a post of high responsibility.

[55] *H.M.C., Salisbury Papers*, VII, 206–7.

[56] *Ibid.*, VII, 445–46.

[57] *Ibid.*, VII, 454 (October 30, 1597).

[58] *Acts of P.C.*, 1597–98, pp. 133, 145; *H.M.C., Salisbury Papers*, VIII, 19.

We have already observed that Essex and his party held him in high esteem. Raleigh, on January 16, wrote to Cecil that he did "exceedingly well allow of the gentleman,"[59] and Cecil personally recommended him to the attention of the Queen. Two days later Parker, "a man of verie approoved experience and service in . . . . warres," was appointed commander at Falmouth and deputy lieutenant for Cornwall.[60] A fortnight later he received his commission from the Queen, with the rank of colonel, to fortify the Falmouth area and to assume a general military responsibility in the western region.[61]

But the government, with typical Elizabethan parsimony, did not lend full support to Parker in the Herculean task he had undertaken. The new commander informed Burleigh on February 27, 1598 that he was employing four hundred workmen on the fortifications at Pendennis Castle at a charge of £80 a week, but complained that he had been given only one piece of ordnance and that his garrison was very weak.[62] A few days later he forwarded to the Council his own charges for three months of service in plotting the fortifications at Falmouth and Plymouth in the amount of £97 for moneys expended and 3*s.* 6*d.* per diem for his own living expenses.[63] Although this sum was paid promptly,[64] Parker was soon irate because the Council was drawing on the reservoir of men which he had trained for the defense of the west in order to send additional forces to the Netherlands.[65]

The Queen was disturbed by the charges that were accumulating for the defenses which Parker had been instructed to prepare and, during the summer of 1598, at least, was not persuaded that a state of alarm was warranted in southern England. In late April the Council, at the express command of the Queen, informed Parker of the royal displeasure because £1,000 had already been expended without bringing the defenses to completion and required him to submit an itemized statement of what remained to be done.[66] This somewhat peremptory communica-

[59] *H.M.C., Salisbury Papers,* VIII, 18.
[60] *Acts of P.C.*, 1597–98, p. 245.
[61] *S.P. Dom., Eliz.*, cclxvi, 45.
[62] *Ibid.*, cclxvi, 74.
[63] *H.M.C., Salisbury Papers*, VIII, 64.
[64] *Acts of P.C.*, 1597–98, p. 281.
[65] *Ibid.*, pp. 302–3.
[66] *Ibid.*, pp. 425–27.

tion was followed by an order stripping Parker's command of his trained garrison for service in Ireland, to such an extent, indeed, that he frantically reported that he had only fifty men left for the defense of Falmouth.[67] These discouraging decisions were taken by the government despite the fact that Sir Nicholas was reporting hostile men-of-war off the coast during these weeks and begging that scouting vessels be placed off Land's End in order to give him adequate warning in case an attempt should be made to land Spanish troops.[68]

The fact was, of course, that the government, during the summer of 1598, had been obliged by the spread of serious civil war in Ireland to begin preparations for the dispatch of a large army in order finally to crush the uprising. Essex did not leave on his ill-starred expedition until March, 1599, but for months before that date the energies and resources of the nation were being mustered. Parker was one of a group of royal servants expressly excluded by the Queen's command from the expeditionary force, one would suppose because his presence was required in the west.[69] A few months later (May, 1599) the government evinced new interest in the western defenses by advancing another £1,000 for the half-completed works at Falmouth, with an appropriation of 10*s.* per day for Parker "till he is advanced to a plan of better profit," together with a stipend of £40 for attendance at court.[70]

Parker was endeavoring to execute an extremely difficult commission in the west under grave disabilities because the interest of the government blew hot and cold in strict relation to the Irish crisis and the danger from Spain. During the summer of 1599, while Essex was procrastinating and toying with treason in Ireland, the Council gave evidence of no interest in the works at Pendennis and, in point of fact, not infrequently failed even to acknowledge Parker's frantic communications. He repeatedly complained that his fortifications were without the ordnance

[67] *Ibid.*, 1597–98, pp. 612–13 (July 25, 1598), *ibid.*, 1598–99, p. 13.

[68] *H.M.C.*, *Salisbury Papers*, VIII, 232, 258 (June 23, 1598, July 11, 1598).

[69] *S.P. Dom.*, *Eliz.*, cclxx, 25 (January 31, 1599).

[70] *Ibid.*, cclxvii, 114 (May 17, 1599).

which they had been constructed to mount,[71] his garrison was pitifully small,[72] and his most urgent problems remained unsettled by the Council.[73] He was actively engaged throughout the summer in searching all strange vessels, examining suspected persons, and in reporting mysterious ship movements to London by courier. During the height of the crisis precipitated by Essex's return from Ireland, Parker was called to London, and one wonders, in view of his earlier relations with the Earl, whether he might not have been under momentary suspicion.

During the next two years Parker remained at his post, though the documents of the period would suggest that the Council had few public servants who were quite as stubborn, proud, and crusty as was the deputy lieutenant for Cornwall. He was still examining papists and strangers,[74] reporting real and imaginary Spanish ships,[75] experimenting with his musters, and vigorously seeking funds for the completion of his military works. He complained bitterly and repeatedly that his allowances were insufficient,[76] that his ammunition remained inadequate, that his ordnance was unsatisfactory, and that he was being slandered by his enemies.[77] In December, 1600, he reported that he had brought the fortifications to as good condition as was possible in view of the delay, the scanty provisions, and the want of concern for which the Council must be held responsible.[78]

Parker applied for a leave of absence in order to come to Court early in February, 1602,[79] but it seems doubtful that he was permitted to return to London prior to the death of the Queen in the following year. He proclaimed the accession of James I in the region under his command,[80] and shortly afterward petitioned Ce-

[71] *H.M.C., Salisbury Papers,* IX, 207 (June, 1599), 223–25, 325–26; *S.P. Dom., Eliz.*, cclxxii, 48–49 (August, 1599).

[72] *H.M.C., Salisbury Papers,* IX, 326.

[73] *S.P. Dom., Eliz.*, cclxxii, 48, 49; *H.M.C., Salisbury Papers,* IX, 225.

[74] *H.M.C., Salisbury Papers,* XI, 120–21 (March, 1601), 143, *et passim.*

[75] *Ibid.*, XI, 196; *S.P. Dom., Eliz.*, cclxxii, 62–63, cclxxxii, 45, cclxxxiv, 15, 32.

[76] *H.M.C., Salisbury Papers,* X, 243–44 (July 25, 1600); *S.P. Dom., Eliz.*, cclxxv, 48.

[77] *H.M.C., Salisbury Papers,* XI, 280 (July, 1601).

[78] *S.P. Dom., Eliz.*, cclxxv, 136.

[79] *H.M.C., Salisbury Papers,* XII, 56.

[80] He was certainly at Pendennis during the remainder of the year.

cil for the favor of the new monarch. Sir Nicholas pointed out that he had been in the service of the crown for thirty years, had made considerable outlays from his private funds for his own maintenance and for the fortifications in the west, and now had no recourse save to call upon the generosity of the king.[81]

It is apparent, however, that Parker did not enjoy the favor of the new monarch. After the removal of Sir Ferdinand Gorges, it is true that he was appointed to the command of St. Nicholas' Island and of the new fort at Plymouth.[82] Shortly afterward, too, he was commissioned deputy lieutenant for the county of Sussex,[83] but at this point, in 1604, the record of his active participation in the military affairs of the nation ends. Parker was now fifty-seven years of age, and it is quite possible that the government might have felt that younger men were better equipped to carry on his work. More probably, however, the conclusion of the war with Spain and the new king's utter lack of interest in the maintenance of the defenses of the realm simply led to the complete cessation of the military preparations in the west. It is not certain that Parker was ever formally removed from his command, but we know that he was residing at Ratton from 1607 until his death in 1619.

During these later years Parker resumed an active share in the affairs of his community and family. He renewed his interest in the Free School at Lewes, to which his family had made gifts almost a century earlier,[84] and of which he had become a trustee in 1592.[85] In 1609 he associated himself with four other gentlemen of the county in the purchase of lands which were conveyed in 1624 under a deed of trust for the establishment of a house of correction at Lewes.[86] At about the same time he became a member of the Virginia Company, his name appearing in the third charter of the company (9 James I) immediately preceding that of his kinsman, Sir Edward Culpepper, and following, save one, the name of Sir Walter Coverte, with whom he had long been associ-

[81] *H.M.C.*, *Salisbury Papers*, XV, 50 (April 16, 1603).

[82] *S.P. Dom.*, *James I*, ii, 98 (July?, 1603).

[83] *Ibid.*, vi, 60.

[84] *Sussex Rec. Soc. Pub.*, XXXIV, 157, 159.

[85] *Ibid.*, XXXIV, 160, 162.

[86] *Ibid.*, XXXIV, 152–54.

ated in Sussex.[87] From time to time Parker was instructed by the Privy Council to attend to minor military matters in his county, but it is evident that no considerable responsibility was vested in him.[88] Indeed, in the year before his death the Council, upon receiving a complaint from Sir Robert Killegrew, then in command at Pendennis, that the fortifications which Parker had constructed there almost two decades earlier were not in good condition, authorized an investigation of the expenditures which had been made.[89] The investigation never took place, possibly because Parker died in the following year. But the bluff Elizabethan must, we may be sure, have found sufficient exoneration in the record of inattention which had marked the governmental attitude toward his effort to place the west in a state of defense.

Shortly before Sir Nicholas Parker's death in 1619 his eldest son, Thomas, contracted a highly favorable marriage with Philadelphia Lennard, the sister to Richard (Lennard), Lord Dacre. This marriage, which joined his family with one of the most ancient in southern England, was evidently carefully arranged. Just after the marriage Sir Nicholas conveyed by deed to his eldest son and his wife all his real property. It would seem, indeed, that as the price of this eminently desirable marriage the younger children, of whom there were six, including Henry Parker, were left with a very small patrimony. This conveyance likewise establishes the fact that Sir Nicholas, despite his self-asserted sacrifices in the national interest, had greatly enlarged the family holdings and that he died at the age of seventy-two a very rich landowner. Among the properties bequeathed by Sir Nicholas were the manor of Jevington and the advowson of the rectory, Hidney Court in Willingdon, the manors of Ratton, Ratton Harwards

[87] Alexander Brown, *The Genesis of the United States* (Boston and New York, 1891), II, 545. Sir Nicholas subscribed the sum of £12–10–0 to the company. There has been considerable confusion between Sir Nicholas and a Captain Nicholas Parker, a seaman active in trade with America during this period. It should also be noted that Sir Nicholas' daughter Ann married Adrian Moore, son to Sir Edward Moore of Surrey, who was likewise a prominent member of the Virginia Company.

[88] *Acts of P.C.*, 1613–14, pp. 144–45, 428; *Sussex Arch. Soc. Collects.*, LIX, 118.

[89] *Acts of P.C.*, 1618–19, pp. 165–66 (June 10, 1618). The Privy Council referred to Parker as Sir John Parker, but Nicholas was certainly meant.

and Hame, also in Willingdon, the manors of Jevington and Eastbourne, the manors of Hidney and Ponts, and le Knowle de Hidney in Willingdon.[90]

Sir Nicholas left seven children, all by his third wife, Catherine Temple, who were born after his forty-ninth year. His eldest son, Thomas, was twenty-three years of age at the time of Sir Nicholas' death, while the fifth son, Henry, the subject of this study, was fifteen years of age. Sir Nicholas was buried in the parish church at Willingdon, where an interesting monument, carrying the arms of his wives and their effigies in an attitude of devotion at the base, survives amongst a number of family memorials. The typical Elizabethan epitaph possibly expresses Sir Nicholas' judgment of his own merits:

> . . . . For custom's sake alone,
> Vouchsafe to hear these lines upon thy stone;
> Not for thine own behoof, but mine give way,
> For what thou would'st ont [*sic*] take, I needs must pay,
> In Philopaemon, Greece did teem her last;
> In Cassius, Rome her vigour did exhaust;
> Then blame not aged Britain's feeble womb,
> For in her Parker's birth she did consume
> Her utmost strength. The world will scarce be strong
> For such another brave conception.[91]

We have observed that Sir Nicholas Parker's eldest son, Thomas, had married the sister of Lord Dacre just a year before his father's death. Sir Thomas Parker (1596–1658?), though a rich and prominent member of the Sussex gentry, did not continue his father's active role in the affairs of the nation and the community. Sir Thomas led a quiet and on the whole an undistinguished life, his chief interests centering, it would seem, on the management of his properties, which he considerably enlarged. In 1623 he secured quitclaims from the Earl of Dorset which reveal that important additions had already been made to his patrimony.[92] It is likewise probable that he acquired in this period the manor of St. John, Ocklynge, Rushlake, and Swines, an ancient holding of the Hospitallers which the Parker family

[90] *Sussex Rec. Soc. Pub.*, XIV, 177.

[91] Horsfield, *History of Sussex*, I, 290.

[92] *Sussex Rec. Soc. Pub.*, XX, 493.

was to own during most of the seventeenth century.[93] In the year following his father's death Parker evidently acquired lands in Radmeld-Beverington,[94] while in 1628 he arranged for the lease of certain marsh lands in Willingdon which had been purchased by London merchants.[95]

It is not possible to estimate the value of the estates which Sir Thomas had consolidated well before 1640. There is reason to believe that the old family possessions in the hundred of Willingdon alone were valued at something over £1,000 per annum,[96] and, as we have indicated, Parker held extensive properties in other parts of Sussex. Moreover, Sir Thomas apparently had considerable liquid capital, if we may take as evidence the loan of £500 which he made in 1647 to his somewhat imprudent brother-in-law.[97]

Sir Thomas Parker did not play a conspicuous role in the troubled politics of his generation, nor was he to be especially active in the administration of his own county. He was a deputy lieutenant for Sussex,[98] a justice of peace,[99] and on one occasion was designated a member of a commission appointed to deal with the military condition of the county.[100] But the official documents reveal that Parker was normally not consulted on affairs relating to his county and that the Council did not choose to vest important responsibilities in him. In part this must have been due to his evident want of interest in political life. More significantly, however, it was probably due to the fact that by 1626 Parker had become identified with the popular party which was rapidly creating an organization to carry out a program of opposition to Stuart policy and constitutional theory. One of the earliest indications of this opposition was the defeat in certain boroughs of gov-

93 *Sussex Notes and Queries*, VI, 194.

94 *Sussex Rec. Soc. Pub.*, XXXIV, 111.

95 *Ibid.*, XXIX, 141.

96 *Sussex Arch. Soc. Collects.*, XIX, 28–32, 208. It should be borne in mind that the Parkers did not own all of the manor and hundred of Willingdon.

97 *Ibid.*, XLVIII, 134.

98 *Ibid.*, XL, 2.

99 *Ibid.*, XVI, 31–32 (1631); *S.P. Dom., Charles I*, ccccxxxv, 49, ii (December 8, 1639).

100 *S.P. Dom., Charles I*, lxxxvi, 34 (December 8, 1627).

ernmental nominees and, on occasion, of members of the Council who were standing for parliamentary seats. In the election of 1626, it should be noticed, Parker was returned from the borough of Hastings, despite the fact that the borough had long been subject to royal influence and that his opponent there was Walter Montagu, the son of the Lord President of the Council.[101]

After the period of personal government in England, when the forces of constitutional opposition were without an adequate means of expression and criticism, Parker resumed his rather pedestrian activity as a member of the parliamentary party. He was elected to the Long Parliament as a member for Seaford, Sussex,[102] but does not figure prominently in the debates or committees of that body. It is almost certain that he was already a Presbyterian by this date, and his sympathies certainly lay with the Puritan faction which had so much responsibility for the outbreak of the Civil War. His brother, Henry Parker, the subject of this essay, had become in 1642 the most prominent spokesman for the radical group of theorists, and it would seem that for some months during that year their political views were roughly parallel. Sir Thomas was appointed in November, 1642, a member of a parliamentary commission empowered to put Sussex in a state of defense and to disarm those whose loyalty to Parliament was suspect.[103] This decision had been taken because of the coup by which Sir Edward Ford had seized Chichester for the Royalists six days earlier, though in the next month Waller moved into Sussex and after a sharp engagement at Hayward's Heath recovered the county for Parliament.

During the months that followed the outbreak of the war, Henry Parker moved rapidly to the espousal of the doctrine of parliamentary sovereignty, and, when it became apparent that the Presbyterians hoped to fasten another ecclesiastical tyranny upon England, to the leadership of the Independent bloc which was ultimately to succeed in defeating these orthodox aspirations. It is evident that the brothers were by no means in agreement

[101] *Sussex Arch. Soc. Collects.*, XIV, 101. The other governmental candidate, Sir Dudley Carleton, a member of the Council, was returned from the borough.

[102] *Ibid.*, XXXIII, 89.

[103] *Ibid.*, V, 35.

after 1642. Sir Thomas was a conservative Calvinist in his religious views and like so many of the Puritan gentry shrank from the full implications of revolution as the war progressed. A petition from his own county called his loyalty into question in 1644, though Parliament apparently took no notice of what was simply one in a flood of petitions from divers articulate but confused groups.[104] Furthermore, his own position was extremely difficult, since his daughter, Grace, had been recently married to the gallant royalist officer, Sir William Campion, who was subsequently killed in the operations around Colchester. His wife's family were moderately parliamentarian in their sympathy, and there is abundant evidence that his relations with Lord Dacre, his wife's nephew, remained intimate.[105] Parker excused himself from further attendance at Parliament in October, 1648 on the plea of illness, though his continuing loyalty to Parliament is attested by his report, communicated in the same year, of disaffection in Sussex.[106] Later in the same year, he was probably excluded from Parliament as a Presbyterian. During the whole of the Interregnum Parker resided quietly at Ratton, taking no part in the affairs of the new government until 1656, when he was again returned to Parliament.[107] He died two years later at the age of sixty-two, leaving his extensive properties to his eldest son, Sir George Parker.[108]

[104] *Ibid.*, V, 72; C. Thomas-Stanford, *Sussex in the Great Civil War and the Interregnum, 1642–1660* (London, 1910), p. 161.

[105] The two families continued to visit each other throughout the revolutionary period (*Sussex Arch. Soc. Collects.*, XLVIII, 124).

[106] *Historical Manuscripts Commission, The Manuscripts of . . . . the Duke of Portland, preserved at Welbeck Abbey* (London, 1891——), I, 501, 719.

[107] *Sussex Arch. Soc. Collects.*, V, 102, XXXIII, 91.

[108] It remains, in establishing the background of Henry Parker's thought, to sketch the history of his family during the next century. Like so many of the landed families that had risen to wealth and some distinction in the period prior to the Civil War, the Parkers gave little evidence of vigor in the management of their estates or of prominence in public life during the remainder of their history.

Sir Thomas Parker, the elder brother of Henry Parker and the head of the family, had fourteen children by his wife, Philadelphia Lennard. His eldest son, Sir George Parker (1620–1673), was married to Mary, the second daughter of Sir Richard Newdigate, first baron of Arbury, Warwickshire (George Edward Cokayne, *Complete Baronetage* [Exeter, 1900–1909], IV, 63–64). Parker matriculated at

During this rather uneventful career, Sir Thomas Parker's more distinguished brother, Henry, had lent steady service to the revolutionary government as a civil servant and far more important support as the most vigorous and advanced political theorist of his age. It will be well at this point, therefore, briefly to sketch the life of Henry Parker, leaving his thought for later consideration in the appropriate place.

Henry Parker was born in 1604, probably at Ratton, the fourth son of Sir Nicholas Parker and the younger brother of Sir Thomas Parker, whose career we have just reviewed. His mother, Catherine Temple, was the daughter of John Temple of Stowe, Buckinghamshire, a family whose rise to wealth and eminence was similar in so many ways to that of the Parkers. Parker's father was absent from Ratton during the child's boyhood for long periods

---

St. Alban's Hall, Oxford, in December, 1637. He apparently studied at the university for only one year and then entered Lincoln's Inn, where his uncle, Henry Parker, had also studied, where he remained as a student for a short season (Joseph Foster, *Alumni Oxonienses, etc.* [Oxford, 1891–92]). There is no evidence that he participated actively in the Civil War or in the affairs of the Commonwealth. Parker was returned to Parliament from the borough of Seaford in 1658, and was elected to the Restoration Parliament in 1660 from the same borough (*Sussex Arch. Soc. Collects.*, XXXIII, 93; *ibid.*, VII, 110). He was appointed a commissioner for the collection of the subsidy in Sussex in 1660 and was named a justice of the peace some time before 1663 (*ibid.*, IX, 106, VI, 242). Parker enlarged his family estates by the purchase, in 1662, of the manor of Radmeld-Beverington from Lord Abergavenny. This property was held by the family for barely two decades, being sold in 1682 by Sir Robert Parker (*Sussex Notes and Queries*, VI, 74).

Sir Robert Parker (1655–1691), who succeeded to the family estates in 1673, was apparently a man of somewhat more vigorous personality. Sir Robert was a student at Oxford, having matriculated at Lincoln College in 1672(?), at the age of seventeen. The evidence for this matriculation seems clear, despite the fact that Foster (*Alumni Oxonienses*) has him entered as Richard Parker under the date 1675. He attended the university for about one year and then entered Gray's Inn. He was married shortly before his father's death to Sarah Chute, daughter of George Chute, of Brixton-Causeway, Surrey, at St. Giles, Camberwell, London (*Sussex Notes and Queries*, VII, 162). Parker was created a baronet in May, 1674, at the age of nineteen (Cokayne, *Baronetage*, IV, 63–64). Sir Robert sat in three parliaments where, it would seem, he was a fairly consistent supporter of the royal policy. First returned from the borough of Hastings in 1678, he was elected from the same borough to the parliaments of 1679 and 1680 (*Sussex Arch. Soc. Collects.*, XXXIII, 98, 99, 100). Parker was listed in the memorandum prepared by Montagu in 1688 as one of the gentlemen in Sussex who could be expected to support the abolition of the Test Act and of the penal statutes against Catholics (*ibid.*, XXXI, 14). It does not seem,

when his duties at Pendennis Castle required his attention. John Culpepper, to whom the Parkers were distantly related, at his death in 1607 bequeathed to Henry, "son of my good friend, Sir Nicholas Parker, and my godsonne, a colt or £5."[109]

We have previously noticed that Sir Nicholas Parker died in 1619, when Henry Parker was fifteen years of age, having somewhat earlier bequeathed his estates to his eldest son. Provision was apparently made for the education of Henry, but there is evidence that financial want harassed him during most of his career. He was matriculated at St. Edmund Hall, Oxford, in February, 1622, and graduated B.A. from the university in 1625. It seems probable that Parker studied law at Lincoln's Inn during the next several years, since he was a member of the Inn in 1628 when he took his M.A. at Oxford. It is possible, though the identification is by no means conclusive, that he was married to one Jane Cannon in February, 1634.[110] Nothing is known about his career

however, that Sir Robert was again returned to Parliament. He died in 1691 at the age of thirty-six, his widow surviving until 1708.

Very little is known about Sir George Parker (1677–1726), who succeeded to the title following the death of his father. He was married in 1692 to Mary Bagot, the eldest daughter of Sir Walter Bagot, of Blithfield, Staffordshire, by whom he had one son and three daughters. Sir George was twice elected to Parliament as a member for Sussex, in 1705 and again in 1710 (*ibid.*, XXXV, 138, 141). He was, as members of his family for six generations had been, a justice of the peace in Sussex and was appointed a commissioner of roads in Sussex in 1709 (*ibid.*, XV, 146). Sir George died in 1726 at the age of forty-nine, his wife dying in the next year.

The last of the line, Sir Walter Parker, was born at Ratton, probably between 1693 and 1695. He was betrothed to Elizabeth Barham, of Sussex, who died in 1712 at the age of sixteen (*ibid.*, LVI, 158). It seems probable that Parker was deeply affected by this personal tragedy, since he never married. His life was singularly uneventful, without any record of public service and without any apparent interest in his estates. Sir Walter gave a peal of five bells to the Willingdon church in 1732, and in 1737 gave to the church a beautiful silver flagon which bears his family arms (*ibid.*, XVI, 229, LV, 157). Parker's three sisters were alive in 1727, but it seems probable that only the younger sister survived at the time of Sir Walter's death in 1750 (*ibid.*, XXV, 198). The family estates passed to Philadelphia Parker, who had married one Nathaniel Trayton of Lewes, and thence by descent to the Fuller family, which held Ratton during most of the nineteenth century.

[109] *Sussex Arch. Soc. Collects.*, XLVII, 75.

[110] *A Calendar of the Marriage Licence Allegations in the Registry of the Bishop of London* Vol. I: *1597 to 1648* (Vol. LXII of "The Index Library," issued by the British Record Society, Ltd.) (London, 1937), p. 116.

during the next three years until he was called to the bar from Lincoln's Inn in January, 1637.[111]

Parker had already come to hold radical political opinions when the Long Parliament assembled in 1640. His first book, *The Case of Shipmony Briefly Discoursed*, published in the month in which Parliament was convened, vigorously assailed the royal prerogative and maintained that the good of the people and of the nation must be regarded as the supreme law before which all other laws must yield. During these critical months he was actively engaged in enlisting support for the parliamentary cause by means of his pamphlets and his letters to friends. Thus he rebuked his distant cousin, Sir Ralph Verney, in November, 1641, for his refusal to lend support to either side of the controversy then rending England. He warned Verney that neutrality would be impossible in the impending struggle and that a choice must be made between the two sides on the basis, not of absolute, but of relative right. When, in late 1643, Verney declined to take the Covenant, Parker wrote to him again. "In my opinion you steere a course wherein there is almost no hope of indemnity on either side, but certaynty of greate losse and blame from both."[112] Men must in periods of great crisis "adhere to that cause which is dictated to them to bee the better and the more harmlesse by the light of nature and the most forcible indications of reason." Men of intelligence and status cannot escape the responsibility of decision in periods of cultural crisis. The human mind can never be in precise equilibrium when great moral and political issues, crying out for decision, confront it. Hence, "if ether scale have but one od grayne in it to sway you, you are as much bounde to obey that sway, as he is that has the strongest propension of judgment."[113]

[111] *The Records of the Honorable Society of Lincoln's Inn: The Black Books* (London, 1897–1902), II, 345.

[112] *H.M.C., Reports*, VII, 449. Verney replied somewhat plaintively in December, 1641, that he could not in conscience take the Covenant. Unable to support either side, he had retired to the country. The result had been that the king had sequestered his estates and that Parliament was daily threatening to do the same.

[113] Frances P. Verney, *Memoirs of the Verney Family during the Civil War, etc.* (London, 1892), II, 211–12.

In his correspondence with Verney, Parker raised a moral issue which troubled the best minds of England during the difficult period when a violent civil war was brewing in the realm. Men were deeply disturbed because they discovered right in both parties and because they detected in both a fanatical extremism which repudiated the traditions of political and religious development of the past two generations. In particular, the great moderate party, to which Verney belonged, and which, though unorganized and undecided, included the finest spirits in the realm, drew back from the bath of blood to which the extremists beckoned them.[114] Henry Parker, on the other hand, was the leading intellectual amongst the parliamentary extremists. He defined and accepted the full implications of constitutional revolt long before the greater leaders in Parliament and in the army quite admitted the principles upon which an assault on the crown and its prerogatives had of necessity to be based. Yet, if we may trust the sincerity of his correspondence with a kinsman, he had made his choice with the full realization that moral decisions are never precisely defined, that men and societies progress by choosing that course which offers the greater good and the larger hope.

Shortly after the outbreak of hostilities, Parker was appointed secretary to the army which Essex had just been designated to command.[115] There is no evidence to suggest that Parker held this post for very long and certainly none to indicate that the appointment afforded him an opportunity to increase his "paternal property."[116] In November, 1643, Parker petitioned Parliament for appointment to the lucrative post of registrar of the prerogative office which had recently been sequestered. The House of Commons, later testimony reveals, promised him that he would be considered for this or some comparable post. But in July, 1644, his claims were ignored when Michael Oldsworth was appointed. Three years later Parker complained that a committee designated to investigate the whole matter had never reported

[114] *Vide* W. K. Jordan, *The Development of Religious Toleration in England* (London, 1932–40), II, 349–421, for a discussion of the thought and program of this party.

[115] *Journals of the House of Lords, 1509*—— (*s.l.*, *s.a.*), V, 206, 208 (July 12, 1642).

[116] Horsfield, *History of Sussex*, I, 289.

and that he had incurred heavy expenses in his endeavor to secure a hearing. In July, 1649, Parker protested after his return from Germany, that he had "attended with counsel often before I went abroad, and have often crossed the seas about it, and have maintained agents these five years, and [have] suffered so much that, unless I live long, the place will hardly make me reparation."[117]

Parker's petition and his important contributions to the success of the parliamentary cause were responsible for a belated consideration of the whole problem. After hearing a report from a committee in July, the Commons declared the post of registrar sequestered and confirmed the appointments of Parker and Oldsworth to the position with joint enjoyment of its profits.[118] There were other claimants as well, but the committee cut through a tangled mass of conflicting evidence in order to secure the reward of the two parliamentary stalwarts.[119]

During the period prior to his appointment to the registrarship, Parker had lent valuable services to Parliament. His pamphlets were molding public opinion and his thought had always been a spearhead well in advance of political reality. Moreover, he had given faithful service in a more concrete sense. He and John Sadler were appointed secretaries to the House of Commons in June, 1645, with instructions to prepare a statement on the recent rupture of the negotiations with the King at Uxbridge.[120] This assignment was considerably enlarged when a number of important royal documents were captured during the decisive battle of Naseby in June, 1645. Thomas May, the historian, was then appointed to serve with Parker and Sadler in the preparation of a declaration designed to discredit the royalist cause.[121]

[117] *Calendar of the Proceedings of the Committee for Advance of Money, 1642–1656, etc.* (London, 1888), p. 687.

[118] *Calendars of State Papers, Domestic Series* [*during the Commonwealth and Protectorate*] *1649–1660, etc.* (London, 1875–86), ii, 45; *Calendar of the Proceedings of the Committee for Advance of Money, 1642–1656*, p. 687.

[119] *Calendar of the Proceedings of the Committee for Advance of Money*, pp. 688–89.

[120] *Journals of the House of Commons, 1547–1714* (*s.l., s.a.*), IV, 187.

[121] W. C. Abbott, *The Writings and Speeches of Oliver Cromwell, etc.* (Cambridge, 1937——), II, 85.

The co-operative work of the three parliamentary secretaries was soon published anonymously (1645) under the title, *The King's Cabinet Opened.* This pamphlet, prepared with extraordinary skill, was to be disastrous to the royalist cause. The authors stated in the preface that they intended to let the documents prove by their own weight and substance that Charles was entirely indifferent to the fate and welfare of his realm. The thirty-nine documents were, however, interspersed with annotations which sought to prove by unimpeachable evidence the parliamentary contention that the Queen exercised a vicious influence over the King, that Charles had long been swayed by Catholic advisers, and that he had bent every effort toward raising an Irish army to be employed for the subjugation of England.[122] Parker was rewarded for this and other services by a grant of £100 from Parliament in January, 1646.[123] Shortly afterward another grant in the amount of £50 was voted to him as an honorarium for having brought the news of the fall of Chester.[124] This would suggest that Parker had returned to the army as secretary, though if this were the case his service must have been brief.

Sometime in 1646 Parker accepted an appointment as secretary to the Merchant Adventurers' Company at Hamburg. It is difficult to understand how the active and deeply interested theorist could have been persuaded to leave England just as the Civil War was being brought to a successful conclusion and when a victorious Parliament faced the task of forming a stable government. We do know, however, that he had been unsuccessful in his quest for a profitable political appointment, and it is certain that his new post offered a substantial economic reward. We know, too, that Parker was an agent for the Council during his stay in Germany, so it is probable that his appointment had

[122] The style of the preface would suggest that Parker was not the author, though internal evidence makes it seem probable that he had much to do with drafting the annotations.

[123] *H.M.C., 6th Rep., H. of L.*, VI, 95.

[124] *Ibid.*, VI, 97; *L.J.*, VIII, 121, 147.

quasi-diplomatic implications. He continued to carry on his controversial writing while abroad,[125] and to this period belongs his most important economic tract, *Of a Free Trade*, written at Hamburg.[126] In March, 1649, the Council of State thanked Parker for his loyalty to Parliament and asked him to continue his "care of discovery and information" and to "direct the same to this Council."[127]

Parker returned to England shortly after receiving this letter of commendation from the Council. He probably arrived in London in May, 1649.[128] Clement Walker, the violent Presbyterian protagonist, in the second part of his *Anarchia Anglicana*, published in 1649, remarked that "Harry Parker, the observator is returned from Hamborough, and highly preferred to be brewers clerke (alias secretary) to Cromwell; to whose designes he hath prostituted his pen."[129] In June (1649) the Council asked Parker to supply them with information concerning the progress of military preparations in Sweden and Denmark,[130] and, as we have previously noticed, confirmed his appointment, with Oldsworth, to the registrarship of the Prerogative Office. At about the same time, Parker was named a commissioner for the collection of the parliamentary tax which had been levied by ordinance in March,

[125] Three pamphlets, all relatively unimportant, were written during this period of his career: [Henry Parker], *The cordiall of Mr. David Jenkins; or his reply to H. P. Barrister of Lincolnes Inne, answered* (London, 1647); H. P. (i.e., Henry Parker), *An answer to the poysonous sedicious paper of Mr. David Jenkins* (London, 1647); H. P. (i.e., Henry Parker), *Severall poysonous and sedicious papers of Mr. David Jenkins answered, etc.* (London, 1647).

[126] *Of a Free Trade*, it should be noted, was a defense of the chartered companies which were then under abusive criticism.

[127] *S.P. Dom., Commonwealth and Protectorate*, i, 25.

[128] Parker, writing in 1650 against John Lilburne, indicated that he had not yet returned to England when that worthy was arraigned before the Council on March 28, 1649 on charges of seditious libel. Moreover, he wrote that his health was poor at the time of his return and that he remained infirm for several months thereafter.

[129] [Clement Walker], *Anarchia Anglicana: or, the History of Independency. The Second Part* (London, 1649), p. 199.

[130] *S.P. Dom., Commonwealth and Protectorate, 1649–1650*, 185.

1648,[131] and, on May 14, 1649, he was designated a member of a commission for the levying of an assessment.[132]

It is apparent that Parker, whose services had gone unrewarded in the early years of the Civil War, enjoyed the full confidence and favor of the Commonwealth. He had been vested with a number of remunerative commissions during the spring of 1649 and was able to purchase a sequestrated property in Wales.[133] In May he was questioned concerning the disposition of jewels, plate, and other valuable properties which had belonged to the late Earl of Worcester and which Serj. John Glynn declined to deliver from his lengthy custody. Parker testified that he and an associate had been instructed by the Committee of Safety to search Worcester House in 1643. There they had seen goods worth £2,000 but had been unable to prepare an inventory because Glynn had refused to surrender the keys to all the rooms.[134]

This and other public missions must have occupied all Parker's time during the summer of 1649, when the peace of the young Commonwealth government was gravely disturbed by the spread of civil war in Ireland. The English position was deteriorating so rapidly that Cromwell was obliged in early August to proceed to Ireland in order to assume personal command. Henry Parker was appointed secretary to the Irish army, and hence to Cromwell, probably arriving with him on August 15, 1649.[135] The Council, on October 25, wrote to Parker expressly instructing him to keep it fully informed concerning Irish affairs.[136] Parker, it may be assumed, assisted with the preparation of the terse and triumphant dispatches which flowed back to England in a steady stream as Cromwell struck at the roots of rebellion. Cromwell left Ireland in May, 1650, but Parker remained behind as secretary to the army and to the parliamentary commission appointed to assist Ireton, who was left in command as Lord Deputy.

[131] C. H. Firth and R. S. Rait, *Acts and Ordinances of the Interregnum, 1642–1660* (London, 1911), I, 1113.

[132] *Ibid.*, II, 120.

[133] *Calendar of the Proceedings of the Committee for Compounding, 1643–1660*, p. 1602.

[134] *Calendar of the Committee for Advance of Money*, pp. 215–16.

[135] Abbott, *Cromwell*, II, 85.

[136] *S.P. Dom., Commonwealth and Protectorate, 1649–1650*, 364.

We know very little about the few remaining months of Parker's life. It is probable that he was the author of the anonymous *Cheif Affairs of Ireland Truly Communicated*, a narrowly controversial work on Irish politics published in 1651. Parker died, presumably in Ireland, in late 1652. A few weeks later, on January 18, 1653, the Council favorably entertained a petition from his widow, Jane Parker, for arrears of pay due for her husband's services in Ireland.[137] His widow was further assisted in October, when the Council conferred on her the joint tenure, with Oldsworth, of the registrarship of the prerogative court.[138] In the next year, however, the widow found it necessary to petition the Council again in her own name and that of her two children.[139] This request was apparently buried in committee, and Jane Parker and her children immediately dropped into obscurity.

These brief and unexciting annals comprise all we know concerning the career of one of the most vigorous and original thinkers of a period teeming with genius. It is not evident that Parker possessed political or administrative gifts of any particular distinction. But in the sphere of ideas his fertile and courageous mind ranged widely and made contributions of the first order to English thought. He was the most interesting and significant of a group of English thinkers who were molding the shape of a revolutionary government, who were cautiously exploring the frontiers of the liberal society of the future.

[137] *Ibid.*, xxii, 46.

[138] *Ibid.*, xli, 74, xlii, 4.

[139] *Ibid.*, lxxi, 50.

III

HENRY ROBINSON (1605–1673?): ANTECEDENTS AND LIFE

HENRY PARKER was a member of an old, established, and prosperous landed family; Henry Robinson was descended from an old, prolific, and rich merchant family. Both families had attained stability and wealth during the early Tudor period and both were in a true sense of the Tudor gentry, the one of land and the other of commerce. The two men were practically the same age, Parker having been born in 1604 and Robinson in 1605; both men were students at Oxford at the same time, where they probably met; both resided in London during most of their mature lives; and there is a remarkable similarity between them in the power, freshness, and originality of their thought. There is no evidence that they knew each other intimately, though they were connected with the government in similar capacities at about the same time, but there is every evidence that each was strongly influenced by the writings of the other.

Henry Robinson's family had been London merchants of very considerable wealth for almost a century before his birth. Moreover, they had been for about two generations among the richest, if not the most prominent, of the landed gentry of Staffordshire. During this landed interlude, however, the members of the family in whom the lands were vested remained citizens of London and active mercers. An incomplete study of the Robinson family indicates that ten of its members were prosperous merchants and members of various London companies during the period 1520–1660, while three of the daughters married merchants of similar status. The family, including most of its branches, resided for at least a century and a half in the then prosperous parish of St. Helen's, Bishopsgate. It was apparently a family with very close-

THE ROBINSONS OF LONDON AND DRAYTON BASSETT, STAFFORDSHIRE

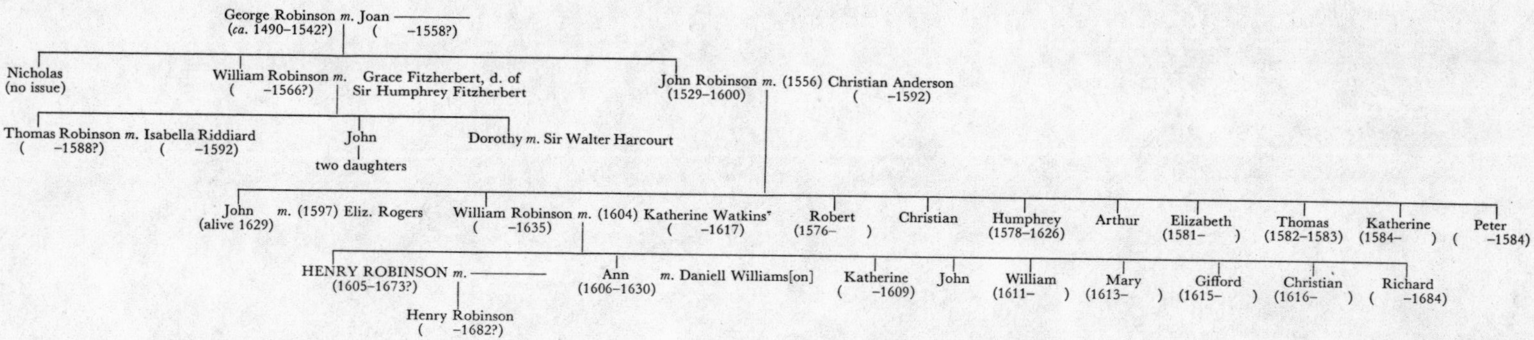

ly knit interests and sympathies. Younger sons seem to have become quite as prosperous as the eldest, brothers were not infrequently joined in trading ventures, and marriages of daughters must have been carefully arranged. The records of St. Helen's, Bishopsgate, suggest that the Robinsons were during about a century one of the leading families in a rich parish. Their charities within the parish were numerous, and substantial bequests were made to the companies in which numerous family fortunes were made. It is very rare indeed during this period to find a merchant family with as long and unbroken a record of prosperity or with as consistent an interest in trade.

The founder of the family fortune was George Robinson (*ca.* 1490–1542?), who seems, however, to have entered commerce with a substantial patrimony which had been considerably increased by speculation in land. Robinson was a member of the Mercers' Company as early as 1520, when he appears in the records of the society as one of a group associated in the financing of a voyage.[1] There is abundant evidence that he was a disputatious and stubbornly independent man who throughout his career was always insisting on receiving just a little more than his due rights. In 1523 the company was obliged to intervene in a dispute between Robinson and a fellow-member involving a house which belonged to the former.[2] Just a year later the master-wardens found it necessary to adjudicate in a controversy between Robinson and one of his apprentices in which the sympathy of the wardens was patently with the unhappy apprentice.[3] Robinson was elected a master-bachelor of the company in 1525, and in the next year assumed an important share in the administration of its affairs.[4] In 1527 he was admitted to the livery of the company.[5]

At about this date Robinson likewise became a member of the Merchant Tailors' Company.[6] For four successive generations his

[1] Laetitia Lyell and F. D. Watney, *Acts of Court of the Mercers' Company, 1453–1527* (Cambridge, 1936), p. 528.

[2] *Ibid.*, p. 675.

[3] *Ibid.*, p. 679.

[4] *Ibid.*, pp. 740, 760, 762.

[5] *Ibid.*, p. 768.

[6] Charles M. Clode, *The Early History of the Guild of Merchant Taylors, etc.* (London, 1888), II, 100.

family were members of both these great merchant companies. Robinson had apparently acquired great wealth by 1535 when he was assessed the sum of 2,000 marks, one of the heaviest levies imposed on any citizen of the capital.[7] One would suspect, however, that this heavy imposition was in part at least a form of blackmail levied at the instruction of the chief minister, Thomas Cromwell, in order to bring the wily and stubborn Robinson to heel. We know that Cromwell's agents were scouring London for the rich merchant in August, 1535,[8] while later in the same month one of Cromwell's henchmen reported that he had found Robinson and had upbraided him because of the incomplete assessment of the merchant's goods in the recent levy.

The inordinate curiosity which Cromwell exhibited concerning Robinson's affairs during the next few years is to be explained by the fact that the merchant had the temerity to balk the minister's plan to acquire as inconspicuously as possible the valuable manor of Drayton Bassett in Staffordshire. This manor, which had been conferred on Turstin de Bassett about 1086, remained in the hands of the Bassett family until the end of the fifteenth century.[9] During the reign of Richard II it passed, following the death of the last male member of the Bassett family, to Thomas, Earl of Stafford, whose wife was the next of kin. The estate, with the other great holdings of the Stafford family, escheated to the crown on the attainder of the second Duke of Buckingham in 1483 and was apparently not restored by Henry VIII in 1509, when the third duke regained the royal favor. In any event, the estate does not appear in the detailed inventory of the Stafford properties which reverted to the crown in 1521 after the execution of the third duke on charges of treason. The probability that the manor remained in royal hands for some time after 1483 is supported by the fact that the notorious Edmund Dudley was appointed steward of the property in 1506,[10] and that the mano-

[7] *Letters and Papers, Henry VIII*, viii, 478. [8] *Ibid.*, ix, 172.

[9] John A. Langford, C. S. Mackintosh, and J. C. Tildesley, *Staffordshire and Warwickshire, etc.* (London, *s.a.*), I, 136; *Collections for a History of Staffordshire. William Salt Archaeological Society* (London, 1880–97; 1898–1909; 1910——), XI, 242.

[10] *Cal. Pat. Rolls, 1494–1509*, II, 464.

rial tenants certainly recognized his son, Sir John Dudley, as steward as late as 1531.[11]

The manor seems to have been acquired by George Robinson, probably under a long lease, shortly before 1531.[12] At that time the estate was not only highly productive but was likewise relatively large. The arable lands amounted to 2,000 acres, meadows to 200 acres, pasture to 2,000 acres, woodlands and marshes to 800 acres, and heath to 2,060 acres.[13] There were seventeen freeholders possessed of 325 acres and a considerably larger number of copyholders on the property, whose total extent was 7,060 acres.[14] The manor house, which dominated the central property in Drayton Park, was an imposing mansion described in the eighteenth century as a "curious specimen" of ancient simplicity, constructed of wood and plaster, "with a rude old hall."

The rich London merchant, now suddenly elevated to the position of a prominent country gentleman, removed to Drayton Bassett in 1531 to administer his property and to discipline his tenants, who had been very laxly handled, to the performance of their legal responsibilities. The short-tempered and stubborn Robinson soon found himself involved in altercations which were not entirely settled during his lifetime. He lodged an eloquent complaint with the Star Chamber in 1531, alleging that though he was "lawfully seised and possessed of the manor and park of Drayton Bassett" for a term of years, his premises had been invaded by a band of villagers and yeomen who would have "beten, murdred, and slayne" him had he not been rescued by his friends and servants.[15] The principal culprits, in their rejoinder, contended that they were simply protesting against the arbitrary action of Robinson in depriving them of customary offices and rights vested in them by the former owners of the property.[16] They submitted, moreover, that they had not tried to prevent

[11] *Salt Arch. Soc., Collects.*, 1910, pp. 25–26; *et cf.* Stebbing Shaw, *The History and Antiquities of Staffordshire, etc.* (London, 1798, 1801), II, 5.

[12] Langford, *Staffordshire and Warwickshire*, I, 136–37.

[13] *Salt Arch. Soc., Collects.*, XII, 185.

[14] *Ibid.*, XII, 185; Shaw, *History of Staffordshire*, II, 9.

[15] *Salt Arch. Soc., Collects.*, 1910, pp. 22–23.

[16] *Ibid.*, 1910, pp. 23–24.

tenants from paying rents and fees legally due, as Robinson alleged, but, as bailiffs for the property, had rather sought to collect them in the customary manner for the new proprietor. The Londoner, who all evidence would indicate was extremely unpopular in the neighborhood, had abused the defendants, had ordered them off the premises, saying he was "to bygge" for them, and as a parting gesture had fitted an arrow to his bow in a menacing manner.[17]

That Sir John Dudley, whose servant the bailiff at Drayton Bassett claimed to be in 1531, still retained a shred of title to the manor is indicated by a letter to Cromwell, dated December 10, 1532, which mentions a dispute between Robinson and Sir John regarding the presentation rights for the parish. Both men claimed full right of possession, and so bitter was the misunderstanding that it seemed probable that the presentation might "fall into the king's gift by lapse."[18] The altercation had not been settled in the next year and may well have precipitated the violent dispute between Robinson and Cromwell regarding the possession of the manor.

The tangled affairs of Drayton Bassett were presumably resolved when in 1535 Sir John Sutton, whose previous connection with the manor is obscure, sold the title to Robinson for the sum of £2,000.[19] This sale, which was apparently designed to be nothing more than a formality, was actually consummated upon the basis of a private agreement by which Robinson was to convey the property to Sir John Dudley, who, in turn, was to hold it for ultimate conveyance to his master, Thomas Cromwell. Cromwell's share in this complicated and purposely obscure transaction is clearly reflected in his private accounts which record that the sum of £1,333–6–8 had been paid by Dudley, acting as Crom-

[17] *Ibid.*, pp. 25–26.

[18] *Letters and Papers, Henry VIII*, v, 676 (#1624). In 1533 Dudley was sued by Sir Edward Seymour, Sir Thomas Butteler, William Harwoode, *et al.*, as deforciant of the manor of Drayton Bassett and other properties. Dudley acknowledged the right of the complainants and paid them the sum of £2,000 (*Salt Arch. Soc., Collects.*, XII, 185).

[19] Cf. *Letters and Papers, Henry VIII*, xii, pt. i, 1263.

well's agent, to Robinson as part, it seems safe to assume on the basis of subsequent developments, of the full purchase price.[20]

Robinson, however, failed to honor his commitment and apparently defied the powerful and unpopular minister to force the conveyance. As we have seen, a discriminatory tax had thereupon been laid against Robinson, and further retaliation had been threatened. The merchant, to add insult to injury, had removed to Staffordshire where he remained in full and aggressive possession of the property. In early 1536 an extraordinarily suspicious indictment was returned at Lichfield by a court in which Sir John Dudley was one of the justices. Robinson was accused of having received stolen horses and of having permitted the thieves to escape.[21] Dudley reported the accusation directly to Cromwell with the comment that the justices had "done well in the king's service."[22] It seems entirely safe to assume that the charge against Robinson had been carefully arranged, one would suspect by Sir John Dudley. Further pressure was applied when Robinson's name was included on a small list of London merchants who could be required immediately to pay larger sums to the government.[23]

The charges against Robinson were not pressed but were evidently being held in hand in order to force the recalcitrant merchant to surrender the property to the minister who was threatening his agents with dire punishments unless they brought the affair to an immediate and satisfactory conclusion. Nothing further could be done for the time being, however, and one is surprised to note that Robinson, together with Sir William Pickering and George Harper, was granted the houses, lands, and site of the late priory of Stone, Staffordshire, in April, 1538.[24]

This grant may well have been a peace-offering designed to induce the tough-spirited Robinson to agree to transfer Drayton Bassett to the angry and dangerous chief minister. Moreover, it

[20] *Ibid.*, ix (1535), 137, 172, 193, 478.

[21] *Ibid.*, x, 272 (February 7, 1536).

[22] *Ibid.*, x, 291 (February 11, 1536).

[23] *Ibid.*, xi, 1419 (iii).

[24] *Ibid.*, xiii, pt. i, 329. This property was owned by the Robinson family as late as 1596, when John, the youngest son of George Robinson, was engaged in litigation concerning it (*Salt Arch. Soc.*, *Collects.*, XVI, 163).

was by this time abundantly clear to Cromwell that Dudley's hands had not been wholly clean in the complicated transaction which had left Robinson in full possession of the manor at a charge to Cromwell of upward of £1,300. One Thomas Pope, a friend of Robinson's, admitted in a plaintive letter to Cromwell, that he had acted as Robinson's agent with the full knowledge of Dudley. Robinson had asked Pope to act for him in the purchase of the manor, since most of his funds were at the moment invested in goods, and the merchant had actually advanced only £400 of the purchase price of £2,000.[25] Drayton Bassett had accordingly been purchased and had then been conveyed to George Robinson for a term of ninety-nine years.

The frightened Dudley wrote immediately to Cromwell admitting that he had known of the arrangement between Robinson and Pope.[26] Pope, now thoroughly alarmed, wrote to Wriothesley on July 29, 1538, asking the councilor to intercede with Cromwell on his behalf and promising to meet all the chief minister's wishes in the matter.[27] Cromwell was now employing a new agent, Polstede, to bring all possible pressure to bear on Pope with the expectation that he might be able to compel the irascible Robinson to surrender the title.[28] Pope capitulated entirely in August, 1538, but found it impossible to persuade Robinson to yield until November, 1539, when the wily London merchant, after Cromwell had paid him 400 marks as the debit balance due on the total purchase price, finally agreed to surrender the title.[29] Actually, however, Robinson simply pocketed this additional payment and then despite incessant pressure managed to retain full possession of the property until Cromwell's fall from favor relieved him of further anxiety in May, 1540.[30]

George Robinson apparently remained in the quiet possession of his Staffordshire properties during the last two years of his life. He died in late 1542, having arranged shortly before his death for

[25] *Letters and Papers, Henry VIII*, xiii, pt. i, 1472.

[26] *Ibid.*, xiii, pt. i, 1473.

[27] *Ibid.*, xiii, pt. i, 1488.

[28] *Ibid.*, xiii, pt. i, 1499; xiii, pt. ii, 28.

[29] *Ibid.*, xiv, pt. ii, 782.

[30] Robinson was returned from Drayton Bassett in the Staffordshire muster roll for 1539 (*Salt Arch. Soc., Collects.*, IV [N.S.], 231), and, as a reference in the state papers would indicate, was residing there in December of the same year.

an additional purchase of lands from the Chancellor, Audley, who had recently received them as a grant from Henry VIII. The conveyance was not executed until June, 1543, when extensive former monastic properties were alienated by Audley to George Robinson's widow, Joan. The holdings consisted of the priory at Avecote, Warwickshire, together with landed possessions in Shittington, Reycote, and Avecote in the same county and additional tenements in Marsham, Derbyshire, and Bramston, Leicestershire.[31] Joan Robinson, who lived until 1558, was an entirely independent and competent lady who was active in the management of the family holdings and who, with her "landed son," William, purchased still more lands in Warwickshire in 1555.[32] Some years earlier she had vigorously asserted her rights as guardian of the heir of Sir Thomas Drake, who had held lands in Drayton Bassett, and pressed charges of trespass and riot against certain of Drake's tenants.[33]

George Robinson was survived by three male heirs, the eldest of whom, Nicholas Robinson, died, probably in 1550, without heirs. His extensive and rich estate was divided, following his widow's death, between the "landed son," William (d. 1566?), and the merchant son, John Robinson (1529–1600), with whose line we are principally concerned.

William Robinson inherited the properties at Drayton Bassett and the holdings which had been acquired in Warwickshire and Lincolnshire since his father's death.[34] Though he resided in Staffordshire most of his life, he none the less maintained a keen interest in commerce, being for most of his mature life a mercer and a citizen of London.[35] He seems likewise to have inherited the quarrelsome temper of his father, the Star Chamber having been obliged on one occasion to take account of a pitched battle between Robinson and his servants and the servants of one Walter

[31] *Letters and Papers, Henry VIII*, xviii, pt. 1, 802 (#12).

[32] *Cal. Pat. Rolls, 1554–1555*, 246.

[33] *Salt Arch. Soc., Collects.*, 1912, pp. 177–78; *ibid.*, 1938, pp. 94–95.

[34] *S.P. Dom., Eliz., 1547–1580*, 285; *Cal. Pat. Rolls, 1554–1555*, 246.

[35] *Salt Arch. Soc., Collects.*, 1917–1918, p. 355.

Horton.[36] Late in his life William Robinson attained a more secure social status in the county by his marriage to Grace, the daughter of Sir Humphrey Fitzherbert of Uphall, Hertfordshire,[37] and by his appointment as a justice of the peace.[38]

John, the younger son of George Robinson, with whose line we

[36] *Ibid.*, 1912, p. 153.

[37] Following William Robinson's death (1566?), his widow married, as a second wife, Sir Simon Harcourt. Sir Simon's son, by his first wife, was later to marry Dorothy Robinson, his then wife's daughter by William Robinson.

[38] *Salt Arch. Soc.*, *Collects.*, 1912, p. 323; *ibid.*, 1915, p. 371; *et vide ibid.*, pp. 85–87. The remaining history of the elder, and landed, branch of the Robinson family may be very briefly sketched. William Robinson was survived by three children. As we have seen, the daughter, Dorothy, married Sir Walter Harcourt, a member of a family of some prominence. The younger son, John, was apparently a farmer at Drayton Bassett. The elder son, Thomas, to whom the extensive properties of the father descended, died about 1588, his wife Isabella (Riddiard) surviving until 1592.

Thomas Robinson was apparently extravagant in his habits and unsuccessful in his efforts to administer his sprawling properties. In 1578 he "mortgaged or sold" Drayton Bassett to one Richard Paramore, who in turn sold the property to the Earl of Leicester, thus, curiously enough, returning it after some fifty years to the Dudley family (Langford, *Staffordshire and Warwickshire*, I, 136–37). Paramore discovered when he sought to take possession of his property in October, 1578, however, that Thomas Robinson was quite as irascible as his father and grandfather. He complained that Robinson and his servants entered the house and defied the new owner in his effort to take possession of the property. The dispute, which was apparently chiefly concerned with the ownership of the growing crops, the livestock, and the furnishings, could not be amicably settled, and Paramore was obliged to call upon Lord Stafford and the sheriff who, we are informed in what must be an apocryphal account, employed "7000 people" to lay siege to the house whose "garrison" surrendered after the fifth day (*Salt Arch. Soc.*, *Collects.*, 1912, pp. 206–7). Thomas Robinson had apparently not lost his other holdings in Staffordshire, since he paid a heavy assessment for the subsidy of 1583 (*Salt Arch. Soc.*, *Collects.*, III, 20), but his fortunes were at a low ebb when he died about 1588.

Thomas Robinson having died without issue, his younger brother, John, inherited his properties and his quarrels. In November, 1588, Robinson made forcible entry into Drayton Bassett to which he contended he had title. The property, which had been purchased by Leicester, had been bestowed by him upon his wife, Lettice, the widow of the first Earl of Essex, who now sought the support of her son, Robert, the second Earl of Essex, who already stood high in the Queen's favor. Essex sought aid against Robinson (*H.M.C.*, *Reports*, IV, 329 [2]), and in subsequent proceedings in the Exchequer was finally able to silence the claims of the persistent Robinson family. The elder branch of the Robinson family dropped rapidly into obscurity after this date; parish records make it clear that they were during the next half-century relatively well-to-do farmers in the neighborhood of Drayton Bassett.

are concerned, apparently inherited the London business of the family together with the properties in Stone and Darleston acquired by his father in 1538, which he retained throughout his life and which were inherited in turn by his son, John Robinson, Junior.[39] John Robinson, who was evidently a far more placid citizen than his progenitors, acquired great wealth in trade and assumed a leading role in the commercial and municipal affairs of the capital during the Elizabethan era. He was during his mature life a mercer, a merchant of the staple, and a merchant tailor. In 1556 he married Christian Anderson, the daughter of a prominent London grocer,[40] by whom he had a family of nine sons and seven daughters.[41] Of this family, at least five of the sons were to become prosperous merchants in the City, while two of the daughters married leading London merchants.

John Robinson was chosen warden of the Merchant Tailors' Company in 1585, serving until 1590.[42] It would seem that most of his commercial activity was centered in this company in whose affairs he was likewise chiefly interested. He was elected alderman for the ward of Aldgate in 1592,[43] and possibly served a second term toward the close of his life. Robinson was one of a group of six merchant tailors who subscribed the sum of £56 each in order to create a permanent trust fund for the benefit of six widows of the company,[44] and in 1594 he assumed personal responsibility for the maintenance of one additional widow.[45] He bequeathed by will a tenement near the Tower to his parish church with the provision that the sum of £5–4–0 should forever be paid out in weekly amounts in order to provide bread for the

[39] *Salt Arch. Soc., Collects.*, XVI, 163.

[40] *London County Council, Survey of London*, Vol. IX, pt. i: *The Parish of St. Helen, Bishopsgate* (London, 1924), pp. 64–65.

[41] *The Publications of the Harleian Society Registers*, Vol. XXXI: *The Registers of St. Helen's, Bishopsgate, London* (London, 1904), *passim.*

[42] Clode, *Merchant Taylors*, I, 170; II, 342–43.

[43] Alfred B. Beaven, *The Aldermen of the City of London, etc.* (London, 1908–13), I, 11.

[44] C. M. Clode, *Memorials of the Guild of Merchant Taylors of the Fraternity of St. John the Baptist, in the City of London* (London, 1875), pp. 292–93, 367–68.

[45] *Ibid.*, p. 367.

poor of his parish.[46] Robinson died on February 19, 1600, at the age of seventy-one, his wife having died eight years earlier.[47]

We have previously observed that at least five of John Robinson's sons were London merchants. Humphrey Robinson, who was born in 1578,[48] married Anne Pyott, the daughter of a well-known London merchant, Richard Pyott.[49] Pyott, the son of a Staffordshire landowner, was at one time an alderman and in 1610 was named sheriff of Middlesex. Humphrey Robinson, who was a charter member of the newly organized Levant Company,[50] remained an active member of the Mercers' Company until his death at the age of forty-eight in 1626. Another younger son, Arthur, likewise a mercer, married Elizabeth Walthall, the daughter of a prosperous member of the company, and probably resided in the parish of St. Peter's, Cornhill.[51] A third son, Robert, was also a mercer. He was born in 1576, was a churchwarden of St. Helen's, Bishopsgate, from 1610 to 1612, and died prior to 1618. His widow, Mary Robinson, bequeathed by will the sum of £500 to the Mercers' Company, the income of which was to be paid to four poor scholars at Cambridge to assist them in preparing for the ministry.[52]

The eldest surviving son of John Robinson, John Robinson, Junior, inherited the largest portion of his father's estate and as early as 1595 was a prominent member of the Staple and of the Merchant Tailors' Company. He married in 1597 Elizabeth Rogers, the daughter of Sir Richard Rogers of Blandford, Dorset, a member of a family of no little wealth and antiquity.[53] This

[46] J. E. Cox, *The Annals of St. Helen's, Bishopsgate, London* (London, 1876), pp. 75–76. The property was subsequently acquired by the Carpenters' Company. Later it was sold to the East India Company, which used the site for its warehouse. The annuity is still paid by the Carpenters' Company.

[47] Beaven, *Aldermen of London*, II, 44; *Registers of St. Helen's, Bishopsgate.*

[48] *Registers of St. Helen's, Bishopsgate.*

[49] *Salt Arch. Soc., Collects.*, V, pt. ii, 248.

[50] *P.R.O., F. A. Levant Co.*, #107 (1605).

[51] *The Publications of the Harleian Society*, Vol. XXV: *Allegations for Marriage Licenses Issued by the Bishop of London, 1520–1610* (London, 1887), p. 276.

[52] The fund in 1914 yielded £44 per annum for each of the exhibitioners (John Watney, *History of the Mercers' Company of the City of London* [London, 1914], p. 174).

[53] *Allegations for Marriage Licenses*, p. 241 (August 27, 1597).

marriage, which was typical of the fusion taking place between the county and the commercial aristocracies, did not last long, since Elizabeth Robinson died in 1600.[54] She left a son and a daughter to her husband, who apparently did not marry again. Robinson was shortly afterward appointed a "searcher at the customs," a post which he was to hold for some years. In 1605 he was nominated an alderman, but the nomination was rejected by the court because customs officials had been specifically exempted by act of parliament from aldermanic responsibility.[55] A few years later (1611), John Robinson's already diverse trading activities were enlarged when he was named a member in the original charter of the Company of Merchants Trading in France.[56]

Robinson was evidently a stubborn and self-willed merchant. Thus he declined to accept office when in 1613 the Merchant Tailors' Company elected him a warden of the society. The post was expensive alike in time and money because of the elaborate entertainments which were periodically provided and because of the attention which had to be given to the details of administering an ancient corporation. Not only did Robinson flatly decline the honor but he retired to his country estate in order to escape the jurisdiction of the local civic authorities. The company laid him and certain other recalcitrant members under bond, but Robinson, finally appearing in court, refused either to serve or to pay a fine. The Lord Mayor thereupon intervened with the ruling that the merchant should pay a fine of £100 by the next day or go to prison.[57] Only then did Robinson consent to negotiate, and the controversy was settled by his paying a fine of £50 with the understanding that he would be relieved of the necessity of serving as a warden for a period of two years.[58] Nothing more is known concerning this John Robinson save that he was alive in 1629, when

[54] *L.C.C.*, *Survey of London*, IX, pt. i, 39.

[55] Beaven, *Aldermen of London*, I, 158; *et cf. ibid.*, I, 246.

[56] C. T. Carr (ed.), *Select Charters of Trading Companies, 1530–1707* (London, 1913), p. 65.

[57] Clode, *Merchant Taylors*, I, 331–32.

[58] *Ibid.*, I, 332–33; Clode, *Memorials*, p. 246.

he was upward of fifty-five years of age. There is reason to believe that his children did not survive him and that most of his considerable estate passed to his next brother, William Robinson, with whom he was long associated in business.

William Robinson, the father of Henry Robinson, was probably the third son of the elder John Robinson, and was born in St. Helen's parish, possibly in 1575. Like most of his family, he married rather late, taking as his wife in June, 1604,[59] Katherine, the daughter of Giffard Watkins, a Northamptonshire gentleman. Nine children were born to this union before Henry Robinson's mother died in childbirth in March, 1617.[60] Robinson was a mercer with large interests abroad, and we know from his son's account that he not infrequently paid lengthy visits to the Continent. The pass issued by the Privy Council to William Robinson, gentleman, and one servant for a business trip to the Low Countries in 1619 almost certainly refers to him.[61] He was a churchwarden of his parish from 1610 to 1612[62] and, in sharp contrast to his elder brother, seems to have taken a keen interest in the affairs of his company. During the reign of James I, Robinson and one Zouch Allen were granted a reversionary interest in the post of registrar of affidavits in the Chancery. Robinson assumed this post in 1629, as the survivor, petitioning the crown to issue a new grant in his name and that of his elder brother, John.[63] Robinson gave a small altar to his church in 1633, inscribed: "The gift of Mr. William Robinson, mercer." He died two years later, in January, 1635,[64] having bequeathed to his church "a messuage or tenement and two yard lands, and a quarter of a yard land in Staveton-upon-the-Hill," Northamptonshire, all his other lands in that community, and one annuity of £2–11–0, to be delivered to the poor of St. Helen's parish "in good sweet wheaten bread" every Sunday.[65]

59 *Registers of St. Helen's, Bishopsgate*, p. 120. 60 *Ibid.*, p. 277.

61 *Acts of P.C.*, 1617–1619, p. 479 (June 19, 1619).

62 *Registers of St. Helen's, Bishopsgate.* 63 *S. P. Dom., Charles I*, clii, #24.

64 *Registers of St. Helen's, Bishopsgate*, p. 289.

65 The payment from the trust amounted to a shilling per week during the seventeenth century.

as water seeks its level, religion has ever followed the whim and policy of the sovereign. If England has any doubt on this score, it need only reflect on the reign of Mary Tudor, when evidently the ruler's stubborn caprice carried more decisive weight than the zeal of a thousand ministers.[50]

These were harsh and unpalatable facts, Parker realized, but they must be accepted if peace and unity were ever to be restored in England. Blind zeal in religion, he maintained, has brought both state and church to the precipice of ruin, though it is not too late to restore sanity and stability within the nation. The truth is that the religious sentiment has long mastered and inflamed men; it must be disciplined, and the church must be restored to its proper place of subordination within the larger interests and preoccupations of mankind. Consequently, the church must be ordered in the interests of the whole of the state of which it is part. We may assume that the state will impose upon the sects the peace of tolerance, not so much because there is philosophical or religious virtue in tolerance as because society can no longer permit the warring of presumptuous communions which strive to rivet their authority upon mankind and seek to invade the heart of sovereignty itself.

The whole history of the clergy would suggest, however, that they will not willingly accept the proper role of the purely spiritual office. For too long they have striven to expand their true function into dominance. They must therefore be tamed and chastened by the firm hand of the civil magistrate. "Let them not contend for supremacy in the highest offices of devotion, but like humble servants let them account it their most supreme service, to attend upon that supremacy. . . . . Let them be jealous of themselves, that no part of honour due to the independent power of princes, may rest upon the secondary instruments but returne to the first and highest movers."[51] They must be sharply punished when they transgress by a hair's breadth the narrow sphere of their proper office. For their relation to the awful majesty of the civil sovereign must be clearly and finally defined. "Peter as a citizen of the common-wealth is a servant to Nero, and though in

[50] *Ibid.*, p. 62.

[51] *Ibid.*, p. 63.

the meere consideration of a Christian, hee has not dependance upon Nero further than is to be testified by suffering under him in ill commands, yet in all civill things, and things indifferent, his dependance remayns undissolved." The civil ruler may not compel the minister to contravene a commandment of God, because the minister, if he be truly righteous, will follow the dictates of his conscience while meekly accepting the punishment of the magistrate. In this extreme instance the violence of the prince is tyrannous, but the authority upon which it rests is not tyranny. "For the same sword which offends one defends many still, and if one here be defended, many must be offended, and the good of the many is to be preferred before the good of one."[52]

Parker's discussion had reduced to narrow limits indeed the power and competence of the clergy and of the ecclesiastical system of which they were the guiding members. The sphere of their capacity was further and sharply limited by his contention that the clergy did not even possess the power to discipline and cleanse the church by administering the penalty of excommunication. This power, as it has developed historically, Parker shrewdly points out, assumes an infallible ability to judge between truth and error and an authority to purge the world of sin and evil which no sane or honest person would dare pretend to possess.[53] The penalty of excommunication, he contends, has simply been used by a clerical caste to enslave mankind and has been lifted as a threat against the power of the prince. It has been nothing more than a kind of private war waged against the integrity and stability of government. It is the foundation upon which the clergy have posited their spurious and vicious claim to supremacy over mankind, and it has brought the church into frontal collision with the whole face of sovereignty. They have ever pretended to possess the power to excommunicate the prince, as if it were possible within law or reason for an inferior power to prevail against the stronger from which the inferior is derived.[54] These men have warred against the majesty of the prince, forgetting that "princes are sacred in respect of their supreme rule, and spirituall in respect of their spirituall rule, and that priests have

[52] *Ibid.*, p. 23. [53] *Ibid.*, pp. 67–69. [54] *Ibid.*, pp. 70–72.

no proper rule at al over mens spirits, or in any ecclesiasticall cases, but derivative. . . . . I may conclude, that there can be no office, nor action so sacred upon earth, for which princes are incompetent in respect of personall sanctity."[55]

In these shrewd and bitter passages, Henry Parker may be said to have laid the intellectual foundations upon which the great Erastian party, composed of lawyers, military leaders, sceptics, and moderates, was to build itself as the Civil War wore on and as the danger of Presbyterian domination in England became steadily greater.[56] Some years before this party began to take effective form under the pressure of political circumstances, Parker had grasped in its full implications the fact that the dynamic of the Civil War involved the repudiation of the organic concept of the Christian society. It should be observed that Parker's remarkable contribution to the religious discussion was made in the early days of the war; that he opened up lines of consideration which were to be exploited and applied by later writers of the Erastian and Independent persuasions. Parker was one of the few men of his generation who belonged to no religious party; indeed, his whole intellectual position would suggest that his only religious interest was comprised in the principle that the civil society must erect adequate safeguards against the divisive effects of religious controversy and sectarian striving for dominance. The whole complex of his thought and the weight of his argument make his intellectual position strikingly similar to that of Francis Osborne and James Harrington, who were to make their contributions some years later.[57] Far more important, however, was the influence which Parker's thought probably had on the greatest of the intellects of the revolutionary era, Thomas Hobbes. There is no evidence that the men knew each other, but there is every evidence that Hobbes accepted not only the basic philosophy underlying Parker's treatment of the religious problem but

[55] *Ibid.*, p. 64.

[56] *Vide* Jordan, *Religious Toleration*, III, 53–57, 64–74; IV, 265–329, for the rise and thought of this group.

[57] For the thought of Francis Osborne, *vide* Jordan, *Religious Toleration*, IV, 240–49; for Harrington, *ibid.*, IV, 281–91.

whole segments of the structure of Parker's argument.[58] Parker sketched in clear and precise outlines the political theory which Hobbes, with one of the most lucid and powerful minds that England has ever known, was to expand into a systematic and documented structure.

Parker, like Hobbes, was interested in religious thought only because of the inseparable connection which it had with political theory during the seventeenth century. He was keenly sensitive to every threat to the stability and strength of the civil society. His reading of history and his observation of the forces of his own age persuaded him that religious institutions, unless restrained by the firm hand of the civil magistrate, offered nothing save danger to mankind. Perhaps no thinker in England before him was quite as bitterly consistent in his distrust and dislike of the clerical mentality, which had for so long guided the thought and molded the political morality of Europe. Certainly no Englishman before him had embraced Erastianism so completely in all its ultimate implications. Parker was almost incidentally to make a notable contribution to the development of religious toleration, not so much because he was persuaded of its philosophical desirability as because he realized, as did few of its proponents, that it was a necessary corollary to the proposition that the state disavowed responsibility for the spiritual welfare of its subjects because it had assumed larger responsibilities for the maintenance of stability, the betterment of the material lot of its citizens, and the ordering of a more complex and delicate society. With a kind of prescience, Henry Parker delineated the thought of a new civilization, a harsher and more realistic civilization, which was to disavow the ethic which had prevailed in western Europe for rather more than a thousand years.

2. HENRY ROBINSON

Henry Robinson made a considerably greater contribution to religious thought than did his contemporary, Henry Parker. It will be observed that both men wanted much the same issue from the civil war which was in progress when their numerous religious

[58] For a discussion of Hobbes's thought, *vide ibid.*, IV, 291–320.

pamphlets were composed: the shattering of ecclesiastical power, the triumph of a lay society, and the establishment of a system of legally imposed religious toleration. But they approached these desired ends by intellectual paths which were quite dissimilar. Parker wished to vest complete responsibility for religious matters in the civil magistrate, in whose Erastian judgment he reposed an almost naïve confidence; Robinson vehemently denied that the magistrate possessed any power whatsoever in spiritual concerns and looked forward to a religious society which would be broken into fragments of opinion and doctrine when liberty of conscience were once established. Parker viewed religion coldly as a dangerous and virulent infection which wasted the sinews of the state; Robinson better understood the nature of faith and the yearnings of the religious mind, and was consequently more realistic in his proposals for the chastening of zeal and the protection of the tender conscience. Both men disliked the clerical mind, both dealt effectively and savagely with Presbyterian intolerance, both reflected the fears and aspirations of the lay mind, and both men were vigorous, bold, and courageous in the range and depth of their writing.

Robinson was more closely allied with sympathetic groups, which had been pressed into some cohesion by the centrifugal force of Calvinistic rigidity, than was the stalwart and somewhat contemptuous Parker. Though quite evidently a member of no religious group, Robinson allied himself with the Independents, who, as we have previously observed, were called into existence as a party to oppose the threat of Presbyterian intolerance and the insistent Calvinistic demand that an exclusive church, supported by the power of the civil magistrate, be erected in England.[59] This group was amorphous, having been drawn from many elements in English political and religious life. But it was quickly united in defense of the principle of religious toleration. Moreover, Robinson was closely associated with a number of men, belonging to no religious party, whose temper was rationalistic and sceptical. He was disposed, in view of his grave concern for the

[59] *Vide* Jordan, *Religious Toleration*, III, 347–451, for a discussion of the rise, contribution, and decline of the party.

future of English religious life, from 1643 to 1646 to ally himself with any men or any group which would vigorously oppose the Presbyterian ambition and, as a corollary, which would lend support to the high end of attaining freedom of worship.

Robinson's thought on the complex problems of religion was at once mature and catholic. He saw issues clearly, met them with singular courage, and discussed them with persuasive skill. It is probable that he made the most significant of the theoretical contributions to the principles of religious liberty in an age which discussed the problems involved in a vast, learned, and stimulating literature. Certainly he was the first Englishman, without the interest of a particular communion in mind, to lend systematic philosophical defense to religious liberty. And, it should be emphasized, he pleaded for religious liberty and not for toleration.

Above all else Henry Robinson was the apostle of the lay intelligence which during the revolutionary period was able finally to secure leadership in English thought. Perhaps no development in the history of modern culture is quite as significant as the passing of moral and intellectual leadership from the clerical to the lay society. In particular, the discussion and solution of the complex problems imposed upon the nation by a long and bitter religious conflict were during the era of the Civil War taken over, rather violently, by laymen unversed in the niceties of theological debate and unsympathetic with the traditions and aspirations of the clerical mind. The lay mind was to triumph in England during this period, and Henry Robinson must be regarded as one of the most important of the powerful and influential group of laymen who sought successfully to dispose of questions which for a millennium had been regarded as without the province of secular thought. Robinson confessed, reminiscently, in his *Briefe Considerations, concerning the Advancement of Trade and Navigation* (1649), that in the recent conflict when liberty of conscience was at stake he had published his most powerful writings anonymously, "not so much for safety of my person, which yet could not escape," as because the people at large still expected these transcendent questions to be discussed and resolved by the clergy.[60]

[60] Henry Robinson, *Briefe considerations, concerning the advancement of trade and navigation, etc.* (London, 1649), Pref.

Robinson was deeply persuaded that religious dissensions and conflicts had already ruined much of the Continent and that they threatened the integrity and stability of his own beloved England. He was convinced that the new society which he envisaged, liberal in government, active in trade, progressive in social policy, and tolerant in religion, could be attained only by the subordination of institutional religion to the larger and more compelling needs of mankind. He realized that the modern world had grown at once complex and fragile; that the good life must now be conceived in terms which bore little relation indeed to the medieval civilization which was past. Robinson, like Parker, saw the outlines of the future with startling clarity and prescience.

Henry Robinson's numerous religious pamphlets were all written during the critical period 1643–1646, when it seemed probable that an intolerant and disciplined national church would be imposed by the Presbyterians upon a nation which had only recently risen against the lesser tyranny of the Anglican Establishment as administered by Laud. Since all these works were published anonymously, it will be appropriate to discuss in some detail the list of books which we have attributed to Robinson.

His first pamphlet, published anonymously in 1643, was entitled *Liberty of Conscience: Or, the Sole Means To Obtaine Peace and Truth.* This rather lengthy work (10+62 pp.) marks Robinson's greatest contribution to the religious discussion of the generation and should be regarded as one of the three or four really great pleas for liberty of conscience as a philosophical and moral right.[61] The work was first attributed to Robinson by the Presbyterian protagonist, Thomas Edwards,[62] and, somewhat later, by Prynne. Robinson probably had this tract particularly in mind when he mentioned in 1649 that he had published anonymously numerous

[61] Gardiner, who attributed the work to Robinson, held it in very high esteem. He remarked that the pamphlet "serves as a high-water mark of the controversy on religious liberty in the seventeenth century" (S. R. Gardiner, *History of the Great Civil War, 1642–1649* [London, 1904–5], I, 290).

[62] Thomas Edwards, *The first and second part of Gangraena, etc.* (London, 1646), I, 96. In his list of sectaries, and other dangerous men, Edwards mentions "Mr. Robinson who is commonly reported to be the author of that book called Liberty of Conscience, printed in the yeere 1643, and by Mr. Pryn spoke of as the supposed author of many other scandalous books."

defenses of liberty of conscience.[63] Firth, in a careful article in the *English Historical Review* in 1894, established the attribution with reasonable certainty.[64] Later bibliographers and historians have all agreed that Robinson was the author of this remarkable treatise.[65] Moreover, the internal evidence and numerous, if somewhat inconclusive, references in Robinson's economic tracts would seem to establish his authorship.

Four pamphlets were published anonymously in the next year, 1644, which may be ascribed to Robinson with some certainty. The important *John the Baptist* was regarded by the Presbyterian leaders with quite as much enmity as they bestowed upon Robinson's earlier work. It was answered by the great Calvinistic divine, George Gillespie, in his *A Late Dialogue betwixt a Civilian and a Divine* (1644) and in his *Wholsome Severity Reconciled with Christian Liberty* (1645), but Gillespie was evidently uncertain concerning its authorship. Samuel Rutherford attacked it venomously in his *A Free Disputation against Pretended Liberty of Conscience* (1649), linking Robinson as a libertine with other notable protagonists of religious liberty.[66] He charged that the author was "sure a wilderness man void of reason," who was promulgating a doctrine which could have no other issue than the destruction of society.[67] Modern commentators have been in agreement in attributing this work to Robinson, an ascription which would seem to be confirmed by a careful examination of the text.[68]

[63] Robinson, *Briefe considerations*, Pref.

[64] C. H. Firth, "An Anonymous Tract on 'Liberty of Conscience,' " *English Historical Review*, IX, 715–16.

[65] The Thomason catalogue, the B.M. catalogue, the McAlpin catalogue, the *D.N.B.*, and William Haller, *Tracts on Liberty in the Puritan Revolution, 1638–1647* (New York, 1934), are all in agreement on this point.

[66] Rutherford linked Robinson with John Austin, the Catholic author of the notable *Christian Moderator* (*vide* Jordan, *Religious Toleration*, IV, 446–52), Roger Williams (*ibid.*, III, 472–506), and John Goodwin (*ibid.*, III, 376–412).

[67] Samuel Rutherford, *A free disputation against pretended liberty of conscience tending to resolve doubts . . . . contending for lawlesse liberty, or licentious toleration of sects and heresies* (London, 1649), pp. 342, 343–48, 349.

[68] The McAlpin catalogue, the *D.N.B.*, and Haller, *Tracts on Liberty*, I, 67, agree in ascribing the work to Robinson.

The other works published in 1644, which have been ascribed to him, *An Answer to Mr. William Prynn's Twelve Questions concerning Church Government*, *Certain Briefe Observations and Antiquaeries*, and *An Answer to Mr. John Dury His Letter Which He Writ from the Hague*, were almost as certainly written and, for that matter, published by Robinson. The point of view is almost identical with that expressed in his earlier works, there is strong evidence that the author of the first and third of these pamphlets had lived abroad, and all are animated by the secular spirit so typical of Robinson. Moreover, the consensus of bibliographical opinion seems agreed in attributing these pamphlets to Robinson.[69]

We may be reasonably sure, as well, that three important pamphlets were written and published by Robinson in 1645, when the controversy between the Presbyterians and the Independent-Erastian bloc was at a fever heat. These treatises were *A Short Answer to A. S.*, *A Moderate Answer to Mr. Prins Full Reply*, and *The Falsehood of Mr. William Pryn's Truth Triumphing*. On internal evidence the first of these works may almost certainly be at-

[69] Prynne flatly accused Robinson of having written the *Answer to Mr. William Prynn's Twelve Questions* (Prynne, *A fresh discovery*, p. 4) and of having published it on his private press (*ibid.*, p. 6). Similarly in his *Truth triumphing over falshood, antiquity over novelty, etc.* (London, 1645) he denounced the author as being "destructive to the very fundamentall power and being of parliaments," because he would deny all religious authority to the magistrate. Moreover, he accused Robinson of having been a libeler of the Presbyterians, the Scots, and those who desired the imposition of order in religion (Prynne, *Truth triumphing*, *Epist.*, pp. 125, 149, 152). This work is likewise ascribed to Robinson by *H. & L.*, the Thomason catalogue, the McAlpin catalogue, Firth (*E.H.R.*, IX, 716), and Haller, *Tracts*, I, 67. The B.M. catalogue errs in attributing it to Henry Burton. Robinson is not at his best in this work, which was hastily composed, repetitious in content, and turgid in style.

The *Certain briefe observations and antiquaeries* is attributed to Robinson by the McAlpin catalogue, the *D.N.B.*, and the Newberry catalogue. The pamphlet was answered by Prynne in his *A full reply to certaine briefe observations and antiqueries on Master Prynnes twelve questions about church government, etc.* (London, 1644). Prynne made no attempt to identify the author, save to suggest that he was an Independent, a generic term of abuse as employed by him.

The *Answer to Mr. John Dury* was almost certainly written by Robinson, who knew Dury and who was closely associated with Samuel Hartlib, whose views are in part under discussion in this work. The McAlpin catalogue, *H. & L.*, the *D.N.B.*, and the Thomason catalogue agree in attributing it to Robinson. The B.M. catalogue attributes it to Henry Burton, while Haller (*Tracts*, I, 65) is inclined to attribute it to someone in the Independent party.

tributed to Robinson, though there has been considerable bibliographical confusion on the question of attribution.[70] The second pamphlet, though attributed to John Goodwin by the Huntington Library catalogue, the British Museum catalogue, and other sources, was likewise probably written by Robinson.[71] The third was without doubt from Robinson's pen,[72] since Prynne in his *Fresh Discovery* named him as the author and publisher.[73] The pamphlet was vigorously attacked by Edwards in his *Gangraena* and by Bastwick in his *Independency Not Gods Ordinance*, though neither of these writers attempts to identify the author. Firth accepted Prynne's attribution on the ground that similarity of style and temper of argument proved that Robinson had written the pamphlet.[74] Most of the modern commentators on the subject have accepted this conclusion.[75]

Finally, Robinson published in 1646 his *Some Few Considerations Propounded*, a compilation of letters exchanged between him and John Dury. Though published anonymously, the title-page itself clearly indicates that Robinson was responsible for the pamphlet, which is perhaps the least valuable of all his numerous works dealing with the problem of religion.

In 1646, when it became apparent that the dominant position

[70] The B.M. catalogue and the Bodleian catalogue agree in attributing it to Robinson. Haller likewise attributes it to him without hesitation. The McAlpin catalogue ascribes it to John Goodwin, probably because of confusion of the title with Goodwin's *A reply of two of the brethren to A. S., etc.* (London, 1644) and because of Prynne's incorrect attribution to that author (*A fresh discovery*, p. 4).

[71] My judgment on this attribution is tentative. The pamphlet certainly could not have been written, as has been suggested, by John Goodwin, since the conception of the church elaborated in the work in no sense agrees with the very definite views entertained by him on that subject in 1645. The style and vocabulary, the repetitive argument, and the piling-up of evidence are strongly reminiscent of Robinson's known works. But the tone of the pamphlet is too theological and the point of view too specifically sectarian to lend incontrovertible support to the attribution to Robinson.

[72] This view is supported by almost conclusive evidence in Robinson's *Briefe considerations*. The *D.N.B.*, Dexter, and the McAlpin catalogue likewise attribute the pamphlet to Robinson.

[73] Prynne, *A fresh discovery*, pp. 4, 6.

[74] Firth, *English Historical Review*, IX, 716.

[75] The *D.N.B.*, the McAlpin catalogue, the Thomason catalogue, the B.M. catalogue, and Haller (*Tracts*, I, 67) agree in ascribing the work to Robinson. Internal evidence in the pamphlet would seem to me to be conclusive on the point.

so long exercised by the Presbyterians in Parliament and in the counsels of the revolutionary party was rapidly disintegrating, Robinson turned from absorption with the religious issues of his age to the political and economic problems with which he was personally more vitally concerned.[76] It will be observed that the weight of Robinson's influence and his masterly skill in controversy were thrown into the struggle against ecclesiastical tyranny during the months when the danger was greatest. His contribution to the development of the theory of religious toleration was of cardinal importance, and it was made at a critical moment in English history when courage, vision, and an almost intuitive perception of the momentous issues at stake were required. It would be difficult, indeed, to overestimate Henry Robinson's significance in the history of English thought during this seminal era.

Robinson and Parker were in complete agreement in their fervent devotion to the principles of religious toleration and in their earnest desire to bring religious dissension to an end by curbing with steely secular restraints the restless clerical mind. But here the agreement ends. For Parker was completely Erastian, exhibiting little understanding of or sympathy for the religious emotion and proposing only that it be strictly restrained by the civil authority. Robinson, on the other hand, within the framework of the lay individualism which was destroying the structure of religious institutions in England, was evidently a religious man, who found a solution for the problems which harassed England in complete religious freedom, in the fragmentization of religious institutions, and in the complete withdrawal of the civil magistrate from any responsibility for the spiritual welfare of the nation. Parker proposed as his panacea a national church, sternly ordered by the sovereign, devoid of spiritual vitality, and harmlessly administered as a department of state. Robinson, on the contrary, suggested an essentially anarchical solution which ex-

[76] Robinson has occasionally been regarded as the author of three additional pamphlets. *The araignement of Mr. Persecution, etc.* (London, 1645), *Martin's Eccho: or a remonstrance, etc.* (London, 1645), and *A sacred decretall, or hue and cry, etc.* (London, 1645?) have occasionally been attributed to Robinson because of Prynne's incorrect ascription in his *A fresh discovery* (pp. 9–10). The first two items were certainly by Richard Overton, who subsequently acknowledged the authorship. The third may tentatively be attributed to Overton as well.

ploited the institutional liberty of Independency and which, in the final analysis, reduced faith and organized religion to a completely individualistic basis.

Robinson's thought was animated by a deeply rooted rationalism and by a brooding scepticism typical of the radical group of secular intellectuals of which he and Parker were leaders. The London merchant was persuaded that the ideal of an exclusive church based upon a complete and infallible body of truth was quite fantastic, simply because men do not possess capacities wherewith truth may be finally known. He was therefore impelled to the conviction that truth can have none other than a subjective meaning—that it is most effectively advanced when the individual conscience is left free to seek it. This wholly individualistic philosophy was of course in flat denial of the organic conception of truth to which most Englishmen still lent lip service and which underlay the strong conviction that some ordered national church must replace the episcopal establishment. Moreover, Robinson's theory of the nature of truth and his noble defense of the sanctity of the individual reason formed the basis of his theory of religious liberty, a theory which he expressed unequivocally because he was firmly persuaded that religion must in the last analysis be regarded as a lonely quest which each man makes for the elusive substance of truth.

The honest search for truth, Robinson submitted, is actually more important than its attainment, since truth is relative as between men and ages and, for that matter, within the individual's own experience. No guide can accompany and direct man in his quest for truth save the reason with which God has so richly endowed him. Reason is inviolable and is the most precious of all the gifts which providence has bestowed upon us. Hence, "ought [not] such as goe about to fasten a yoake of their owne doctrine and opinions on others, be accounted the most ignorant, absurd, presumptuous, and the greatest enemies both to God and man of any people under heaven; deserving death more then a murderer or traitor?"[77]

[77] [Henry Robinson], *An answer to Mr. William Prynn's Twelve Questions concerning Church Government, etc.* (London, 1644), pp. 4–5.

The individual man, then, lies under the grave responsibility of searching throughout his life for truth, a responsibility which he cannot possibly discharge unless his mind and body are freed from all compulsion and restraint. If this precious freedom is granted him, he will find at least saving truth, though his conclusions may differ radically from those of his fellows and from the formulations of the organized churches. The orthodox have ever erred, and that impiously, in their persuasion that religious truth may be easily ascertained and that it may be congealed in the molds of creed. The Bible is so vague, our capacities are so limited, and our eyes so dim that we can do no more than work out our own salvation, fully aware of the fact that our delineation of truth has none save a subjective validity.[78] Truth, Robinson submitted, is actually "a jewell which lyes out of sight . . . . in the bowels of many reasons."[79] The totality of truth and knowledge is in the mind of God, while its substance amongst men is broken into individual particles which, none the less, have their due place in the mosaic of the whole.[80]

The fact must be recognized, Robinson insists, that men for a full thousand years have been pitifully wrong in their persuasion, born at once of pride and fear, that they could define and enforce an infallible system of truth. But the shattering of this delusion and the emancipation of reason should occasion no misgivings. For it is probable that God has obscured the face of truth in order to "make us more diligent and inquisitive in the search for truth, that we might not be over confident and presumptuous of our opinions," and to persuade us that every man must enjoy a perfect liberty in his solitary search for saving faith.[81] Hence the man who has found truth sufficient unto his own needs will be quietly

[78] [Henry Robinson], *John the Baptist, forerunner of Christ Iesus; Or, a necessity for liberty of conscience, etc.* (London, 1644), p. 43.

[79] [Henry Robinson], *Certain briefe observations and antiquaeries: on Master Prin's twelve questions about church-government* (London, 1644), p. 1.

[80] This argument is startlingly similar to that of Donne's (John Donne, *The poems of John Donne, etc.* [Oxford, 1912], I, 156–57; John Donne, *Fifty sermons, etc.* [London, 1649], p. 214 *et passim*), though there is no evidence that Robinson was directly influenced by him.

[81] [Robinson], *John the Baptist*, p. 43.

confident in his own mind, but will be infinitely humble and charitable before God and his fellows. For truth is necessarily sure of itself, "passion and railing were never wont to be her companions; peace, gentlenesse, and meeknesse ever attended her as handmaids."[82] Such a man will know that truth is held relatively and that he himself may tomorrow discover that the truth of today is faulty and incomplete. "God reveales more and more of the gospel every day in a fuller and clearer manner," as men and churches grow in knowledge, maturity, and spiritual stature.[83] Truth, then, is organic, and the presupposition which we have about it, whether as men or as institutions, must be fluid and tentative. To define the body of religious truth rigorously and intolerantly may well be branded as an assault upon God and as an impious attempt to destroy his church and truth.

We move slowly and haltingly toward fulness of knowledge, learning by our errors and advancing in quite direct relation to our personal scepticism. The ideal of a perfect truth, like that of a perfect church, should be steadily before our eyes, but we must not and dare not freeze into rigid formulas the imperfect knowledge of any particular time or place, or prescriptively declare that the Kingdom of God has been attained. We have prated too shrilly of one true religion, one way to salvation, and of one faith. "The papists, Lutherans, Calvinists, all Episcopal and Presbyterian disciplined men generally are of this opinion; each of them, whole nations and people, damn for the most part hand over head, all other professions but his own." This intolerance is at once destructive to the vitality of the church and ruinous to the pursuit of truth. "Would it not be wonder," Robinson warmly exclaims, "if this circumference, this little continent of earth, should satisfie the vast desires of such, who seeme to think, that the heavens so infinitely more capacious, were only made for them and some few of their familiars."[84] When we rule so im-

[82] [Henry Robinson], *A moderate answer to Mr. Prins full reply to certaine observations on his first twelve questions . . . . a short description of the Congregationall way discovered. Some arguments for indulgence to tender consciences modestly propounded* (London, 1645), p. 1.

[83] *Ibid.*, p. 3.

[84] [Henry Robinson], *A short answer to A. S. alias Adam Steuarts second part of his overgrown Duply to the two brethren, etc.* (London, 1645), p. 26.

periously and infallibly in our definition of truth, we are guilty of the shocking impiety of excluding from salvation, indeed from the hope of salvation, all the pagans, the Jews, the Muslims, the Catholics, and the protestant communions that differ from us. No sane man would brand his faulty conscience and his imperfect mind with such an hideous intolerance.

Above all, we must not so narrowly and rigidly draw the ambit of our definitions that if we happen to be in error it will be impossible to extricate ourselves.[85] Robinson maintained that this had actually happened at various times in European history when the "beast of persecution" ranged abroad beyond control. No reasonable man can deny this allegation when he recalls that men have, on the whole, lived and died in the religion in which they were born, whether that faith happened to be true or false. Men have exhibited quite as zealous devotion to error as to truth and have been quite as willing to die martyrs for falsehood as for truth. This has been true simply because they have never had an opportunity to try all faiths freely and to examine doctrines sceptically, and because they have been despoiled of that integrity of mind which is the birthright of all mankind.[86] Men must enjoy a complete emancipation of reason, therefore, if religious vitality is to be restored and if we are to progress in the quest for truth. No man can go faster than his own reason takes him. "God hath put the understanding in a man, to be a light to his path; a mans understanding is to a mans practice, as the eye to the body, without which it cannot walk safely."[87]

The search for truth, to which we have been commanded by God, consequently requires an untrammeled liberty of conscience and a complete freedom of worship. The orthodox will immediately allege that such a policy will unchain error and bring about the ruin of the church. But these inflamed spirits must not be heeded, since they understand neither the meaning of truth nor the nature of the church. Error and heresy are already rife in

[85] *Ibid.*, p. 28.

[86] [Henry Robinson], *Liberty of conscience; or the sole means to obtaine peace and truth. Not onely reconciling his majesty with his subjects, but all Christian states and princes to one another, etc.* (London, 1643), p. 4.

[87] [Robinson], *A moderate answer*, p. 37.

England. But error does no harm and, when vigorously expounded, possesses the positive virtue of stimulating discussion and causing all men rationally to measure their own beliefs.[88] It is better, far better, that "many false doctrines were published, especially with a good intention and out of weaknesse only, then that one sound truth should be forcibly smothered or wilfully concealed."[89] And it is infinitely better that men should be reasonably wedded to an error than that they should entertain no rational convictions whatsoever.[90] Many an heretic has gladly delivered his body to be burned as the token of a sublime faith; surely truth may meet error with an equal confidence.[91] No man who walks abroad in the light of reason in patient and honest search for truth should be without our compassion, because such a man is a true and earnest son of God and is in the way of salvation.

The seventeenth century has bequeathed to us no more noble defense of the integrity and sovereignty of the human reason. Robinson, it will have been observed, was evidently a sceptic in his conviction that religious truth could never be exactly or fully ascertained. He wrote persuasively at a time when men in England were being compelled by the harsh tuition of history to abandon reluctantly the age-old conception of an infallible body of dogma. Robinson would have freed the human mind from all external restraints, and he boldly maintained that the error into which men must fall had not only a subjective but a social value. He was contemptuous of those theological tags, those surviving religious mores, which his incisive intelligence taught him had neither meaning nor relevance in the modern world.

As one might expect, Robinson defined the true church in terms which accented not only the subjective nature of truth but which required that the institutional frame of man's worship must be voluntary in origin and tolerant in practice. He submitted that a true church under the gospel was "a company of believers, joining themselves together in the name of Christ, for the enjoy-

88 [Robinson], *An answer to Mr. William Prynn's Twelve Questions*, pp. 17–18.

89 [Robinson], *Liberty of conscience*, p. 56.

90 *Ibid.*, pp. 51–52.

91 *Ibid.*, pp. 58–59.

ment of such ordinances, and exercise of such spirituall government, as the Lord hath apointed for his worship and honour, and their mutuall edification."[92]

Neither the institutions nor the doctrines of such a church can be rigidly or exclusively defined, and it is for that very reason that the senseless disputes over these matters have been so virulent and exhausting. Gradually, however, reasonable men have become less certain of their infallibility. They have come to realize that "no church can possibly be sure to be without a mixture of errour and superstition," since God reveals his truth to us but partially and gradually.[93] No church and no man must dare to place limits upon the free play of the gospel or the restless search of free men for truth, until it can be demonstrated that a particular church enjoys, self-evidently, perfection of truth. Faith, then, is organic; men and churches grow slowly in spiritual stature and knowledge; to place restraints upon the search for truth is a violation of the very nature of the Christian religion.[94]

This is not to suggest, however, that particular churches do not possess the capacity to determine whether those persons who voluntarily seek membership in their communion are deemed to enjoy Christ's grace.[95] Furthermore, the congregation evidently has the power to maintain internal discipline by excommunicating those who, by its definition, sin or fail to exhibit the marks of grace. But this discipline is limited to the congregation, it is not buttressed by civil penalties, and it is applied only to those who have voluntarily submitted. In England, sinful and religious men alike have been tyrannously pressed into a church which, in a frenzied search for a dead uniformity, corrupted itself and neglected the true discipline with which it was vested. Only gradually can any church attain purity and perfection; it need not and must not concern itself too rigorously with defining the line which

[92] [Henry Robinson], *An answer to Mr. John Dury his letter which he writ from the Hague, to Mr. Thomas Goodwin. Mr. Philip Nye. Mr. Samuel Hartlie. etc.* (London, 1644), p. 1.

[93] [Robinson], *Liberty of conscience*, pp. 48–49.

[94] *Ibid.*, p. 50.

[95] [Robinson], *An answer to Mr. John Dury*, p. 2.

separates truth from error. It can only hope to consist of those who "can be judged by the saints to be elect. If men be not saved, its not because the church is deceived, but themselves: the Church goes only on these probable rules of judging by which the word prescribes."[96]

In the true church, therefore, emphasis will be laid at all times on enlarging the opportunities for gaining truth and for preaching the Word of God; not upon the negative and destructive obsession of ferreting out uncertain errors by uncertain criteria of truth. The formal organization of the true, visible church is of very slight importance indeed. The true church is constituted by the separation of men not content with the stature of the truth which they possess from the corruption of churches in which salvation may be gained, but which do not provide perfect opportunities for worship and for the eternal quest for truth.[97] Men must ever be free, therefore, to separate from existing churches in order to join what seems to them a purer communion or, if necessary, to walk alone.[98] For the responsibility vested in us to seek truth and to attain salvation is so intensely personal that it cannot be discharged by a formal and ignorant compliance with the dicta of any church, however pure it may be.

Robinson here propounds and defends an individualistic conception of religion and faith which may be regarded as the central pillar of his religious philosophy. He would dissolve the hard shell of institutional religion, which in his view had been responsible for erecting and defending an arbitrary and intolerant tyranny over men's minds and souls, by declaring that the individual man was the highest common denominator in all matters of faith. The church, in his judgment, could in the last analysis be defined as an individual man, earnestly seeking truth and salvation, whom conscience had constrained to separate from all existing communions. Robinson, in sharp contrast to Parker, denied that the magistrate could treat with religion on any other terms. Robinson resolved the troubled question of the national church and its discipline by declaring that neither existed.

[96] [Robinson], *A moderate answer*, pp. 29–30.

[97] [Robinson], *An answer to Mr. John Dury*, pp. 4–5.

[98] *Ibid.*, p. 12.

Robinson therefore regards the febrile discussions of the form of the national church which should replace the shattered episcopal structure as at once pointless and dangerous. The concept of a national church is, in fact, contrary to the nature of the church and the spirit of Christianity. "Doe we thinke that Gods salvation is also nationall," Robinson enquired.[99] Those orthodox spirits in England who labor so earnestly to secure the erection of still another rigid and intolerant national church simply prosecute intensely personal ambitions, not God's design. They absurdly maintain that seas and rivers can form the boundaries between the churches of God, between truth and error.[100] They violate the letter and spirit of the scripture in a desperate search for sanctions with which they may bind the conscience of the nation in chains to be riveted on by the civil magistrate at their command. They would require England to walk sedately and cheerfully to gallows which they erect for the extinction of faith and freedom. They search the New Testament in vain for precedents which will shore up the national church which they desire to found and for the engines of persecution with which they would defend it. These men have demanded that the state prostitute itself to their infamous ends and have raised the cry of sedition against those who require freedom as the badge of human dignity and the guaranty of a free conscience. They quite forget that the Christian, as Christian, has no interest in the form of the civil power so long as sovereignty does not invade the area of religious freedom which must remain sacrosanct if a society is to be denominated Christian.[101]

This conception of the nature of the church and of the sanctity of the religious conscience caused Robinson to view with the greatest alarm the steady and persistent efforts of the Presbyterians, supported by the weight of the Scottish alliance, to impose upon England a rigidly defined, exclusive, and intolerant ecclesiastical system. Robinson, with Parker, was one of the first and most effective of the thinkers who launched against the Presbyterians, then high in prestige and authority, a ceaseless, con-

[99] [Robinson], *Liberty of conscience*, p. 27.

[100] [Robinson], *A moderate answer*, p. 4.

[101] [Robinson], *An answer to Mr. William Prynn's Twelve Questions*, pp. 11 ff.

centrated, and skilful attack. Robinson's works were, as we have seen, profoundly disturbing to the champions of orthodoxy, who were quick to join him in bitter controversy. In the ensuing controversy, Robinson rendered signal service by providing the Independent-Erastian bloc, both in and out of Parliament, with a theory of the church and a conception of the religious society which made it possible to rally the overwhelming weight of English opinion against the vociferous Presbyterian minority and which was to be of profound significance in shaping revolutionary policy in ecclesiastical affairs under the Commonwealth and Protectorate.

The Puritan party, out of which Presbyterianism in England had been derived, had been completely inconsistent, Robinson maintained, in its attitude toward the problem of the national church and in its theory of uniformity. Before the convention of the Long Parliament, no group in England denounced religious intolerance so fervently or defended spiritual freedom so manfully. Now, however, he declares, they have apparently forgotten that the Puritans were driven from England to "carry with them their gifts, arts, and manufactures into other countries, to the greatest detriment of this commonwealth." They do not recall, Robinson sharply reminded England, that a systematic effort to extirpate their communion failed, just as all similar repressive undertakings must fail. Certainly men who so recently labored under such a yoke can scarcely have the arrogance to reply that God delivered them out of persecution in order to make them a scourge against their brethren.[102] It is incredible that these men, who a few short months ago denounced the bishops in such ringing phrases, now regard themselves as ordained "to establish a dragon on his throne in stinting the whole worship of the great God of heaven, in manacling the conscience of His saints their brethren, and not suffering them to pay their very tythings, or perform the least parcell of their duty unto the only creator of the world, save in such manner as they allow of, and impose upon them."[103]

[102] [Robinson], *Liberty of conscience*, pp. 31–32.

[103] [Robinson], *John the Baptist*, Pref.

The Presbyterians have speedily cast their intolerant pretensions into a systematic theory of an exclusive church, supported by deliberate and vigorous persecution, which, if permitted in England, would bring ruin to the nation and render frustrate every aim of the Civil War. They have no better proposal than to take up the bloody cudgels of force so recently laid down by the papists and the prelates.[104] England would be mad indeed were it to permit men crazed by such delusions and tormented by such disordered dreams to cast the design of its future. Moreover, the Presbyterians have ignored the fate of the persecuting systems which have so recently been shattered in England. They quite forget that they expose themselves to an appalling danger when they seek to found their system upon the insecure approbation of the civil power. For the magistrate will not for long tolerate their arrogance, their contriving, and their ruinous war upon dissenting opinion. The ruler will say, as logically he must, "These Presbyterian churches are growne corrupt, their way of government was never apostolical and good, they tyrannize over their brethren insted of feeding them, aiming at no reformation soe much as to get themselves into the fattest benifices," and hence the state may best be preserved by banishing them from the nation.[105] If the Calvinists are constrained by no instincts of piety and charity, they should at least be sobered by the reflection that they too are likely to perish from the edge of the sword which they would now wield against those who differ from them.

Far more important than these politic considerations, however, was the fact that the Presbyterians threatened England with a virulent and almost mad spiritual arrogance. They displayed a temper which was extremely dangerous not only to the fabric of the civil society but to faith as well. The mark of blood, Robinson soberly alleges, is upon them. They have explicitly revealed in their writings and in the formulations of their Assembly at Westminster that they require the assistance of a puppet magistrate who will banish or destroy all those whom they choose to brand as heretics. These men, blinded by an incredible arrogance,

[104] [Robinson], *Liberty of conscience*, pp. 32, 36.

[105] [Robinson], *A short answer to A. S.*, p. 8.

cheerfully assume the moral responsibility for persecution. They seem quite careless of the fact that if blood be shed "by their authority or approbation," it must be "accounted for by them, as if they themselves had sat upon the bench, passed sentence, and beene executioners."[106] Neither Christianity nor reason confers upon any group of men such hideous and demoniacal power. The Presbyterians offer no better prescription for the cure of the wounds which have so weakened England than to override and destroy opinions and points of view held by Christian men endowed with quite as much faith, devotion, and tenacity as their own.[107] They would, for example, destroy their Independent brethren, from whom they scarcely differ in doctrine, by precisely that authority which the papists pretend for the scourge of persecution with which they laid waste a continent.[108] Nor, Robinson concludes, are the orthodox pretensions empty rhetoric, for in New England the rigorous party, having laid hands upon the civil sword, have systematically sought the extirpation of all dissent.[109] This is the paradise of harmony and Christian fellowship to which the divines at Westminster and their supporters have beckoned a free and pious nation.

Robinson charged with acid eloquence that the Presbyterians could advance no other claim to such "murderous authority" than their own spiritual rigidity. They have wrenched and violated the scriptures without exhibiting an iota of authority to support the punishment of heresy by the civil power. Surely they would not suggest that their Assembly orders faith for the Christian world; surely they do not seek to "condemne the whole world into spirituall captivity, because their phansies tell them it is for Gods glory and the churches weale that it should bee so."[110] They have advanced the most outrageous claims to a spiritual authority which can hardly be granted by England just because the Presbyterians desire to wield it. It "rests on you," Robinson exclaimed, "to prove, or not require obedience as though the

[106] *Ibid.*, pp. 9–10.

[107] [Robinson], *An answer to Mr. William Prynn's Twelve Questions*, pp. 14–15.

[108] [Robinson], *A short answer to A. S.*, pp. 21–22.

[109] *Ibid.*, pp. 23–25.

[110] *Ibid.*, pp. 15–16.

Holy Ghost were in your bosom, were at your beck."[111] Reasonable men will know that, when God chooses to speak through an assembly, its formulations will be transcendently clear to all Christian men and women. The Presbyterians have no other recourse, so long as men of tender conscience cannot accept the truth which they so imperiously proclaim, than earnestly and patiently to persuade. But their divines do not exhibit these Christian virtues. "They are the Presbyterian doctors whose asses must passe for trumpeters, and whose geese are swans; whose wares must be thought better, and payde for deerer than any of their neighbours; whatever they say must be accounted seraphical; and mechanicks, all lay-men wave their owne reason and religion whilst they worship theirs."[112]

No seventeenth-century writer assailed the Presbyterian pretensions with such cold fury as did Robinson. He does not display, as did Parker, a pronounced anticlerical bias. But he was even quicker than his contemporary to detect the danger inherent for society in the rigid and calculative design of a Puritan minority which had been pressed into an extremist position during the Laudian regime. Robinson steadily maintained that the Civil War had as its objectives the widening of English freedom in the three great areas of the religion, the constitution, and the economy of the nation. He almost intuitively realized that the Presbyterian design for the church lay squarely athwart the revolutionary aspirations which molded his thought. He accordingly entered the lists against Westminster at a very early date with an extraordinarily effective pen. The great danger with which England was threatened by Presbyterian orthodoxy was, he averred, the studied design to impose a spiritual tyranny upon the nation—a design far more dangerous than the prelatical because it was more systematic, more ruthless, and more capably led.

The Presbyterians, Robinson alleged, have been blinded by their zeal and confounded by their ambition. They maintain, on the one hand, that the church must be national and catholic in scope and membership, while, on the other hand, they seek to impose upon that church a far more rigid discipline than any

[111] *Ibid.*, p. 16.

[112] *Ibid.*, p. 17.

national church has ever exercised. This means, if it means anything in reason, that they would forcibly erect a national church which they would then decimate by wholesale excommunication and persecution.[113] This position is completely illogical in theory, while its application would be disastrous in fact.

Equally fantastic is the fact that the Presbyterians have framed their entire structure of government and discipline from the spe cial mandates of God for the Jewish people. They seek to apply the Old Testament literally in the modern world, insensible of the truism that with Christ's coming the Law gave way to the Gospel.[114] Indeed, they have ransacked the Bible in their search for precedents and have violated the meaning of Holy Writ in order to support a preconceived design which has no relation whatsoever to Christianity. They have deliberately sought to discover ways and means for enslaving the magistrate in order to impose upon him and his people the arbitrary will of an irresponsible clergy.[115] They have taken advantage of the distraction of a weary nation to propose the peace of slavery and to fasten their glosses upon the Christian conscience. Their vaunted godly order consists of nothing else than that yoke of persecution which has for so long stifled the vitality of Christian faith.[116] It would be far better for England to enjoy liberty of conscience under a tolerant Catholic or under a reasonable Turk than to submit to the governance of the godly.

In his sharp controversy with the doughty Prynne, Robinson attacked with great vigor and effectiveness the spiritual tyranny which the Presbyterians sought to impose. He reminded England that the true ministers of Christ had ever been gentle and charitable, whereas the "prelaticall presbytery, the pretended ambassa-

[113] [Robinson], *A moderate answer*, pp. 30–31.

[114] "Under the gospel its otherwise; Christ being come himselfe, as king of his Church, hath made a covenant with no nation under heaven, but in every nation he that feares him is accepted with him; his laws being onely spirituall, and that concerning the conscience" (*ibid.*, p. 9).

[115] [Robinson], *A short answer to A. S.*, p. 8.

[116] [Robinson], *John the Baptist*, Pref.

dours of Christ in these times, wee know to bee wolves that worry, sterve or fle[ece] the very lambes of Christ alive."[117] The Presbyterians endeavor to enslave England with a spiritual authority which has no scriptural validity, which invades and usurps the proper functions of the civil state itself.[118] They seek to absorb *in toto* the full authority of the prelates, whom they so recently and so vehemently denounced, as if it availed England "to have the head of one lordly episcopall prelate cut off, when a hydra, a multitude, above 77 times as many Presbyteriall prelates succeed instead thereof."[119] These are dangers which England must face with clear and resolute courage; these are the enemies of freedom which she must overthrow.

Moreover, Robinson submitted, the Presbyterians must be denounced as men who seek to destroy the vitality of faith and the institutions which permit men to worship freely and sincerely. They propose to erect an exclusive system which would utterly destroy the free and voluntary churches which are spiritually and politically necessary in England. They offer instead "a composure and frame of divine service pieced up together into a body by some men, which must serve insteed of gifts to all men and for all times . . . . they doe not only set their posts by Gods posts, but they lay aside his, and enjoine theirs only to be used as fitter for the building." Their purposes and their conceptions are consequently inimical to the vitality of Christianity and lay in ruin the fabric of the Christian Church. It is inconceivable that a nation which has so recently risen in arms against one spiritual tyranny would willingly embrace another.

Indeed, Robinson explicitly affirmed, if England were confronted with the possibility of honest choice between the restoration of episcopacy and the establishment of the Presbyterian system, it would and should choose the prelates. Robinson, like Parker, had no philosophical objection to the episcopal system save that under Laud it had assumed powers not vested in it legally or morally. It may well be, he submitted, that those moderates who

[117] [Henry Robinson], *The falsehood of Mr. William Pryn's Truth Triumphing, in the antiquity of popish princes and parliaments, etc.* (London, 1645), p. 3.

[118] *Ibid.*, pp. 5–6.

[119] *Ibid.*, p. 9.

in the early sessions of the Long Parliament desired simply to chasten the bishops were correct in their judgment. For a moderated episcopacy is infinitely to be preferred before an intolerant Presbyterian establishment.[120] Even Laud, Robinson pointed out, was revealed in his *Diary*, recently published by Prynne, as a man of "a morall noble pious minde, according to such weake principles as hee had beene bred up in"—as a man endowed with a charity which Robinson could not discover in the intransigent Presbyterian party.[121] The ruin which Laud and his prelatical faction brought on the Church of England was entirely occasioned by the "depraved principle of enduring no body of any other religion or opinion but his owne," and by embracing the hideous doctrine of persecution in order to compel the nation to his judgment.[122] In other words, the unlawfulness of episcopacy proceeded not from its form or constitution, but from its frightened espousal of persecution of conscience as a religious instrumentality.[123] These facts the Presbyterians and all England should ever remember; certainly they should persuade even the most zealous of the godly not to plunge England into a new and senseless conflict. And, if the tuition of a religious conscience will not convince them of the necessity of liberality and tolerance, they should at least be given pause by the patent fact that England is still soundly though moderately Anglican at heart.[124] Persecution under any circumstance is an unmitigated evil, but it is insane when an arrogant minority deliberately adopts it as a cardinal principle of policy and faith.

We have observed that Henry Parker hoped to curb clerical arrogance and to temper sectarian strife by vesting in the civil ruler an absolute control over religion and its institutional manifestations. Parker was completely Erastian because he was confident that the lay spirit and the intuitions of sovereignty were sufficiently powerful to ensure in the revolutionary government a

[120] [Robinson], *A moderate answer*, p. 15.

[121] [Robinson], *The falsehood of Mr. William Pryn's Truth Triumphing*, pp. 9–10.

[122] *Ibid.*, p. 10.

[123] [Robinson], *A moderate answer*, pp. 16–17.

[124] [Robinson], *The falsehood of Mr. William Pryn's Truth Triumphing*, pp. 11–12.

religious policy which would be posited upon the principle of toleration and which would bring under tight restraint the divisive religious forces which had been loosed in England. In part Parker was a traditionalist who was thinking in terms of the Elizabethan settlement; in part he was reposing confidence in his own conviction that the secular spirit had already triumphed in England. He was consequently wholly prepared to surrender unlimited religious authority to the magistrate because of the implicit certainty that men would be ensured freedom and tolerance by the administrative policy of cold, sane, and cautious government.

Henry Robinson, on the other hand, shared none of this Erastian confidence. He was explicitly anti-Erastian because his reading of history, his estimate of sectarian strength and determination, and his analysis of the political situation during the period of the Civil War persuaded him that conscience and freedom would find no bulwark in the sword of the magistrate, that a complete fragmentization of religious institutions was necessary as the consequence of legally enforced religious liberty before either the individual or the state could be secure. Robinson was personally a religious man, though his own beliefs and conceptions fitted into none of the numerous seventeenth-century doctrinal niches. He understood better than did Parker and most of his contemporaries the dangers to which England lay exposed because of the savage strife between mutually exclusive and hostile sects, each of which was determined to be a church, and hence he elevated the theory of religious liberty into a principle of faith and politics. In so doing, he contributed not a little to the formation of a loosely allied group of forces which gradually won control of Parliament and the army; which gained powerful support from the mass of sober and cautious Englishmen who stood apart from the civil conflict; which was able to frustrate the Presbyterian plans for the imposition of a godly order upon the nation.

Robinson denied categorically, thereby repudiating not only medieval but sixteenth-century political theory, that the magistrate had any responsibility in, or power over, the Christian Church. This view is explicitly propounded in all his religious works and must be regarded as a central doctrine in his thought. He held this view because history taught him that, when the magistrate assumes power in the church, that power must inevitably result in the creation of an intolerant national church. As we have noticed, Robinson maintained that a national church could not possibly be a true church, while history has demonstrated again and again that the organized clergy of such an institution despoil the power of the prince, use his sword for the extirpation of opposition, and lay waste the substance of civil order and religious freedom. This, he insisted, was the plainly announced intention of the Presbyterians, whose arrogant ambition could be thwarted only by expressly withdrawing the civil sword from their grasp.

There can certainly be no doubt, Robinson maintained, that the prince has consistently intervened in ecclesiastical causes and that his power has supported great religious institutions. But these facts by no means establish his *de jure* right to order religion. The spiritual authority of the magistrate, if it exists at all, must be inherent in rulers as rulers rather than as members of any one of the innumerable sects, and hence whatever spiritual power is vested in one must be vested in all. In other words, "the power is given to them as magistrates and princes, not as Christians; otherwise they might be deposed at any time if they became antichristian, which is exploded for a popish doctrine."[125] Historically, the clerical groups have consistently striven to found and maintain a power which they impose on the magistrate. They have held that "the Church hath power over states and kingdomes, for the Church is to deale in all matters of religion most powerfully," when they have been able "to get states to be their servants" and to fasten their will upon mankind.[126] Actually, of course, the various Christian communions have welcomed and accepted the spiritual power of the state only if the ruler were pliable to their will and have lent obedience to him only when his religious persuasions and actions happened to enjoy their approval. This is conclusively proved by the fact that the Puritans prior to 1640 vigorously denied the religious power of the ruler,

[125] *Ibid.*, p. 14.

[126] [Robinson], *A moderate answer*, p. 19.

while directly after that date, when their own dominance seemed at hand, they as vehemently championed it.

Very evidently, then, this vicious teaching has been rooted in convenience rather than in principle. It has ever menaced the stability of civil government and has made a shambles of the church. It has meant in historical practice that truth, about which the orthodox prate so piously, can have no other definition than that opinion enforced by competent power at a particular time and place; truth has been quite precisely a corollary of political power.[127] Thus the clergy have dictated to the civil ruler concerning what is and what is not heresy, their own imperious determinations having been scarcely masked by the hollow façade of magistracy. This is the power which the Presbyterian divines strive to gain in England. How, Robinson enquired, unless they enjoy the "spirit of infallibility," can they "be more certaine then the Papists or Jewes in crucifying againe our Saviour in his Saints?"[128] It is an awful, an hideous power for which they strive, for "whosoever attributes to any man or magistrate a power of imposing anything upon the consciences of others in matters of religion, does justify them in whatsoever they impose, though it be erroneous, so they impose according to their owne judgements and understandings, condemning the other for not submitting, though it be unto erroneous impositions."[129]

The evil teaching that the civil ruler may and should frame and govern the church has had no other consequence, Robinson asserted, than that religion has been placed at the mercy of erratic historical circumstances and that successive waves of persecution have swept across the face of Christianity.[130] No scriptural foundation for this power can possibly be adduced from the New Testament, and certainly any reasonable man would agree that it has been ruinous in practice during more than a thousand weary and bloody years. Robinson submitted that for his part he

[127] [Robinson], *John the Baptist*, p. 43. [128] *Ibid.*, p. 45.

[129] [Robinson], *The falsehood of Mr. William Pryn's Truth Triumphing*, p. 15.

[130] Robinson emphasizes this point in several of his works: *vide The falsehood of Mr. William Pryn's Truth Triumphing*, pp. 18–19; *Liberty of conscience*, pp. 43–44; *John the Baptist*, pp. 66–68; *A short answer to A. S.*, pp. 1–2.

could discover no legitimate function for the magistrate in the church beyond the pious hope that he might set a salutary example by his own life and conduct. This is all we dare concede to the ruler, for "since the magistrates weapons are coercive, [ma]teriall, carnall, if they take upon them the vindication of spirituall neglect or defect, each state setting up its own, a different worship; men must from time to time take that to be the truest, and subject their consciences to that which hath the sharpest sword to fight for it, still changing religion according to the event of warre."[131]

The Presbyterian rejoinder to this argument, and it was one which impressed a frightened and bewildered England, was that to withdraw religious power from the prince was to invite a ruinous spiritual and civil anarchy. This plea, Robinson asserted, was viciously specious. The complete liberty which the state should grant the subject does not involve a grant of civil license. When actions which are pretended to spring from religious causes threaten the civil security of the state, they may be and should be punished for what they are—infractions of civil law. He insisted that within their proper civil sphere the laws of the state are absolute and that they bind every subject. There can be no reservations placed upon sovereignty, but, similarly, those who concede spiritual power to the sovereign must likewise make the cession absolute, and that no sect in Christian history has ever been prepared to do. Therefore, "there remaines no medium, either a liberty of conscience must be permitted us to enjoy our owne opinions in matters of religion, or else there is a necessity of being liable and subject against conscience, whensoever the civill powers which surely are no more infallible then ecclesiasticall, shall happen to enact or stablish any thing else, lesse consonant and agreeing to the Word of God."[132] Upon reflection, England will surely see that the dark past which has so vitiated the vitality of faith and so circumscribed the enlargement of truth must be expressly and finally repudiated. This can be done only if the state abandons without reservation any claim to responsibility for the ordering of the church and the salvation of its

[131] Robinson, *Some few considerations*, p. 5.

[132] [Robinson], *Liberty of conscience*, p. 44.

subjects. Those inflamed spirits who would "pin the Gospel with its propagation and whole affaires upon civill powers; the greatest share, or major part, whereof . . . . is in the hands of Turkes or infidels," must be repudiated as dangerous and irresponsible.[133] All sane men must now realize that faith and salvation have meaning in no terms larger than the individual. They must know, after so terrible a tuition, that divisions, bitterness, and the scourge of war have been the persistent fruit of the effort to enforce exclusive and infallible systems of truth by the sword of the magistrate. They must at last be persuaded that no other solution is left, whether we wish it or no, than the guaranty to all Christian men, of whatever ecclesiastical persuasion, of an unlimited liberty of conscience and freedom of worship prescribed in and enforced by law.

By careful and solid reasoning Robinson had firmly laid the foundations for his great plea for religious freedom. As we have previously suggested, this systematic defense of spiritual liberty was the most persuasive and impressive of all those advanced in England during this fruitful period and must, indeed, rank as one of the greatest of all time. Robinson's defense of tolerance is invested with peculiar strength because it was so evidently propounded by one who had no special interest in the fate of any particular sect. His thought, though molded in the heat of internecine conflict, remains objective, reasoned, and good-tempered. He was inspired by a passionate belief that the human mind and spirit were sacrosanct, that it was the prime function of government to provide unlimited scope for the play of the honest and enquiring mind. At the same time, Robinson was a cool and careful pragmatist in politics who was deeply convinced that the modern state could not survive, could not realize its illimitable potentialities, unless ways and means were found to tame the brawling sects, to attain through legally imposed toleration the stability and order which the merchants of London and Bristol required for the prosecution of their designs, and to free the lay spirit which was feverishly, if somewhat naïvely, engaged in preparing the blueprints of the future European society.

Before passing to his great defense of religious freedom, Robin-

[133] [Robinson], *The falsehood of Mr. William Pryn's Truth Triumphing*, p. 21.

son lent careful attention to the problem of heresy and error. Perhaps no question so perplexed responsible opinion in England during the early years of the revolutionary era as the rapid spread of radical and eccentric sectarianism. Men were gravely disturbed by the obvious fact that the immediate result of the disintegration of the episcopal structure was a shattering of the body of faith into countless particles. The centrifugal forces operative in English religious life frightened conservative Englishmen of every persuasion and lent much support to the Presbyterian plea that only the imposition of their discipline could prevent the complete decay of order and Christian truth. The reply of the sectaries to this contention was weak and unconvincing prior to 1646; the tone of their defense was apologetic; and their treatment of the problem of heresy was normally restricted to an attempt to prove that their aberration from doctrinal orthodoxy was not in fact heretical.

Robinson, on the contrary, faced the issue with courage and intelligence during these early years when the country at large was almost hysterically alarmed because of the spread of strange opinions. Nor was there any evasion in his consideration. By heresy he meant not variations from the Calvinistic core of dogma upon which the traditional groups were in fundamental agreement but error, persistently held and openly maintained, in those fundamentals of faith generally accepted by his age. This, he maintained, was heresy, and the peace and religious vitality of the nation depended upon securing to these eccentrics protection against the savage arm of persecution.

This position, Robinson admitted at the outset, had not been accepted by those communions which in the past had held a dominant position, nor was it consonant with the views of those which hoped to secure ecclesiastical power in revolutionary England. In other words, he admitted that his attitude toward heresy enjoyed no support in history but—and this is a matter of some importance—it happened to enjoy the clear sanction of the Bible. Nothing is more explicitly indicated in scripture than that heretics are to trouble the church and that they may not be molested by the civil arm. The true church is commanded to cast them out of its communion in order to keep the body of its faith pure, but this action represents the ultimate limit of its punitive authority. The question of their final punishment, or salvation, must be left in the hands of God, who has not chosen to relinquish this authority to men fallible in judgment and weak in knowledge.[134]

The orthodox in England have rested their plea for a persecuting ecclesiastical discipline on the time-worn argument that heresy, if left unmolested, will destroy the church. This position is a strange and a vicious perversion of truth, which holds in low esteem the strength and assurance that faith gives to the Christian man. It must be evident, upon reflection, that God "spares not these erronious beleevers or hereticks that they might seduce and pervert the faithfull, for that is impossible, but that the faithfull might in due time reduce the misbeleevers unto the truth."[135] Thus it must be granted that heresies have the positive merit of stimulating the vitality and animating the evangelical strength of the church, while they offer no threat whatsoever to the man of resolved conscience. Heresy, or what we call heresy, can be vanquished in no other way than by permitting it "to bee with all possible freedome examined and debated, which must necessarily infer the most acknowledged truths themselves, to be subject to the same proceeding, in that what one man, church or nation takes to be truth, another perhaps accounts no lesse then heresie."[136]

There has been a tragic tendency for Christians to employ as the weapon of the church the fire and slaughter of the Old Testament which Christ so patently and specifically repudiated.[137] The spiritual weapons with which Christ has endowed his church have throughout its bloody history been neglected because the clergy have been fascinated by the sharpness of the magistrate's sword. They have entirely forgotten the obvious fact that none but spiritual weapons will prevail against heresy; that men's

[134] [Robinson], *John the Baptist*, pp. 62–63.

[135] [Robinson], *Liberty of conscience*, p. 12.

[136] Robinson, *Some few considerations*, p. 7.

[137] [Robinson], *Liberty of conscience*, pp. 13–14.

minds are changed by argument and not by destruction. No man can be won to truth, no spirit can be cleansed of error, until God has touched the mind and heart.[138] Consequently, the punishment of heresy enjoys no spiritual sanction and certainly it can be supported by no rational argument. For it must be admitted that if the convicted heretic repents upon the scaffold, he ceases, in so far as our limited knowledge discloses, to be an heretic at all, and the grounds for his destruction have ceased to exist. The process of conviction and abjuration can go on until the day of doom, because the state of another man's grace is if anything a little more uncertain than that of our own. We proceed dangerously and sacrilegiously indeed when we constrain other men for what we crudely, inaccurately, and uncertainly choose to denominate as heresy.[139]

Heresy, Robinson would seem to hold, cannot possibly harm the content of Christian life and doctrine. There can be no doubt that it exists and that it will continue to exist, since, for reasons that are not entirely revealed to us, God happens to find it desirable for his inscrutable purposes. But we are not permitted to levy war against God by arming ourselves for its extirpation. The sober truth is that we possess neither knowledge nor insight sufficient to determine accurately when it exists in other men, much less to predict when the heresy of another man will in due season give way to truth. Heresy has long been an ill-defined and frequently malicious term with which we insult those who err only in the fact of disagreement from us. It has been the convenient excuse of sect after sect that has sought nothing else than its own aggrandizement under the spurious claim that it intends to impose righteousness upon a nation.

The enemy of Christianity and the great danger to the stability of the social order, therefore, is to be found, not in heresy, but in the arrogant presumption of the sects. Every church is blindly convinced of its own infallible truth and savagely condemns all persecution save that which it plots to impose upon the dissentient conscience. This, Robinson submitted, is an absurd posi-

[138] *Ibid.*, Pref.

[139] [Robinson], *John the Baptist*, pp. 63–65

tion. Quite clearly, "if it be lawfull for any people or religion to persecute or keep inquisition houses . . . . 'tis lawfull to all alike."[140] All sensible men must agree upon reflection that an express repudiation of the orthodox theory of persecution is essential for the survival of Christianity. This is patently true, since it is apparent that no sect can dare claim infallibility in these matters of spiritual judgment. "How," Robinson demanded, "can you bee infallibly assured that a man is sufficiently convinced, if he himselfe denyes it? How know you which is Gods houre for convincing of a man? May not you likewise possibly interpret a dulnesse of apprehension in him, or your owne want of truly and well informing him, to bee his obstinate wilfull rejecting of the truth?"[141] Even the most intransigent amongst the Presbyterians can return no satisfactory answer to these questions. They have, in fact, avoided dealing frankly with problems that are central in the Christian ethic; by subtle shifts and evasions they have defended the preposterous claim which they so arrogantly advance to the moral and spiritual right to extirpate what they choose to call heresy. We may be very sure that if any church possesses the right to put any heretic to death, "they need not use any Machivillian stratagem to prevent the peoples censuring them of cruelty, or make so nice to fowle their fingers with the blood of such as they put to death deservedly."[142]

The Presbyterians, like all the rigorous and persecuting churches before them, stand convicted of an impious arrogance and a dangerous phobia against dissent. They possess no special grace which enables them accurately to determine what is and what is not heresy. But, granting they were vested with this divine wisdom, they would have no right to punish even the most wilful and vicious heretic. Even the angels of heaven are expressly forbidden to pull up the tares before the day of God's judgment. We have at least an intimation of God's purpose in his stern commandment, when we reflect that had he "given leave

[140] *Ibid.*, p. 87 (mispaged).

[141] [Robinson], *A short answer to A. S.*, p. 10; *et cf.* [Robinson], *Liberty of conscience*, pp. 38–39.

[142] [Robinson], *A short answer to A. S.*, p. 11.

unto the true Church to pull up the tares, each false church pretending to be the only true one, would have appropriated the commission . . . . and so have gone to worke pulling up more wheat then tares."[143] The conscience of the heretic is ringed round with a freedom, with an inviolable dignity, which God himself has seen fit to bestow upon every human being.

The truth is, of course, that the orthodox in England are animated not with zeal for truth but with a shattering fear. They talk of heresy when they are thinking of shifts which will secure and maintain their own dominance. They neglect entirely the teaching of history which so evidently demonstrates that heresy has ever flourished when it lay under severe repression; they forget that "that which is opposed and cried out against, men will the more prye into; Bishops made more Puritans against their will, then ever was before; and it will be so in other things too: men will be doubting whether that power be lawfull, which is so cruell: errors are like camorile, the more you tread them downe, the more they will grow, let them alone they will fall off themselves."[144]

Those, therefore, who are sincerely interested in the cure of heresy will be quick to realize that an unconditional liberty of conscience is essential to secure those ends to which the orthodox have pretended to aspire. Heresy is a disease which can be cured by no other means than by the cool salve of persuasion. When we press the heretic, we drive him deeper into his error, while destroying the fabric of our own faith and piety. It would be infinitely more salutary simply to ignore heresy than to attempt its destruction.

Robinson, it will have been observed, dealt carefully and honestly with the problem which, more than any other, so grievously troubled his age. His remedy, drawn from the New Testament, posited on history, and armed with common sense, was ultimately to prevail in England and western Europe, but it appeared radical and incendiary to his own age. He attacked the traditional attitude toward heresy with unremitting vigor on the ground that

143 [Robinson], *John the Baptist*, p. 89.

144 [Robinson], *A moderate answer*, p. 39.

it could not be accurately diagnosed, that we have in any event no authority for its extirpation, and that those who levy war on heresy are animated by an ethic which cannot be described as Christian. From a theoretical position thus strongly fortified he launched a notable and sustained assault upon the classical doctrine of religious persecution.

Robinson endeavored to vindicate his bold treatment of the problem of heresy and to prepare the ground for his remarkable theory of religious liberty by a careful examination of the nature of persecution and by a thoughtful analysis of its effects upon the individual, the church, and the state. His frankly secular mind was peculiarly sensitive to all species of religious pressure, whether labeled with the Anglican plea of uniformity, the Calvinistic insistence upon discipline, or the sectarian assertion of certainty of grace. As always, Robinson brought freshness and vitality of treatment to a problem which had been carefully and vehemently discussed by his own and earlier ages. He vastly enlarged the definition of persecution by including not only the corporal and economic pains laid against dissent but likewise the subtle and more effective force of institutional pressure persistently exerted against the individual conscience. Robinson's conception of freedom, his sense of the dignity and sanctity of the human soul, were remarkable, whether viewed in terms of his own or subsequent centuries.

In numerous pamphlets Robinson argued that history teaches us that those churches and individuals who have suffered under the lash of persecution have normally exhibited the most certain evidences of grace. Christ foresaw that the true church would be persecuted and accordingly sought to prepare it for the cruel test of violence.[145] While indignantly denying the fact, those churches which have striven to gain or defend dominant positions in the state have always employed the arm of persecution for the maintenance of their perquisites and honors. The result has been that all spiritual vitality has been dissipated and such churches have come to enforce their decrees and discipline by bodily pains which do violence to the true offices of religion.

145 [Robinson], *John the Baptist*, p. 49.

The persecuting churches have intuitively realized that the mere accident of possessing power lent no ethical support to the use of persecution and hence have been obliged to invent sources for an arrogated and wicked authority. The scriptures have been twisted, the historical past misinterpreted, and councils convened in an effort to encase the naked edge of the civil sword with a sanction which at least appears decently spiritual. The formulations of the councils and synods have in point of fact simply expressed the determination and ruthless ambition of the powerful, who are searching for more imposing sanctions.[146] The clergy have deliberately incited those whom they have duped with a mad zeal against dissent, which they have condemned with the awful name of heresy. Thus the church and its leaders have strayed farther and farther down the "by-paths" of zeal until they have quite separated themselves from the veritable foundations of Christianity.[147] Gradually, therefore, the fraud and impiety which have characterized the persecuting policy of dominant groups have broken down of their own weight and, more recently in history, have been further weakened by the slow triumph of the spirit of toleration which has summoned men to a true understanding of the nature of faith and to a valid conception of the nature of the Christian Church.[148]

The persecuting spirit, Robinson would suggest, has defamed and ruined the church not only because of the conspiracy of those who seek power but because there is in all of us an imperious disposition to place too high a value upon our own opinions. Directly this psychological tendency is armed with institutional power and sanction, persecution is embraced as a settled religious policy. The Christian world, Robinson lamented in his *John the Baptist*, is simply unable to adjust itself to the fact that men and their consciences stand unchained before God. The aim of persecution has steadily been to create a uniformity of belief "which never hath been yet, nor never is to be expected while we are here; for as long as men have reason in them, and a free under-

146 [Robinson], *Liberty of conscience*, pp. 46–47.

147 [Robinson], *John the Baptist*, pp. 57–58.

148 [Robinson], *Liberty of conscience*, pp. 47–48.

standing, there will be different apprehensions of things."[149] Therefore it would destroy the very nature of man and render impossible the pursuit of truth, if men were to be forced into any mold of definition and behavior. The ideal of uniformity must consequently be regarded as nothing more than a conspiracy to destroy freedom and truth in the interests of a dominant clerical caste. This infamous design, which has writ in letters of ruin the history of western Europe, must at last be repudiated and forever extirpated from the Christian ethic. Persecution must be recognized for what it is—"the greatest hindrance of knowledge and growth in religion that can be; for it puts out mens own eyes and judgment, and ties them to see by others; every man . . . . will be affraid to read the scriptures, or search them throughly, for if God should dart in any light from them, or his own ingenuity thorough the strength of his reason should be forced to dissent from the multitude, either he must stiffle in the birth his divine conception . . . . or else he must dissemble his judgment, and wound his conscience."[150]

Men have for so long been bound with the cords of persecution and compulsion that their limbs are wasted; churches have for so long been animated by the lust of zeal and arrogance that they reflect but dimly the gospel and tolerance of Christ. Christians of his own age, Robinson wrote, were "not much unlike to people suddenly waked out of a deep sleep by the hideous crying of fire, fire, whose eyes being dazled with the sight thereof, and their understandings surprised . . . . forthwith cast themselves downe staires, or out at window to their destruction."[151] Thus England, weakened and dazed by the tyranny of the prelates, seems only too likely to accept the equally ruinous tyranny of the presbyters, for these men clearly aim at the erection of an exclusive national church which they openly announce they intend to impose upon the nation by the sword of persecution.

Surely, at this late date and after such tragic consequences, the claims of any communion to an infallible truth which must be supported by the sword of persecution will be critically and

[149] [Robinson], *A moderate answer*, p. 43.

[150] *Ibid.*, p. 44.

[151] [Robinson], *John the Baptist*, p. 58.

sceptically examined. For these men propose to make force, not truth—compulsion, not persuasion—the weapons of Christ for the erection of his church. The application of this teaching in the modern world would have terrible consequences. It neglects completely the patent truth that men can be bound by no ties other than their own consciences, that they can see the will and truth of God with no eyes other than their own. They may be lost and confused in error, but persecution cannot recover them, since God has never "sanctified it to such an end: nay, there is nothing more hardens men in their error then such a course, and makes them more refractory and incorrigible: men will be led and not drawn; few or none ever were recovered, with whom such course[s] have been taken."[152] Those weak men whom the lash of compulsion can whip into stupid conformity to a particular faith may be too easily whipped out again by as "many lashes more."[153] England will court civil disaster and spiritual ruin if she heeds the siren voices of the orthodox, who seek nothing else than to recover the lash which has fallen from the weakened grasp of the prelates.[154]

England, Robinson repeatedly maintained, was poised on the brink of momentous decision. All the blood and treasure consumed in the Civil War would be spent in vain, all the hope for a future which ensured peace, stability, and freedom would be frustrated, should she not repudiate decisively and finally the ruinous doctrine of force in religious causes. The Bible, the instruction of history, and the calm persuasion of common sense inform us that men's opinions and religious beliefs can be changed in no other way than by spiritual tuition. Hence, "if Gods word must doe it, and that in the last day; whence [have sprung] these consistories, inquisition houses, High Commission Courts, with all their humane ordinances and canons which anticipate or antidate Gods

[152] [Robinson], *A moderate answer*, p. 42.

[153] [Robinson], *John the Baptist*, p. 59.

[154] Indeed, Robinson strongly urged that Presbyterianism was a greater threat to tolerance and freedom than was Episcopacy. He held that it was more rigid and arrogant, that responsibility under the ecclesiastical system it proposed was dangerously diffused, and that its formulations were marked by evident symptoms of irresponsibility (*ibid.*, pp. 59–60; *et cf. ante*, pp. 105–8).

judgements?"[155] The human soul is too tough, the nature of truth too elusive, the content of Christianity too spiritual, for compulsion to effect the changes which the orthodox so imperiously and impiously require. Men throughout history have dissembled, have evaded the issue, or have died the martyr's death, but still no mind has been changed by the instrumentality of brute force. This must be true simply because religion is spiritual in nature and can therefore be propagated by none save spiritual means. Most men, even the proudest, really know this even when they mutter the threats of the persecutors. We say that heretics should be put to death, yet when concrete cases present themselves we know that neither good nor mistaken men can be made to suffer for the sake of conscience. Instinctively, reasonable men have shrunk from the implications to which their theory has committed them. But England, to be free and to face the future with equanimity, must make sure that the barbarous possibility of persecution is swept from the body of law; must remove the constant threat that war, perjury, and brutality will not suddenly well up in a burst of insensate persecuting rage.[156]

Nor is this all. England likewise owes a larger responsibility to mankind in making certain that the teaching and practice of persecution be destroyed. For the iniquitous engine of persecution has been the greatest of the impediments which have weakened the vitality of Christianity and prevented the spread of faith to all mankind. Heathen nations have not dared embrace Christianity lest they too be contaminated with this fatal virus. The Jews, whose conversion must be accomplished before biblical prophecy can be fulfilled, would rather yield their lives than their souls unless the weight of compulsion be lifted from them. No unbeliever, no one lost in error, no heathen people, could on the basis of reasonable observation and prudence be persuaded to accept a faith which for so many centuries has been disgraced by religious wars, by the blight of persecution, and by the consuming zeal of imperious spirits.[157] England, consequently, must dis-

[155] [Robinson], *John the Baptist*, p. 14.

[156] [Robinson], *Liberty of conscience*, pp. 5–7.

[157] [Robinson], *John the Baptist*, pp. 14–20.

charge a grave responsibility not only to herself and to her own future but to humanity as a whole. She must cleanse herself of the contamination of persecution, must base her political and religious future on an untrammeled freedom for the human conscience, if she is to be worthy of the destiny to which history has summoned her.

Robinson dealt carefully and critically with the manifold problems which must underlie any significant consideration of the theory of religious toleration. He wrote with a warm and eloquent style which betokens his deep devotion to the cause of religious liberty; his thought was careless of doctrinal niceties and repudiated boldly and incisively postulates concerning the Christian Church and society which had stood firmly embedded in political philosophy for a full thousand years. He required men to consider the myths, the traditions, and the ideals of the past in terms of the complex structure of modern society and warned them that accommodations must be made in thought and institutions which would secure free room for the play of the secular mind. Robinson built his structure of theory slowly and solidly: he was now prepared to rear the edifice of his plea for unlimited religious freedom upon stones of reason that had been firmly joined with the cement of historical necessity. All his religious pamphlets, written in those years when liberty of conscience was in desperate dispute, are dedicated to the principle of unrestricted freedom of conscience and worship. His thought, in its totality, may be regarded as one of the most significant of all the contributions made to the defense of the dignity and freedom of mankind.[158]

Robinson sought critically to consider the problem of toleration from every angle from which attack could be launched by the orthodox. He first addressed himself to the ideal of unity, which, in his judgment, was implicit in every persecuting philosophy and which, it was generally believed, the proponents of religious toleration repudiated. The dominant churches have

[158] The discussion of Robinson's contribution to the theory of toleration (pp. 124–35) rests heavily upon this writer's earlier analysis of Robinson's religious thought (Jordan, *Religious Toleration*, IV, 140–76, and esp. 166–76). It would seem pedantic, even in a few instances where direct quotations have been employed, to give the customary page references.

throughout history, he submitted, neglected the true spiritual unity which binds them to Christ in order to erect a formal unity, which they have endeavored to maintain by the brutal destruction of all who dissent from the arbitrary and meaningless definitions of truth which they have propounded to suit their own needs and ambitions. Hence sect has been pitted against sect, church against church, kingdom against kingdom. Dissension, persecution, warfare, and ruin have been the bitter fruits of this impious pursuit of the phantom of formal unity. Men have discovered that there is little to choose indeed "betwixt being persecuted by an Episcopall or Presbyteriall" clergy, and have at last been persuaded that neither the good life nor a vital faith can exist for long under conditions of intolerance. The Christian world would have fared better under the tolerant and careless rule of the Turk than under the lash of those dominant groups which have scourged Europe in the name of orthodoxy. A wholly fictitious plea of unity has been advanced, which has been belied by the struggling, warring sects that have made Europe their battleground. Even the Protestants dogmatize from forty different translations of the Bible, thereby erecting into ossified systems of creed minor differences of faith that have no bearing whatsoever upon those fundamentals which join the Christian world in a true spiritual unity.[159]

The true unity to which all Christians aspire can be gained in no other way than by building upon the essentials that all churches hold in common. Men have come at last to realize that the effort to enforce a rigid and arbitrary system of doctrine upon a people can have no other result than constant change, perpetual strife, and civil disorder. Men who have tasted of the strong wine of freedom can never again be forced into the rigid molds of a meaningless conformity.[160] They realize that spiritual censures adequately guard the purity of the church's doctrines, which the sharp sword of the magistrate can neither defend nor destroy. Every man and every sect must be left entirely free to find and expound the truth of Christ and to weave more tightly the web of

[159] [Robinson], *John the Baptist*, Pref.

[160] [Robinson], *Liberty of conscience*, p. 5.

unity that binds them as Christians. This unity, Robinson maintained, in a startling section, is more complete than men blinded by zeal have understood. He suggests that the differences between the various Protestant communions and, for that matter, the controversies between Protestants and Catholics, have no connection whatever with the body of truth essential for salvation.[161] Thus he would hold that European Christianity was not "spiritually divided" even on the dread doctrine of transubstantiation. Every man and every sect should be free, entirely free, to limit their conformity to those matters which are so transcendently clear that all men agree to their validity. Hence the freedom of the Christian gains its full scope only when every trace of restraint has been lifted from the hand of reason. "If the scriptures and such reasons as they produce, through my infirmity and weaknesse, cannot satisfie my conscience," Robinson enquired, "has fraile mankinde the infinite power of God at their disposal" to compel the conscience to embrace teachings which the mind is unable to accept?[162]

Truth and unity of faith, we may be sure, have nothing to fear when all restraints upon religion are removed and they are no longer shored up by the formulations of the orthodox. We must ever bear in mind that the precious truth of Christ may be greatly advanced by the "stammering illiterate tongue of some otherwise despised soule."[163] Those who truly seek unity and vitality of faith will gladly grant that "all such as shall propound their thoughts touching any part of the discipline and doctrine of Gods worship and mans salvation" ought not only to be tolerated but to be encouraged, "though they seem never so strange and novel."[164] Those persecuting spirits should be repudiated who seek to implement God's truth "with rods and staves," cruelly destroying those who do not agree with them.[165] When toleration at last prevails, men will discover unity in the common truth which binds them, while the differences that separate them will speedily

[161] [Robinson], *John the Baptist*, pp. 25–26.

[162] *Ibid.*, p. 30.

[163] Robinson, *Some few considerations*, p. 7.

[164] [Robinson], *John the Baptist*, Pref.

[165] Robinson, *Some few considerations*, pp. 8–9.

disappear as free discussion, free preaching, and free enquiry enlarge the circumference of common understanding.

The spiritual unity that the Christian world will gain from religious freedom will be further strengthened by a great rising tide of spiritual and intellectual vitality. Modern Europe, Robinson pointed out, enjoyed in the printing press a unique instrument for the exploration and diffusion of truth. He paid the highest tribute to the services it had already rendered to the enhancement of knowledge and freedom. The Reformation would scarcely have been possible without its assistance, and the remarkable progress which has been made toward religious liberty has been largely brought about by a relatively free press. The orthodox have complained that by it errors as well as truth have been disseminated, but their frantic efforts to stifle thought by placing restrictions upon the press betoken nothing else than a poisoned and stupid mentality. "The necessity of suffering erroneous opinions to be published, lest truth thereby should be stifled, is so cleare and necessary to the eye of reason, as it is for him that hath lost any thing, to seek it where it is not, as well as where it is, if ever he mean to finde it."[166] Absolute liberty is necessary, not only for enlarging the known limits of truth, but for enabling those who are lost to find their way. Once the press has been completely freed by the extension of the liberty which the Christian world requires, a new and fruitful vitality will possess all churches and all searchers after truth and eternal life.

The spiritual vitality that will develop directly a complete religious freedom has been gained will be marked, it should be candidly recognized, by a considerable increase in heresies and eccentric opinions. But this will actually be an extremely salutary circumstance, since it is the inevitable concomitant of a dynamic spiritual life. Christians must be endowed with unhampered freedom to search the scriptures without restraint, to try all doctrines, and to move restlessly across the limitless face of knowledge.[167] These men will occasionally fall into error, but theirs will be an honest and maturing experience which the passage of time will

[166] [Robinson], *John the Baptist*, p. 24.

[167] Robinson, *Some few considerations*, p. 4.

rectify. "Shall we put our selves into such a condition, that if we be in an errour it shall be impossible for us to get out of it againe, unlesse the whole civil state, the men of war, the world doe see it as clearely as our selves? That if as yet wee have but some degrees of truth and knowledge, it shall be impossible for us to attain to greater?"[168] England must be brought to understand, and that quickly, that the horror with which the rigorous view error betrays an essential misunderstanding of the nature of faith and the way in which it must be gained.

It is incredible, Robinson continued, that men have been duped into surrendering to authority their most precious freedom—that of the mind and conscience—that they have been careless of their eternal salvation. We would regard it as an insupportable tyranny should the civil state seek to order the conduct of business, the development of the arts, or the advancement of science, yet how infinitely worse it is to surrender the prescription of our faith to an external power. The area of our faith must be held inviolate, if we are to grow in spiritual stature and if we are to be sure of our salvation. We do not attain salvation by proxy; every Christian must answer for his own talents before God. Therefore, Robinson pleaded, "I desire every Christian heart, in the feare of God, to consider, and resolve in his saddest and most retired thoughts, whether it be not a much safer way in spirituall affaires, for every particular man to understand his owne estate betwixt God and himselfe, and manage his own busines."[169] This precious liberty is absolutely essential for the integrity of man, for the advancement of true religion, and for the health and security of the civil state.[170] In England it is the prime cause that has compelled men to take up arms because they sensed that they had for too long been bound in the chains of a subtle yet implacable slavery. The civil laws, Robinson reminded his countrymen, permit men to defend their estates with arms, "but what kinde of laws are those which expose men naked, to

[168] [Robinson], *A short answer to A. S.*, p. 28.

[169] [Robinson], *Liberty of conscience*, p. 40.

[170] [Robinson], *A moderate answer*, pp. 39–40.

have their religion and consciences assaulted."[171] Men can serve God and themselves in no nobler way than by the defense of the sanctity of their own consciences.

A tremendous strengthening of its evangelical power is a further advantage which will accrue to the church when toleration has been gained. It is doubtful, in fact, whether the church has ever enjoyed its full resources of missionary strength since the days of the apostles. For the Christian world has strayed very far indeed from the simplicity and tolerance of the early church. Every sect has advanced fantastic and intolerant claims that it alone has found and professes the complete truth.[172] Reason, charity, and enquiry have been stifled by men who are, to put it bluntly, murderers of the mind. These men who "goe about to fasten a yoake of their owne doctrine and opinions on others" should be "accounted the most ignorant, absurd, presumptuous, and the greatest enemies both to God and man of any people under heaven."[173] The persecuting churches have alienated all thinking men because they have endeavored to force them into a dead conformity, "as though it were in their power to be converted at their pleasure, whether God would or no; or as if we were able to judge when they were wilfully ignorant, or reprobately hardned."[174] Sober reflection should inform us that papists and unbelievers can never be won until the specter of persecution is laid to rest. Europe has been torn by fratricidal wars that have made the conversion of the New World impossible so long as Christianity is synonymous with barbaric persecution.[175] Men who profess the name of Christ seem to have forgotten that the lost are to be redeemed by preaching, the erroneous won by reason, rather than to be "taken out of the world in their sins."[176] The church, then, has been gravely weakened by the virus of persecution, its ends and purposes have been betrayed, and its energies have been criminally dissipated because it has been wedded

[171] [Robinson], *Liberty of conscience*, p. 40.

[172] [Robinson], *An answer to Mr. William Prynn's Twelve Questions*, p. 2.

[173] *Ibid.*, pp. 4–5.

[174] [Robinson], *John the Baptist*, pp. 6–7 (pagination irregular).

[175] [Robinson], *Liberty of conscience*, p. 14.

[176] *Ibid.*, p. 15.

to a philosophy of force rather than to Christ's charter of freedom for all men.

True Christians, it should be apparent, above all other men must be engaged in the great work of winning for the church the inestimable benefits of an unconditional religious freedom. They, at least, will realize that no true and perfect church can be formed until the broad and deep foundations of liberty have been laid. "What can be more against the rules of wisdome," Robinson enquired, "then endeavouring to bring into the true church such as are without by a rigorous way of persecution?" Reason and charity inform us that men can be persuaded by none other than gentle and patient discussion. These means "both win and keep the heart fast, whilst violence and constraint can at best, but prevaile upon the body."[177] The human soul has been left immune by Christ from the torments which may afflict the body; has been specifically exempted from that obligation of obedience to which our bodies are bound. Hence no church, no imperious clerical group, can allege anything from "the Word of God which warrants us to imprison, fine, banish, or put to death any one . . . . for difference of opinion in religion."[178] What authority, therefore, can be claimed for all the paraphernalia of persecution and coercion with which every church has frantically equipped itself?[179] These are the crosses which the orthodox have laid on the back of faith; these are the impediments which puny but wilful men have laid athwart the majesty of God's will.

Henry Robinson made his most effective contribution to the discussion of the theory of religious toleration by a careful, direct, and sustained attack on the inconsistency of the Calvinistic position. Since English Puritanism was in 1644 clothed with the mantle of a tight and almost perfectly integrated theological system, this assault was at once courageous and telling. Robinson correctly detected that Calvinistic thought was mortally vulnerable at one point—it was logically inconsistent in applying its central doctrine of predestination to the political fact of widespread and deeply rooted diversity in England. We have observed that Cal-

[177] *Ibid.*, p. 14. [178] *Ibid.*, p. 16.

[179] [Robinson], *John the Baptist*, p. 14.

vinism stood convicted of suspicious inconsistency so long as it clung to the keystone of its dogmatic edifice while supporting at the same time the theory of enforced uniformity with such determined vigor.[180] Earlier thinkers had touched rather gingerly upon this logical inconsistency which Robinson attacked with an incisive and calculated irony.

The Calvinists, he maintained, belie their devotion to the central pillar of their doctrinal edifice by their every action and policy. It must be obvious, if we are honestly persuaded of the fact of election, that men cannot by their actions thwart the will of God. Why, he enquired, "are we so fondly jealous and preposterously carefull, lest the people of God should bee misled and carried away with every wind of doctrine?" Election, by fundamental admission, must be immutable and consequently can hardly be obscured by the mists of error. It is strange indeed that the orthodox require the suppression of heresies which cannot possibly pervert the elect by employing an authority that is even more likely to be used for the persecution of the saints.[181] The orthodox, Robinson suggests, are either pathetically uncertain of their own doctrinal tenets or stand guilty of an heretical and dangerous perversion of their own convictions.

Moreover, it must be granted by the Calvinists that those who have not been elected by God cannot possibly be saved despite the compulsion of the most violent persecution. Uniformity of profession, he caustically reminded the Presbyterians, cannot be confused with certainty of grace. Those who persecute, therefore, may be said to attack the validity of the doctrine of predestination. Those who are truly persuaded of its truth will instantly denounce every species of religious coercion as outright barbarism. For such men will be convinced that "though sects and heresies should multiply never so much . . . . if that one saving truth can but get liberty to shew it selfe, it will at last infalibly vanquish that many headed monster of error." They will earnestly maintain that those who take up the sword of persecution invade the

[180] *Vide* Jordan, *Religious Toleration*, I, 242–43; II, 202–5; III, 308–9, 399–401, 453, 465–66.

[181] [Robinson], *John the Baptist*, p. 35.

"secret closet of Gods eternal predestination," destroying the consciences of the saints and provoking wars and schisms which accomplish the ruin of saint and sinner alike. They will insist above all others, as a consequence of the sublime confidence which they have in truth and in its ultimate victory, that all men of all faiths should enjoy a perfect freedom for the realization of those potentialities with which God has endowed them.

Robinson had dealt at length with the positive benefits which liberty of conscience would bestow upon religion. He had shown that coercive practices were not consonant with the nature of the true church and that persecution defiled and perverted the structure of faith. Religious freedom, he submitted, was necessary if men were to grow in spiritual stature, if the ambit of our knowledge were to be enlarged, if the vitality and evangelical strength of the church were to be revived. He contributed powerfully to this discussion by demonstrating that the Presbyterians, the most determined and the strongest foes of religious toleration in his own age, were themselves required by the very substance of their vaunted doctrine to lend their full measure of support to the emancipation of the human conscience. Amongst the many reasons which demand that the modern world shall be endowed with the priceless benefits of religious freedom, the prime surely must be that religion itself requires it for our own fulfilment as men and Christians.

But this, Robinson insisted, is by no means all. It is equally true that the modern state and the society which it governs cannot possibly survive, much less prosper, unless the anarchical forces of religious dissension and persecution are curbed by religious toleration. Robinson developed this argument, the most persuasive for the seventeenth century, with rare skill and with warm convictions derived from his pragmatic intelligence.

So violent and aggressive have the several communions become, so haughty and inflexible have their definitions of truth grown, Robinson insisted, that the existence of an ordered civil state in Europe is seriously menaced by intolerance. The sects fail to realize that the very fact of their existence means that the age of institutional catholicity, of an enforced uniformity, is past.

They are guilty, in effect, of a nihilistic waging of war on themselves, of a reckless and arrogant ambition which is inconsistent with the facts of European politics and with the certain requirements of the future. Already numerous European states have been obliged, not from choice but out of necessity, to discover that harmonious relations are possible between nations of different religious professions. The next step must now be taken by permitting and protecting a variety of faiths within the confines of each state.[182] It so happens that religion requires this solution, but even more pertinent is the fact that social order and the continued existence of national sovereignty compel it. The problem, consequently, is not so much *de jure* as *de facto*.

The European states must choose between religious toleration and civil dissolution. Wars, the worst of the scourges which afflict mankind, have steadily mounted in number and intensity since Europe embraced Christianity.[183] Men have bound themselves with fanatical zeal to the defense of rigidly defined systems of creed, have become infected with an insane lust which perverts their loyalty and weakens the very pillars of the civil society. So ruthless has their zeal grown that "no man might adventure to call in question the lawfulnesse thereof, or seem backward in supplying without palpable scandall and suspition of luke-warmnesse in religion."[184] The finest sentiments of the human heart have been shamefully exploited for the attainment of sectarian and partisan ends. When one faction within the state has risen up in arms in the name of an infallible and exclusive truth, every other faction has leaped to battle armed with identical war cries and animated by an equal zeal. Thus has sovereignty been invaded and religion ruined; thus has European civilization been brought to the verge of dissolution.

The time has come, Robinson urged, for sane and reasonable men to think honestly and effectively on the necessities which confront them. They must realize that if we concede to the Protestant fanatics the right to propagate by force what they call

[182] [Robinson], *An answer to Mr. William Prynn's Twelve Questions*, pp. 5–6.

[183] [Robinson], *John the Baptist*, pp. 98–101.

[184] [Robinson], *Liberty of conscience*, p. 2.

truth, then "both papists, Brownists, and Anabaptists, even Turkes and very dogs" have inherently the same rights.[185] This view of the nature of religion is at once anarchical and evil, but it has throughout history been implicit in the dissensions which have laid western Europe in ruins. By it the world has been brought to chaos and Christ's gentle gospel has been prostituted to the most evil of all human actions. "What a sad thing is this," Robinson lamented, "that a man for following his judgement . . . . should not be suffered a place in the world; for if one state will not suffer him, why should another?" Religion can never be restored, nor peace regained, nor the civil authority confirmed in its capacities and responsibilities until mankind has demanded for itself that endowment of religious liberty with which the laws of God and reason have vested it.[186] It is quite impossible that "there should be a firme secure peace throughout the world, nay not in a province, city or towne, so long as men make a point of conscience to compell one another to their opinions."[187]

By every test which human reason can devise, then, men and nations are entitled to and will infinitely profit from religious toleration.[188] But we must frankly recognize that when religious

[185] [Robinson], *The falsehood of Mr. William Pryn's Truth Triumphing*, Epist.

[186] Thus Robinson reminded Parliament that "what ever power the principles of Presbytery will give them, the Congregationall way will give them much more: neither have the Parliament truer friends then they, who will be more willing to venture their lives, and sacrifice all they have for them; onely this is desired by them . . . . that the rights and liberties Christ hath purchased by his own precious blood . . . . may not be taken away by the secular power; as that the secular power might not be encroached on by Christian liberty" ([Robinson], *A moderate answer*, p. 24).

[187] [Robinson], *The falsehood of Mr. William Pryn's Truth Triumphing*, Pref.

[188] Robinson was unequivocal in his defense of the right of every conscience of his age to enjoy an absolute religious freedom, save for the Roman Catholics. He states clearly that no pressure whatsoever should be brought to bear on the Catholics to cause them to embrace Protestantism. But they should not, in his judgment, be permitted the free exercise of their religion because they are idolaters and because they menace the civil quiet of the state. None the less, they should be extended a qualified religious toleration and should enjoy the right to worship freely and quietly in their own churches according to their own rites ([Robinson], *Liberty of conscience*, Pref.; [Robinson], *A moderate answer*, p. 45). When and if they repudiate their doctrine of rebellion, they too should be granted complete liberty. Robinson, in other words,

liberty is adopted as a law woven into the fabric of national life, a clean break will have been made with ancient, though evil, traditions and that a wholly different view of religion and of dissent will of necessity prevail. For the theory of religious freedom assumes at bottom that truth and error shall be permitted to exist, to expand, and to advance their claims under conditions of absolute equality and freedom. We must grant that no man can "hold fast the truth, or be fully perswaded in his owne heart of what he does, of what religion he makes choice of; unlesse after he hath searched the Scriptures, and try'de the spirits whether they be of God or no, it be lawfull for him to reject that which shall appeare to him as evill, and adhere to that which seems good in his owne judgement and apprehension."[189] This is the meaning of religious liberty; to hedge it about with reservations and sly exceptions is to destroy its very nature. This bold and startling teaching the enlightened London merchant hurled into the teeth of an extremist group which, it should be remembered, was even then hysterically demanding the extirpation of heresy and error in England.

The bath of liberty will be icy cold indeed for those hot and inflamed spirits who still denounce as error any teaching varying a particle from their imperious formulation. They will protest bitterly, Robinson prophesied, when the state extends to all opinions an equal liberty and an equal protection under the law. But their shrill cries impiously deny the very essence of Christ's commandments; for Christ has ordained that every man should worship Him according to the measure of his enlightenment. "How," Robinson enquired, "can a weake servant of Christ" exercise his measure of faith "if he shall be silenced or imprisoned by a superiour power, for wanting some other parcell of truth, or interweaving therewith some erroneous doctrine."[190] It is true

---

went as far in endowing the Catholics with freedom as did most of the proponents of religious toleration in his century in the liberty which they would extend to the Protestant sects. With this one partial exception, his defense of religious liberty, as opposed to legal toleration, stood complete.

[189] [Robinson], *The falsehood of Mr. William Pryn's Truth Triumphing*, Pref.

[190] [Robinson], *John the Baptist*, pp. 76–77.

that we are commanded to preach our persuasions, but only after we have freely tried all things. The criteria of truth remain intensely and purely subjective. Hence when men teach falsehoods under the apprehension that they are truth, they do no more than faithfully fulfil the commandment of God. Nor, Robinson again insisted, may any man under any pretext lay the hand of restraint or punishment upon such erroneous teachers. Truth and error must be permitted to contest for the loyalty of mankind upon terms of absolute equality: "this combat . . . . must be fought out upon eaven ground, on equall termes, neither side must expect to have greater liberty of speech, writing, printing, or whatsoever else, then the other."[191]

Robinson fully realized that the Presbyterians had been half-successful in persuading England that the firm doctrinal system and the rigid discipline which they offered alone stood between the nation and the further disintegration of Protestant orthodoxy. The courageous merchant therefore dealt at length with this apprehension. Men of firm faith, he urged, have nothing to fear and everything to gain from liberty of conscience and should therefore decline to heed the outraged cries of the orthodox, who raise the alarm of spiritual anarchy and confusion. Reasonable and pious men may rest assured that truth has nothing whatsoever to fear in the free contest with error. They will reflect that "every sect or heresie obtrudes her errours with as great vehemencie, as the professours of the truth . . . . and neither can alleadge one tittle advantage, wherefore any one in humane reason should rather yeeld or be convinced by the other, untill the evidence of truth prevaile upon the conscience."[192] It is repression, not freedom, that wastes the sinews of faith and dissolves the foundations of society. Surely it is better for men of different views to worship peacefully in several meeting places rather than to be forced to assemble within one edifice for the sake of a dead uniformity.[193] No Christian can possibly admit that he or his church has anything to fear from error, much less from diversity. Men have for too long been de-

[191] [Robinson], *Liberty of conscience*, p. 17.

[192] [Robinson], *John the Baptist*, p. 99.

[193] [Robinson], *Liberty of conscience*, pp. 17–18.

luded by the mirage of an ordered uniformity, neither attainable nor desirable. Faith, we should know at this late date, does not come in the neat packages which the orthodox so busily prepare and label. These factious spirits have sought rather a church of members than the "perfect men in Christ Jesus" which God requires in his church.[194] We must walk alone in the search for truth, oblivious of all pressures save that of our own reason which God will so richly illumine once freedom has been gained. Christian men must demand, as the hallmark of their freedom, relief from that greatest of all tyrannies, compulsion of soul.[195]

Robinson submitted that none of the great national churches and all too few of the sects had been willing to face the trial of liberty and the test of free decision. Romanism and Protestantism alike have girded themselves with an intolerance born of fear. "Let all church governments be . . . . brought to a triall" before the conscience and common sense of humanity, Robinson demanded. Let all men see "what the pope can say, Episcopacie, Presbyterie, or any other that stands for compulsive jurisdiction." For though these great churches "mince it never so finely," they fear to submit the certainty of the truth which they so arrogantly proclaim to the light of reason and to the examination of the untrammeled conscience.[196] Yet there is not an iota of proof, Robinson contended, that all the compulsion and persecution which have been brought to bear upon mankind have ever substantially altered the balance of faith. Thus in England, despite the frenzied efforts of the Presbyterians, despite the fact that almost everyone in London has submitted to the *Covenant*, there has been little or no change in the morphology of faith. England has for some years been under the steady and resolute pressure of the Presbyterians, who have enjoyed every conceivable advantage, but it is apparent to any objective observer that the nation is still staunchly disposed toward moderate Anglicanism.[197] Robinson,

[194] *Ibid.*, p. 21. [195] [Robinson], *A moderate answer*, pp. 19–20.

[196] [Robinson], *Liberty of conscience*, p. 24.

[197] *Ibid.*, p. 27. It will be recalled that Henry Parker expressed much the same opinion. It is significant that Robinson and Parker alone amongst the laymen and sectaries opposed to Anglicanism dealt honestly and dispassionately with this delicate matter.

it should be reflected, was for numerous reasons strongly opposed to the Anglican Establishment, yet so completely was he devoted to the cause of religious freedom that he was willing to leave the trial of faith in England to the free decision of every man. No Christian who trusts the validity of his own faith, no man who apprehends the nature of religion, could have any other desire.

The conscience, then, must be completely emancipated; reason must be permitted free sway amongst all men. We must restore to all searchers after God the responsibility for their own faith and must invest them with that freedom which will strengthen them in their solitary quest.[198] Every man must be granted the legal right to hold and expound that truth to which reason has persuaded him. When this has at last been done, religion will be cleansed of the dreadful virus of persecution and the state will be rid of the threat of divisive sectarian conflicts. Moreover, faith will have been loosed from the wheel of historical circumstance. It is patent that in the historical past truth and error have enjoyed their sway simply as the accidental derivative of power.[199] Christ, on the other hand, has ordained that mankind shall enjoy a perfect liberty for testing all things and trying all paths. He is far more concerned with the honesty of our search than with the accidental propriety of our views at any particular moment. We may rest assured that "such as study the variety of opinions, and trie the spirits out of a zeale to truth," are in the way of truth and righteousness though they are for the moment mired in error.[200] Men vested with fulness of liberty may not escape error, "yet truth being therewith permitted to be published and improved, will in all probability, not only gain so many more to God; but any one thus won to God . . . . is worth thousands of those that fall from it."[201]

Robinson, it may be suggested in summary, lent an impressive and noble defense to the theory of religious freedom. He wrote with rare objectivity and amazing dispassion on a subject which

198 [Robinson], *A short answer to A. S.*, pp. 32–33.

199 [Robinson], *John the Baptist*, p. 85.

200 [Robinson], *Liberty of conscience*, Pref.

201 [Robinson], *A short answer to A. S.*, p. 33.

had divided England into warring camps of opposed extremisms. He mustered all the arguments which divinity could present into an impressive statement of the thesis that the vitality of faith and the nature of Christianity require complete freedom for the development of the individual faith and for the pursuit of truth. But he did far more than this. He likewise demonstrated that the society of his own day was imperiled by the festering bitterness of sectarian warfare; that the very fabric of civilization had been torn by the aimless strivings of factions which sought mastery under the guise of truth. Robinson held that Europe must break cleanly and irrevocably with the past. A complete and unequivocal liberty of conscience must be instituted which would protect the weak and chasten the arrogant, which would endow man with that dignity to which his divine origin entitled him, and which would open up to mankind illimitable horizons of knowledge for the free spirit to explore in its insatiable search for truth.

V

POLITICAL THOUGHT

1. HENRY PARKER

HENRY PARKER was the most original and, it may well be argued, the most important political theorist of the revolutionary era. He faced the issues of the Civil War fearlessly and honestly, being perhaps the first responsible thinker to realize that the historical structure of the state had crumbled and that heroic remedies must be adopted if parliamentary resistance were not to result in failure and anarchy. Even before war had actually begun, Parker's political theory was reasonably mature and his pen, during the confused months when all parties moved reluctantly toward open conflict, remained dedicated to the conviction that Parliament must assume a predominant role in the constitution of the nation.

Parker wrote clearly and strongly—there are no subtle evasions in his logic, and there are no evidences of nostalgia in his repudiation of the past. He understood that the Civil War in England had been caused by the fusion of religious and political grievances and that fundamental changes must be made in institutional life in order to accommodate powerful and beneficent forces which were even then dissolving an ancient order of society. It was evident, he wrote some years later, that "religion would make the people more zealous for liberty, and liberty would impower the people the better to defend religion."[1] He stood almost alone during the early and critical months of the conflict in his steady contention that political and religious freedom were inseparable and in his almost harsh insistence that political stability could be gained in England only if the religious emotion were tempered by the Erastian control of the state. Parker's political and religious thought therefore form a unity in which the spiritual life and in-

[1] Parker, *Scotlands holy war*, p. 16.

stitutions of the nation are strictly and completely subordinated to the aspirations of man's secular nature.

Henry Parker's thought was charged with a persuasive pragmatism; his mind was clear, cold, and incisive. From 1640 onward he openly expressed his want of confidence in the integrity of the king, and he systematically endeavored to cut away the foundations upon which monarchical power rested in England. Yet he was no incendiary and was quite as hostile to the democratic extremists as to those who sought to vest the crown with absolute authority. Parker believed that Parliament, the representative of the responsible classes in England, was sovereign, and he taught that this was true *de jure* because it was true *de facto*. His conception of sovereignty was quite as inclusive and elaborately stated as the later definitions of Hobbes, and his political thought in general suggests that the greater philosopher drew very considerably indeed from the contribution of his predecessor. It would be a mistake to exaggerate the influence of Henry Parker's thought, yet it should be pointed out that prior to 1644 he had sketched in detail the course which revolutionary political experimentation was to take and that the few significant royalist theorists of the period recognized in Parker their most dangerous adversary. The trend of constitutional development in England was determined by compulsive historical events which theorists influenced only very slightly. Henry Parker is important because he understood the nature of historical tendencies, and because he analyzed the temper and dynamic of his age with almost surgical precision and with cold and accurate objectivity. Parker was an early and significant harbinger of modernity.

Parker's political philosophy was developed in twenty pamphlets published during the years 1640–1651. It should be noted, however, that twelve of these were published in the early months of the Civil War, and three more before the decisive battle of Marston Moor in 1644. He published three rather slight controversial tracts in 1647 and, after a lapse of three years, wrote two pamphlets, the one in 1650 and the other in 1651, in defense of the existing political system. In other words, Parker's contribution was made during the early and critical months of the struggle when Parliament was engaged in a revolutionary conflict without being quite prepared to admit that revolutionary consequences must ensue.

The first of Parker's pamphlets, published in 1640, was entitled *The Case of Shipmony Briefly Discoursed.* In this brilliant work the king's conception of the prerogative was bitterly and effectively attacked and an exalted theory of the role of Parliament in the constitution skilfully advanced. In the next year he published his *True Grounds of Ecclesiasticall Regiment*, which propounded a startling theory of sovereignty and an extreme statement of the Erastian position.[2]

During the year 1642, in which the Civil War broke out into open flames, Parker published seven pamphlets in which his mature political theory was expounded. The most important of these was his thoughtfully argued *Observations upon Some of His Majesties Late Answers and Expresses.* This original and stimulating work, which has been held in high esteem by numerous modern commentators,[3] provoked a bitter controversy with the royalist champions of the age, whose fundamental position was attacked with such acid logic.[4] The king, in his *Answer to the Petitions of the Lords*

[2] We have previously commented on the contribution of this remarkable pamphlet to religious thought (*vide ante*, pp. 70–85).

[3] Professor Haller has described the work as one of the most important tracts of the Civil War era (Haller, *Tracts on Liberty*, I, 24–26). Mr. Gooch regards the work as a remarkable contribution which had an important effect in hardening the constitutional position of Parliament (G. P. Gooch, *English Democratic Ideas in the Seventeenth Century* [Cambridge, 1927], p. 92). Pease has described the pamphlet as "an original and brilliant attempt" to vindicate the principle of parliamentary sovereignty and as a landmark in political theory (T. C. Pease, *The Leveller Movement* [Washington, 1916], p. 23). Miss Judson, in an illuminating discussion, has dealt at somewhat greater length with the contributions made by this pamphlet (Margaret A. Judson, "Henry Parker and the Theory of Parliamentary Sovereignty" in *Essays in History and Political Theory in Honor of Charles Howard McIlwain* [Cambridge, Mass., 1936], pp. 146–54).

[4] Parker's *Observations* was answered within a few weeks by the anonymous *Animadversions upon those notes which the late Observator hath published, etc.* (London, 1642), a brief but stoutly constructed and well-argued rejoinder, and by *An answer or necessary animadversions, upon some late impostumate observations, etc.* (London?, 1642). In the same year Parker was attacked by William Ball in his *A caveat for subjects, moderating the observator, etc.* (London, 1642), which maintained that Parker had erred grievously in his systematic defense of the ethic of rebellion. Likewise in 1642 ap-

and Commons (July 19, 1642), complained specifically that Parliament had been negligent in protecting the crown from seditious writings of this kind.[5] Parker replied directly to his numerous critics in three pamphlets, all published in 1642. Only one of these, *Contra-replicant, His Complaint to His Majestie,* is of great importance. In this rather angry work, Parker not only attacked the good faith of the king and his advisers but bluntly asserted that parliamentary sovereignty was necessary for the preservation of the nation's fundamental liberties. This position was expanded and matured in his able *A Petition or Declaration, Humbly Desired To Be Presented to the View of His Most Excellent Majestie,* and in the strikingly similar *Danger to England Observed,* both of which appeared in the same year. Parker's prolific writing during this year was completed by the unimportant *Manifold Miseries of Civill Warre and Discord in a Kingdome.*

---

peared Sir John Spelman's *A view of a printed book intituled Observations upon his majesties late answers and expresses* (Oxford, 1642), a carefully argued and impressive defense of the conservative position. Spelman submitted that, of all the spawn of seditious pamphlets, Parker's had been most responsible for intoxicating the vulgar and confusing the responsible of the realm (*ibid.*, p. 3).

In 1643 Parker was assailed in several anonymous tracts, the most important of which were *Christus Dei, The Lords annoynted. Or, a theologicall discourse; wherein is proved that the regall or monarchicall, power . . . . is not of humane, but of divine right, etc.* (London, 1643), possibly by Thomas Morton, and *An examination of the observations upon his majesties answers. Wherein the absurdities of the observators positions, and inferences are discovered, etc.* (London, 1643). Sir Dudley Digges came to the defense of the royalist position in his interesting *An answer to a printed book, intituled, Observations upon some of his maiesties late answers and expresses* (Oxford, 1642), a moderate rejoinder which betrays respect for the power of Parker's logic, and in his *A review of the observations upon some of his majesties late answers and expresses* (Oxford, 1643), published anonymously, though certainly by him. In the latter work Digges suggests that his adversary had expounded a political philosophy consonant neither with the Christian religion nor with English law. In 1643 Bishop Bramhall also replied to Parker in his *The serpent salve, or, a remedie for the biting of an aspe: wherein, the Observators grounds are discussed and plainly discovered to be unsound, etc.* (London, 1643), which criticized the radical's conception of law and which maintained that Parker had made a mischievous assault upon the very foundations of society. The controversy moved out after these publications had appeared to the general issues involved in the conflict then raging in England. Parker, it may be suggested, had opened a momentous discussion.

[5] Edward Hyde, Earl of Clarendon, *The History of the Rebellion and Civil Wars in England Begun in the Year 1641* (Oxford, 1888), II, 235.

In 1643 Parker published two important works which mark the hardening and expansion of his theory of parliamentary sovereignty. The first of these, *A Political Catechism*,[6] is remarkable for a careful analysis of the relations of the king and Parliament; the second, *The Oath of Pacification: or a Forme of Religious Accommodation*, may be regarded as an early statement of the doctrine of ministerial responsibility. Parker published in 1644 his *Jus Populi*, which may be considered the most systematic and persuasive of his numerous tracts dealing with political thought. The work explores in an original fashion the question of the sources of political power, and is an impressive assault upon the absolutist conception of government. Three years later (1647) he published three insignificant and unworthy controversial works in a discussion of political questions with the irascible royalist judge, David Jenkins.[7] In 1650 he appeared in the unusual role of defender of the established political order in a withering attack on the incendiary, John Lilburne, and in the following year he lashed out with wrathful scorn against the perfidy of the Scots and Presbyterians. It is this scattered body of materials which we have now to examine in an effort to bring under systematic analysis the political theory of Henry Parker.

The temper of Parker's mind and the sturdy independence of his political thought were demonstrated by his early and unequivocal attack upon the king and the regality. He was perhaps the first of the parliamentary writers openly to disavow the king and to attack his policy in terms which could scarcely admit of any constitutional compromise. This position was taken at a time when the parliamentary leaders were fighting a civil war under the confused notion that they were waging war upon the evil advisers of the crown. It may be suggested that Parker was the first thinker in England who saw clearly the fact that a struggle for sovereignty was under way in the realm, who dared face with

[6] This writer cannot share Miss Judson's doubts concerning the authorship of this anonymous work. The general point of view, phraseology, and organization all strongly suggest that Parker was the author.

[7] These were *Severall poysonous and sedicious papers of Mr. David Jenkins answered*, *An answer to the poysonous sedicious paper of Mr. David Jenkins*, and *The cordiall of Mr. David Jenkins*.

courageous honesty the constitutional accommodations which must follow upon a parliamentary victory.

The preponderance of political power, Parker maintained in 1642, lies on the side of Parliament. Indeed, it is doubtful if one-third of the realm favors the royalist cause. The king possesses an army which has been able to overawe the "peasantry" in the areas which it dominates, but that army derives its support from the decayed nobility and gentry and from the "lees of the people." On the other hand, "almost all of the yeomenry . . . . and a very choyse part both of nobility and gentry" lent their full allegiance to the Parliament.[8] No king in English history, it may be said, has ever so completely alienated the sympathy and support of the nation. Charles I has fallen from power not so much because of the revolt of his subjects as because the essence of his sovereignty has wasted away.

The Civil War, then, was precipitated when Charles "invaded" the Great Council of the realm, when he abandoned the staff of Parliament for the broken reed of private counsel which had as its design the robbing a nation of its birthright of freedom. Moreover, the king has steadily shifted his constitutional position, has been guilty of duplicity in his dealings with Parliament, and has sought to advance the monstrous argument that it is legally or theoretically possible for Parliament to betray the nation. He has taken up the sword in the name of law against the supreme court of the realm and has provoked civil war in the center of his dominions at a moment when all order and authority lie in ruins in Ireland.

This mad course, this deliberate effort to destroy a nation, can be explained in no other way than by the fact that the king is animated by a blind and feverish thirst for power. And "power being over obtained by haughty mindes, quickly discovers that it was not first aimed at meerly to effect noble actions, but in part to insult over others."[9] Royal power has been so swollen in Eng-

[8] [Henry Parker], *The contra-replicant, his complaint to his majestie, etc.* (London, 1642), p. 20.

[9] [Henry Parker], *Observations upon some of his majesties late answers and expresses* (London, 1642), p. 39.

land that it has disturbed and weakened the fabric of the state. The inevitable result of this unhappy constitutional deterioration has been a revolution directed toward a sharp and beneficent curtailment of a power that has grown arbitrary and irresponsible.[10] Moreover, the revolution in England has been provoked by the king; Parliament and the nation have no other choice than to defend with every energy that can be mustered their most precious birthright, the liberty of Englishmen.[11] No responsible man can deny this when he examines the numerous manifestos of the king, where "we finde professions favouring all of law, right, and limited power . . . . withall intermingled divers positions placing the king beyond all law, right and limitation, and reducing parliaments to lesse power than ordinary courts."[12]

This clear, reasoned, and persuasive analysis of the political situation in 1642 was far more extreme than that then entertained by the generality of parliamentary leaders and theorists. Parker displayed but slight disposition toward constitutional compromise even at this early date because he realized that a revolution was in progress, that the methods of legality had been abandoned, and that either a parliament armed with the spear of sovereignty or a crown vested with the sword of absolute power must emerge triumphant from that struggle. His diagnosis of the causes of the war, his feat of turning the charge of illegality and irresponsibility against the crown, while it oversimplified, and to a degree distorted, a complex historical development, was that ultimately to be accepted by the leaders in Parliament and the army. But even more importantly, in Parker's theory at least, this thesis permitted him to argue that royal sovereignty had been dissipated by the reckless policy of the king, that power had passed into the more competent and responsible hands of Parliament.

[10] *Ibid.*, p. 41.

[11] [Henry Parker], *The danger to England observed, upon its deserting the high court of parliament* (London, 1642), pp. 2–3.

[12] [Henry Parker], *A petition or declaration, humbly desired to be presented to the view of his most excellent majestie . . . . shewing the great danger and inconveniences that will happen both to the king and kingdome, if either his majestie or his people desert his grand and most faithfull Councell, the high court of Parliament* (London, 1642), p. 4.

This deterioration of royal power and of sovereign responsibility had proceeded steadily during the Stuart period, Parker maintained, having reached the point of ruin when the nation was at last provoked to revolution. The crown had been truly strong in England only during those periods when the interests of the ruler and the aspirations of the subject had been inextricably interwoven. This precious identity of interests had been broken by the Stuarts, who were arbitrary, wilful, and dangerous simply because they had been weak. Thus Elizabeth, who was to Parker the ideal sovereign, was guilty of many arbitrary and illegal actions, yet so great was the reverence which her subjects entertained for her, so complete was the identity of interest which bound them to her, that the realm vested in the queen enormous power which she wielded scrupulously for the public good.[13] "Queen Elizabeth by her publick actions doubted not to win her subjects hearts, and being possessed of her subjects hearts, she doubted not but to command both their hands and purses, and what else could she want to make her truly great and glorious."[14] The great queen ruled well and powerfully simply because her policy and actions gained strength in the trust of a nation which reposed absolute confidence in her sovereignty.[15]

Parker, it should be clear, expounded a theory of sovereignty which by its very definitions placed no restraints upon the competence of the magistrate. The allegation which he laid against the Stuarts was not that they wielded an arbitrary power but rather that they had been guilty of political ineptitude and of reckless irresponsibility. They had destroyed their sovereignty by bad government; had led England to the awful edge of anarchy. The Civil War, therefore, should simply be regarded as a struggle whose aim was the permanent transfer of the essence of sovereignty to Parliament, which by a long tuition now stood ready to administer it in the general interest which Parliament itself so perfectly represented.

13 [Parker], *Observations*, pp. 7–8.

14 [Henry Parker], *Jus populi. Or, a discourse wherein clear satisfaction is given, as well concerning the right of subjects, as the right of princes, etc.* (London, 1644), p. 29.

15 [Henry Parker], *A political catechism. Or, certain questions concerning the government of this land, etc.* (London, 1643), p. 5.

This bold and intelligent analysis of the political struggle then raging in England was supported by Parker's view of the origins of political government. He quite declined to be led astray by his royalist adversaries into a morass of speculation about the divine institution of government and of the monarchical establishment. Like Hobbes, he approached the central problems of political theory in a secular spirit utterly contemptuous of the traditional and medieval views on these matters. His discussion was so extraordinarily salutary because he discarded the time-worn shibboleths and attacked the issues of his age with an honest appreciation of the political realities involved and with full concern for the changes which modernity had imposed upon political institutions and political theory.

In the beginning, Parker suggested, "the universe was but one intire" household, and the "raines of government" hung but loosely upon mankind. At some uncertain date the formation of small cities and civil communities began. In this stage of political development, too, authority could be laxly exercised because human relations were at once intimate and uncomplicated. Indeed, Parker remarked with an Althusian nostalgia, if it were not for the scourge of war and the danger of invasion, humanity would be much happier if it were still organized in small political units.[16] But as states became larger and as the danger of foreign invasion increased, monarchical power was established, a stage of development which may be typified by the Jewish kingdom. However, no warrant, no prescription, for absolute monarchy can be derived from that mild government which was directly administered by God. "We must go beyond God and natures workmanship and impressions, before we can discover any thing but parentall majestie, or gentle aristocracie, or compounded or mixed monarchie."[17]

Despotic government is actually an "Asiatic vice," Parker argued, which developed when states grew large and powerful, when their rulers abandoned the prime responsibilities of governance in a mad and ruinous pursuit of expanded dominion. It is a modern phenomenon, unknown to scripture, and the royalists

16 [Parker], *Jus populi*, pp. 43–44.

17 *Ibid.*, p. 47.

have confused the whole issue in England by an almost comic effort to prove that monarchs are divinely ordained and that they must be obeyed as God's lieutenants. This probing into the dim and uncertain origins of political power is actually quite beside the point. Parker insisted that the question which England faced was rather the just extent of monarchical power and whether the subjects had been left destitute of remedy against an irresponsible and incapable ruler.[18] Government and order are divinely endowed, but this does not mean that misgovernment and confusion, cast in whatever form, likewise enjoy God's approbation. Men have been left with freedom of decision. Thus government may be compared with marriage, which is even more explicitly divinely instituted, but this fact does not preclude freedom of choice before marriage or require subjection after the ceremony.[19]

Monarchical government can be shored up by no approbation of scripture or history. The royalists, Parker pointed out, based their case upon the fact that the Jewish kings were anointed, quite conveniently forgetting that the priests and prophets were anointed as well and, for that matter, that the Jewish race was itself holy.[20] They have, in point of fact, sought to apply an exceptional case as a general principle in politics. In so doing, they have identified sovereignty with monarchy so exclusively as to call into question the legality of governments in all republics and in all realms where royal power is limited. This is at once an absurd and a dangerous intellectual position. Any reasonable man must know that royal power, like any other form of government, was "originally inherent in the people, and it is nothing else but that might and vigour which such or such a societie of men containes in it selfe, and when by such or such law of common consent and agreement it is derived into such and such hands, God confirmes that law."[21]

Regality, therefore, enjoys no sacrosanct character, is set apart from any other form of government by no especial virtues. The power of the prince is nothing else than a reflection, a totality, of the power of the society, and he gains and maintains this power

[18] *Ibid.*, p. 2.

[19] *Ibid.*, p. 4.

[20] *Ibid.*, p. 9.

[21] [Parker], *Observations*, p. 1.

by establishing a unity of interests and purposes with his people. The king wields his power in trust for the people, from whom it was derived, and when he violates that trust the very substance of his sovereignty is vitiated by an action for which he alone is morally and politically responsible.[22] And in England, Parliament, the perfect repository of the nation's interests and aspirations, stands as the instrument competent and ready to assume that sovereignty which an irresponsible prince has alienated. Parliament must be regarded as the embodiment of the nation. Princes are its creation, are its designated instruments, accountable in their trusteeship to that organism from which their regality has been derived.[23]

[22] *Ibid.*, pp. 3–4.

[23] It was on this point of the origin of political power and the nature of regal authority that Parker most irritated and frightened the royalists. In reply, William Ball insisted that political power is derived from God and was vested in the people only during the brief moment when they were free to set up whatever form of government they would choose. But the choice, once made, is irrevocable. Hence power in England inheres only in the prince, and limitations upon regal authority are derived from no other source than the grace and honor of the prince (*A caveat for subjects*, pp. 3–6).

The abler Sir Dudley Digges correctly pointed out that Parker had all but taken divinity out of politics (*A review of the observations*, p. 4). When the people by solemn compact deliver political power into the hands of the king, they may not at their discretion forcibly recover it (*An answer to a printed book*, pp. 7–9). It is true that there have been unhappy periods of anarchy when monarchical power has been weakened or overthrown, but this no more proves that power was not originally and sacredly in the monarch than "going upon crutches, after losse of a leg, proves crutches the original and naturall way of going" (*A review of the observations*, p. 4). Digges condemned Parker's *Observations* for its vicious attack on the power of princes, an attack never before equaled (*An answer to a printed book*, p. 16). Parker's whole thesis, he maintained, was based on a narrow, selfish, and reckless concern with the interests of the people which exhibited a complete want of concern with the proper and legal prerogatives of the crown.

The great Spelman also strenuously denied that political power had been originally vested in the people. But even admitting this dangerous hypothesis, he maintained that "if regall power were originally conveyed from the people, they by conveying it over, have devested themselves of it" (*A view of a printed book*, p. 14). To dispute this axiom is to destroy the very nature of government and to deny its continuing possibility. Henry Ferne, in his *The resolving of conscience, etc.* (London, 1642), took precisely this position. Even assuming that power had originally been vested in the mass of men, and "leaving nothing to God in it but approbation, yet could they not therefore have right to take that power away. . . . . Although it were, as they would have it, that they give the power and God approves; yet because [the

Parker sketched brilliantly and persuasively the basic assumptions of modern political theory. His arguments, at once novel and revolutionary in 1642, shocked his royalist adversaries and must have staggered not a little the parliamentary champions with whom he was so intimately associated. It need scarcely be said that Parker's theory ran counter to the whole body of English constitutional thought and that he was in fact proposing an entirely new basis upon which a stable government might be founded. He was one of the first of Englishmen to realize that an ancient society had been dissolved; to understand that history itself required that ultimate responsibility for government must be placed in the hands of Parliament. Having established the propriety and legality of this revolutionary proposal, he was prepared to undertake a careful analysis of the nature of the English constitution and of the proper role of Parliament in the government of the nation.

The ultimate problem in English politics, Parker suggested, was whether the king possessed prerogative powers which made him unaccountable to law and immune to political restraint. As we have already seen, Parker flatly denied the extremist royalist position which endowed the king with a divinely ordained, and hence an inviolable, power. Political institutions, at least in the modern world, are ordered by men for their well-being and security, are designed to meet the requirements of their civilization and the aspirations of particular times and places. Thus the king in England has always possessed "vast prerogatives in doing good, but none at all to do any man, much lesse the whole state, harme."[24] The extent and the limitations of that power are regu-

prince] . . . . is the Lords anointed, and the minister of God, those hands of the people which were used in lifting him up to the crown, may not again be lifted up against him, either to take the crown from his head, or the sword out of his hand" (*ibid.*, p. 15). Morton, in his *Christus Dei*, emphasized much the same argument. The basic impulse of man, he stressed, has ever been to secure his own self-preservation. To this end he has organized commonwealths which "proceed from the common necessity of all mankind, intimated unto them by the law of nature, of which God is the sole cause and author" (*ibid.*, p. 6). Hence the original compact by which plenary powers were delivered to the prince is irrevocable, having been blessed by God, the efficient cause of all commonwealths.

[24] [Parker], *The cordiall of Mr. David Jenkins*, p. 1.

lated, not by God, but by the politically responsible groups within the nation. In England, certainly, there can be no doubt whatever that the prerogatives of the crown lie under very real limitations. For England is a free nation, its sovereign is restrained by law, and he may not, in the event of dispute, sit as a judge in the interpretation of the charters of Englishmen.[25] The power of the king becomes instantly illegal and tyrannous when it ceases to be exercised for the good of the realm.[26]

It had been argued, by royalist extremists, that the prerogatives of the crown are unlimited—are not subject in Parliament to the review of law—because an absolute power has been derived from the Norman Conquest. This contention, Parker submitted, displays an ignorance of history and a perverted kind of logic. We must realize that "if nothing else but the sword had placed William in the chair, nothing else but the sword perpetually unsheathed could have secured him and his posterity therin. . . . . Without some rightfull claime William had been a robber, not a victor, and without the consent of this nation either declaring or making that claim rightfull, the robbery would have lasted for ever, and yet no title had ever accrued thereby."[27] The fact is that the realm consented to the accession of William I and that the Norman rulers were speedily absorbed into the institutions of the land. Hence a valid argument for the unlimited prerogatives of the crown can no more be established in conquest than in the imaginary sanctions of God for an irresponsible regimen.

No other basis can be discovered for a monarchical government than the principle that the king shall rule for the benefit of his subjects. Government, in England at least, is well and truly founded when "the people are subject to the law of the land and not to the will of the prince, and where the law is left to the interpretation of sworn upright judges, and not violated by power; and where parliaments superintend all," and act as arbiter between the king and his people.[28] The prerogatives of the crown are limited by law, and "the good of the subjects is ever to be

[25] *Ibid.*, p. 4.

[26] *Ibid.*, pp. 5–6.

[27] [Parker], *Jus populi*, p. 14.

[28] [Parker], *Observations*, p. 42.

preferred before the monarchical greatness of the king."[29] The peculiar evil of Charles's rule has been that he has been careless of the interests of the realm and has sought to shore up the weakness of his government by a violent overriding of law. Hence perverted views of the constitutional position of the king have arisen which, "instead of giving the subjects a just and compleat propriety in the king, resigne the subject and all that he possesses to the meer discretion of the king, instead of restraining princes where the lawes let them loose, they let loose princes where the law restraines them."[30] The king, it should be repeated, holds his power in trust. When the monarch violates his trusteeship, he acts the "execrable part of a devill" under the majestic robes of a God.[31] For the king is truly the servant of the state, possessed of a greater dignity and authority than the inferior magistrate, but lying under an identical responsibility, for honesty, prudence, and honor.

The prerogative, therefore, is limited not only by law but by the continuing confidence of the realm in the policy of the crown. The whole corpus of written law in England has been created in order to ensure the realm against the possibility of arbitrary government. And it is well that this is true, since "it is more just that we appeale to written lawes, than to the breasts of kings themselves."[32] The prerogative of the prince has been carefully limited in such wise that it will be ample enough to ensure strong government but narrow enough to make the erection of a tyranny impossible. The English constitution, in this respect, may be regarded as effecting a nice balance between the king and the subject, since "the king's power doth not tread under foot the peoples liberty, nor the peoples liberty the king's power."[33] The prerogative has been very carefully defined in terms of law, and any effort on the part of the king to expand regal power at the expense of law can only be regarded as a "mutiny" against the

[29] [Parker], *A political catechism*, p. 7.

[30] [Parker], *Jus populi*, p. 21.

[31] *Ibid.*, p. 22.

[32] [Henry Parker], *The case of shipmony briefly discoursed, according to the grounds of law, policie, and conscience* (London, 1640), p. 5.

[33] *Ibid.*, p. 7.

state.[34] Thus Charles has sought to levy taxes, to govern, and to administer a foreign policy without taking into account the interests of the realm or the express prerogatives and judgment of Parliament. Any nation which delivers its liberties and its property into the hands of a capricious ruler stands in mortal danger, since "princes often vary, but the people is alwaies the same in all ages." When a people surrender the constitutional safeguards upon their liberty, they forget that the alienation of such vast power will either place them in the hands of bad princes or make good princes bad.[35] The king, at least in England, has been given "supreame majesty as to all individuall subjects," but he is none the less "subject to the whole state, and to that supreame majesty which flowes perpetually from that fountaine."[36]

The royal prerogative, therefore, is strictly limited by law, and Parliament, Parker was later to prove, enjoys full power to establish further limitations and, in the event of dispute, to impose its determinations upon the king. The ruler, Parker seemed to believe, enjoyed power only so long as he retained the confidence of the dominant political groups which were, he maintained, perfectly represented in Parliament. Since governance is a sacred responsibility, the prerogatives which accrue to it are forfeited directly the trust which has been reposed in the magistrate has been violated for whatever reason. England, Parker urged, has long been governed by a regulated monarchy, a regimen of law, which stands between the extremes of arbitrary government, on the one hand, and anarchical democracy, on the other. The whole drift of Caroline policy, he was deeply persuaded, had been in the direction of despotism; the Civil War, undertaken to cure this evil, had loosed forces which might bring upon England the curse of irresponsible radicalism unless Parliament gathered the reins of power to itself.

Parker lent careful attention to the dangers of political extremism before turning to an analysis of the proper and harmonious relations which should exist between the king and Par-

[34] "We ought not to presume a prerogative, and thence conclude it a law, but we ought . . . . to cite the law, and thence prove it to be prerogative" (*ibid.*, p. 14).

[35] *Ibid.*, pp. 19–25.

[36] [Parker], *Jus populi*, p. 26.

liament in the English constitution. He believed that states tended to become despotic when they grew too large and when their rulers were imbued with the thirst for conquest. Geography would suggest that the nations of Europe had attained their ideal boundaries in the seventeenth century. When these limits are exceeded, tyranny seems to follow as a kind of corollary, since "great bodies cannot be moved, but with great engines; nor can extensive monarchies be erected or conserved, without extensive prerogatives."[37] For that reason the small state is normally more likely to be able to preserve free institutions and live in peace and quiet than is the great power. Great monarchies have ever been corrupted by war, military rule, and political tyranny.[38]

England, Parker believed, had under Charles I moved rapidly toward the maw of imperial ambition and political tyranny. Absolutism has gained many defenders in the nation amongst men who have not troubled to demonstrate that such a system of government enjoys any validity in the laws or traditions of England. These enthusiasts "must prove that there was cleer law for abjuring liberty, and that the force of the same is universall, and agreeable to that of God and nature."[39] No people can confer more power than it possesses upon any ruler, and no sane man would contend that a nation would willingly destroy those liberties which are its choicest heritage.[40] Nor should any dominion sacrifice itself to the ruthless and insensate lust of any person for despotic power, even though that person should be a king.[41] It is precisely because England has been seriously threatened by an "Asiatic despotism" that the nation has risen in arms to recall from the crown a grant of power that has been grievously abused.

But, Parker made it plain, the Civil War does not mean that the realm will embrace the opposite evil of an irresponsible democracy. For the mark of a democracy has ever been tumult and

[37] *Ibid.*, p. 50.

[38] Parker's brief consideration of this interesting thesis suggests that he may have been acquainted with Johannes Althusius' *Politica methodice digesta, etc.*, first published in Herborn, 1603, and published in its final form in the great third edition, likewise at Herborn, in 1614.

[39] [Parker], *Jus populi*, p. 55.

[40] *Ibid.*, p. 66.

[41] *Ibid.*, p. 30.

violence.[42] The people should be represented by a Parliament which they cannot sway by their passions but which takes into account their interests and well-being.[43] Parker, in his vitriolic attack on the political incendiary, John Lilburne, spoke with scorn of those revolutionaries who would place "mechanicks, bred up illiteratelly to handy crafts," at the helm of the state, thereby debasing men of gentle and aristocratic birth. Such men do not desire free political institutions, but are rather seeking a social and cultural revolution which would lay waste the structure of society. They would "destroy law under the pretext of liberty; and . . . . supplant liberty under pretext of law." This fanatical group would have the "flower of the nation" subjected to its brawn, the gentleman to the peasant, and the judge to the clerk. They desire a democracy which would destroy law, society, and institutions; a liberty which would exceed all "rationall political bounds" and encompass the ruin of the state.[44]

The constitutional genius of England, Parker maintained, had long sought to erect safeguards against the destructive evils of both absolutism and democracy. Hence its monarchy has been "regulated" by law and has been held accountable to law as defined and interpreted by Parliament, the "representative body of the people."[45] Consequently, resistance to any violation of this constitution is not so much rebellion as a defense of the form of government peculiar to the society. The "regulated constitution" of England is an heritage from the past, built upon the experience of history and the wisdom of antiquity. It was molded by Englishmen to fit their particular needs and aspirations; the people, not God, were the original of this frame of government. It is founded upon the Houses of Parliament which "peaceably and sweetly arbitrate betwixt the prince and his poorest vassals, and declining tyranny on the one side, and ochlocracy on the other"

[42] [Parker], *A political catechism*, pp. 5–6.

[43] [Parker], *Observations*, p. 23.

[44] Henry Parker, *A letter of due censure, and redargution to Lieut. Coll: John Lilburne: touching his triall at Guild-Hall-London in Octob: last. 1649, etc.* (London, 1650), pp. 21–22, 28, 39–40.

[45] [Parker], *A political catechism*, p. 2.

preserve to the king the "honour of his scepter, and to the people the patrimony of freedome."[46] Parliamentary government, combining as it does the best elements of all other forms, has provided in England, when the kings have been responsible, the basis for a regimen of great institutional strength which has yet preserved freedom.

The proper functioning of this constitution depends ultimately upon the mutual confidence of the king and Parliament and upon the harmonious pursuit of objectives which have in view the peace, order, and prosperity of the nation. The Civil War was provoked by the evil ambitions of the king to destroy the harmony of the constitution and to arrogate a despotic power to himself. This action, which had no support in law or tradition, precipitated a crisis regarding the ultimate focus of authority in which the "king is to produce his grant (for he hath no more then what was granted) and not the people to shew a reservation: For all is presumed to be reserved, which cannot be proved to be granted away."[47] The king, under the specious plea of emergency, has levied taxes without convening Parliament and has sought to pursue his infamous course of governing without the advice of his Houses. He has forgotten that "the king which is potent in parliament . . . . is as it were so enskonsed in the hearts of his subjects, that he is almost beyond the trayns or aimes of treason and rebellion at home, nay forraign hostility cannot pierce him, but through the sides of all his people."[48]

Charles, then, is the architect of England's ruin. It is he who has sapped the very foundations of the constitution, who has sought to bring a free nation under the galling yoke of tyranny. His advisers have not informed him that the happiness and greatness of England have been built, not upon the king's power, but rather upon the restraints which have hedged about that power.[49] He has forced the realm to choose between the general good and his insane ambitions, has constrained the realm to understand

[46] [Parker], *Observations*, p. 23.

[47] [Parker], *A political catechism*, pp. 2–3.

[48] [Parker], *The case of shipmony*, p. 38.

[49] [Parker], *A political catechism*, p. 3.

that the treason of the subject against the prince is not so evil as the unnatural oppression of the king.[50] Englishmen have been compelled to learn that it "is safer to restrain the king of some power to do us good, then to grant him too much opportunity to do us hurt; and the danger is greater to the people in enlarging the king's power, then in restraining it somewhat."[51] England has been brought by the king to the high necessity of revolution, for he levied dread war upon the institutions of the nation when for many years he sought to govern without Parliament, and, when finally he was obliged to convene it, to bring it to ruin by force, duplicity, and evil counsels.

In still another important sense the king has been responsible for dissolving the fabric of government in the realm, for precipitating a constitutional crisis which has compelled Parliament to gather the reins of sovereignty into its competent hands. No monarch, whatever his pretensions to absolute power, can rule without advisers. Charles, alone amongst English sovereigns, has sought to govern with the assistance of ministers who were at once inexperienced and without the confidence of the dominant political forces of the nation represented in Parliament. Charles has governed both badly and irresponsibly. He has stubbornly fought for the right to follow evil counsels, "though hee bee esteemed inflexible by such as hee hath once judged adverse to his ends, yet hee is much too ductile by those who have once gotten prepossession in his good thoughts."[52] Moreover, the king has persistently assumed so much personal responsibility in the complex and delicate business of government that the structure of sovereignty and administration in England has decayed. "The vast businesse of government, especially where the nation is great, or where many nations are united, is not to be transacted by any one man: Where one man commands in chiefe, the most sublime office of government is attributed to him, but the greatest burthen, and

[50] [Parker], *Observations*, pp. 19–20.

[51] [Parker], *A political catechism*, p. 4.

[52] [Henry Parker], *The oath of pacification: or a forme of religious accommodation: humbly proposed both to King and Parliament. Thereby, to set an end to the present miseries and broyles of this discomposed, almost ship-wrackt state* (London, 1643), p. 11.

most important charge must rest upon the shoulders of thousands, as well in monarchies, as in democracies, or else great obstructions will follow."[53]

Great princes, then, delegate to responsible ministers the actual business of governance and administration. In this way expert assistance is secured, and criticism, when it arises, is addressed not to the crown but to ministers who may quietly be replaced in the event their policy has failed. This, Parker maintained most brilliantly, if prematurely, is the theory of the English constitution, and it has ever been the hallmark of wise rulers. They are truly weak princes who "relish no honour in any thing, but in enjoying their own wills, and their wills they conceive . . . . to be most gloriously fulfilled, when they please themselves by displeasing their subjects."[54] The bitter experience of history has taught us that the welfare of the realm must prevail over the eccentric and prejudicial whims of irresponsible princes. We may truly say, therefore, that the ministers of the crown are "more properly the kingdomes, then the kings ministers," and hence that they should be chosen by Parliament which represents the realm with "utmost perfection."[55] Parliament must be deemed the ultimate repository of sovereignty in England to which the king and his ministers are accountable.

Parliament is vested by the kingdom with the power to punish those who advise the king badly, and it will not heed the inevitable cry of corrupt ministers that they are inviolable since they have served the king. For "the law counts all commands from the king, which are in any way contrary to the law, surreptitiously gotten."[56] Hence the direct command of the king casts no mantle of protection around an unworthy minister. And though such men enjoy the favor, nay the protection, of the king, and even though the king "raise arms" to shelter them against the judgment of Parliament, that supreme body has "power by the law to raise not only the *posse comitatus* . . . . to apprehend them, but also the *posse regni*, the power of the whole kingdom," if that be required to secure a government responsible to Parlia-

[53] *Ibid.*, p. 13.

[54] *Ibid.*, p. 14.

[55] *Ibid.*, pp. 16, 20.

[56] [Parker], *A political catechism*, p. 9.

ment.[57] Certainly it must be said that in no other particular is the authority of Parliament more clearly defined than in the fact that the royal ministers who are charged with the formulation and execution of policy are to be held strictly accountable to it in the administration of their offices. Their tenure of power is the embodiment of the confidence of Parliament; it vanishes instantly when for any reason that confidence is withdrawn.

Parker had advanced a mature theory of ministerial responsibility which shrewdly took into account the basic weaknesses of early Stuart government. He maintained that Charles had erred not only in assuming greater personal power than a modern monarch can exercise but in implementing his policy with ministers who did not enjoy the confidence of the responsible elements in English political life. Parker bluntly asserted that the ministers of the crown should be designated by Parliament and that their policy and tenure of office should be subject to parliamentary criticism and limited by parliamentary confidence. Parker did no little violence to English constitutional history in his contention that this had in effect been the theory of English government in happier ages, but he skilfully diagnosed the constitutional impasse of 1642 and brilliantly outlined the solution toward which the nation was slowly and painfully moving.

In the argument which we have thus far analyzed, Parker was discussing the theory of the English constitution in normal times when the crown worked in reasonable harmony with Parliament and when regal policy took into account the interests and aspirations of the realm. Even in these happy circumstances, as we have seen, Parker vested in Parliament the ultimate source of authority in the English constitution. But the coolly pragmatic theorist was by no means content to pause at this point in his analysis. The central problem in English politics, he submitted, was what could and should be done when the harmony and balance of the constitution were disturbed by a fundamental disagreement between the king and Parliament; when the very essence of sovereignty was threatened by the dissolution of the administrative fibers of government. Parker was perhaps the first

[57] *Ibid.*, p. 10.

English political theorist to submit that England had been plunged into the throes of a revolution which could be terminated only by revolutionary remedies in constitutional theory and practice. Arguments from tradition, reasoning from conditions of normality, flimsy and insincere compromises would be quite incompetent to secure the restoration of order and sovereignty in English political life. The course of historical development in England, Parker strenuously maintained, cried out for heroic remedies for a morbid condition in English political life.

Undergirding Parker's consideration of the revolutionary crisis in politics was a sharp and precise definition of sovereignty, quite as hard and logical as that which Hobbes was to advance in the next decade. Writing in 1641, with the fear of Presbyterianism particularly in mind, Parker sharply maintained that God "hath not left humane nature destitute of such remedies as are necessary to its conservation: and that rule and dominion being necessary to that conservation, where that rule and dominion is granted, there all things necessary for the support of that rule and dominion are granted too." The supreme power in any state must be entire, must embrace all men in order to lend protection to all. The sovereign must stand alone, must control all elements and all forces within the state, must stand inviolate against groups which seek to control or to diminish the essence of sovereignty.[58] In other words, "to be potent hath no terme convertible, but to be potent."[59] Supreme power must specifically be vested somewhere, and it is so entailed in the state that it never dies, ceases, or lies subject to violent alteration. Sovereignty possesses two inalienable characteristics, which may best be described as supremacy and completeness. Thus if Peter possesses more than a capacity to persuade Nero, power in the state belongs by definition to Peter and not to Nero. The scepter cannot be shared, "independence cannot be divided: the people cannot obey both as equall judges whilst their judgments remain contrary, nor serve both as equal lords whilst their commands are contrary."[60]

Sovereignty possesses three essential attributes which can be

[58] [Parker], *True grounds*, pp. 7–8.

[59] *Ibid.*, p. 85.

[60] *Ibid.*, p. 24.

subjected to no restraints whatsoever without incurring destruction of order and the fatal weakening of the state. These are the power to make laws, to interpret them, and to enforce them by competent administrative techniques.[61] The sovereign, then, possesses the totality of power within the state and stands as the symbol and fact of its puissance. Power, Parker wrote, "is as the soule of policy," being of "so exquisite, and delicate sense, that nothing but the wings of cherubims is fit to guard and inclose it, from all rude approaches: vacuity in nature is not a thing more abhorred, or shunned with greater disturbance, and with greater confusion of properties, than the least temeration, and eclipse of power in the state."[62]

Parker had previously demonstrated that historically sovereignty in England had resided in the king in Parliament. The king possessed power by grant from the people; he exercised a regimen which was ultimately subject to the review of Parliament and which in the event of irresponsibility or prejudice to the commonweal flowed back into the great reservoir of parliamentary sovereignty. Charles I had precipitated a revolution, thereby weakening the firm structure of sovereignty by an unnatural and essentially illegal assault upon the constitution. He was therefore in the unenviable position of waging war upon the realm and had thereby created a situation in which a vacuum of sovereignty momentarily existed. That is to say, the king had engendered a conflict in which legality in the narrowly traditional sense must give way to the restoration of sovereignty and the re-creation of a stable basis of order. The political vacuum must be filled, and that at once, by the immense authority, prestige, and genius of Parliament, which has of necessity to gather up all the scattered fragments of sovereignty into its own hands. The king has by his own evil actions and ruinous policy precipitated a crisis in which policy, in which political realities, transcend law and tradition.

This crucial point in his logic Parker maintained with skilful and pragmatic dialectic. Should the state be disturbed by crises and divisions, the safety of the state becomes a matter of prime concern to all men. Common prudence informs us that when

[61] *Ibid.*, p. 86.

[62] *Ibid.*, p. 85.

those that "sit at the head of the common-wealth shall let loose the helm of it, and so let it float at all hazards, or else unadvisedly steere it directly towards rockes and shelves," the commonwealth is empowered and required by natural law to save itself from disaster.[63] This right, for it is the ultimate right of self-preservation, is inherent in every human society and is peculiarly resident in the English constitution, since Parliament possesses in the last analysis the complete potentialities of sovereignty.

In every civilized society the fundamental purposes of law may be described as the protection of the people. In England an inept and reckless king has so far violated the basic principles of governance as to destroy the efficacy of law and thereby has compelled the realm to seek a solution which finds its justification in policy, by which Parker meant prudent necessity. England must face honestly and courageously the fact that policy is the ultimate law of political necessity. Parliament, in other words, has taken refuge in force because no other choice was open to it; a revolutionary solution to the constitutional dilemma must be embraced simply because self-preservation is the supreme law. Therefore, "policy is to bee observed as the only true law, a kind of dictatorian power is to be allowed to her," since he who is compelled to defend himself must be guided by expedient policy rather than by law.[64] This principle of politics, harsh as it may seem, has been evoked by a king who has sought the ruin of his kingdom. Surely "there is nothing more notorious then this, that the peoples safetie is supreme to all judiciall laws . . . . ingraven in our breasts at the creation: so it ought to be the most fundamentall law inrolled in our publick treasuries."[65]

Policy, law, and the necessity for the preservation of social order require that Parliament should take into its own hands the sword of sovereignty. For the political crisis in England, if coolly analyzed, has been patently provoked by the fact that the king has deserted Parliament, has abandoned the foundations upon which his puissance must rest. He has endeavored to make pri-

[63] [Henry Parker], *The observator defended, etc.* (London, 1642), p. 3.

[64] Parker, *Contra-replicant*, p. 19.

[65] Parker, *A letter of due censure*, p. 18.

vate counsels prevail against the public counsel of Parliament and has taken up "the sword against the Parliament, the highest court of law in England," to the consequent wasting of the sinews of legality in his government.[66] He has shrieked that Parliament has betrayed him, completely ignoring the elementary truism that the state cannot conspire against itself and that in all history no Parliament has ever "proved treacherous to the whole kingdome."[67] Since it is the king who wages war against the state, reasonable men can only conclude that it is not the Parliament which "takes up armes against the king, but the whole kingdome in its representative court [which] defends it selfe against such as have seduced, and unjustly incensed the king."[68]

England, in the grave crisis which engulfs her, must move with decision and dispatch; the realm dare not risk the dissolution of all order and legality by involving itself in a senseless discussion of the precise traditional limits of parliamentary authority. The case in England is very clear, Parker repeated. The king has abandoned Parliament, has relinquished the fact and legality of sovereignty, and has abandoned the realm to violence and disintegration. Under these circumstances Parliament, the ultimate reservoir of sovereignty, simply gathers into its own hands the dispersed fragments of power and legality. Its position in such a case is exactly that which would occur if the royal line should come to an end; it would "remaine a living Parliament, and be the supreame power of the kingdome without a king."[69] Sovereignty in England has ever been vested, not in the king, but in the king when he sits in Parliament. Only when he rules in harmony and understanding with the high court of the realm, in other words, does the king possess more than his "owne naturall power, common consent having not derived all power into the king . . . . but reserved much therof till a full union be in parliament."[70] When the king withdraws from this union, he is guilty of desertion, of a kind of voluntary cession of sovereign power to Parlia-

[66] [Parker], *The danger to England observed*, p. 4.

[67] *Ibid.*, p. 3.

[68] *Ibid.*, p. 6.

[69] [Parker], *The cordiall of Mr. David Jenkins*, p. 7.

[70] [Parker], *True grounds*, p. 91.

ment, which must be regarded as the ever constant and ultimately responsible element in national political life.[71]

The royalist political philosophers, Parker wrote in 1647, in contemptuous rebuttal of his critics, held and maintained an ingenuous view of the nature of government. They would suggest that the state is "like a goodly ship, exquisitely decord, strongly man'd, and abundantly riggd with all kinde of tackling; and so built for agility in faire weather, that nothing in that respect can be added to her perfection."[72] Yet they provide her with no safeguards against foul weather, no resilience against the shattering blow of disaster. They choose to forget that the whole frame of government must be designed to withstand the shock of contingency, even though it be as grave and unnatural as the defection of the king from Parliament.

Parliament, then, stands alone, omnicompetently vested in the robes of legality and supported by the requirements of policy, in the governance of England. It was the king, and later the royalist

[71] This argument, which may be regarded as wholly untraditional, raised a storm of protest from Parker's royalist opponents. Spelman reminded Parker that, though the king is greatest when in Parliament, Parliament has neither existence nor competence when separated from him ([Spelman], *A view of a printed book*). Digges, who declined to meet the argument squarely, alleged that Parker had propounded a treasonable doctrine and was deliberately preparing "mens hearts and perswasions, to the receiving of some new forme of government" ([Digges], *A review of the observations*, p. 7). Moreover, he maintained that Parker's reasoning was at bottom anarchical, since it suggests that men may repudiate basic compacts when it suits their convenience. Parker, he insisted, had forgotten that when "one suffers . . . . wrongfully, thousands enjoy the benefit of being protected from wrong. And therefore though it should happen to me in particular, to be condemned by the magistrate without cause, I am bound to suffer patiently, because having made such a bargain, which might have been profitable, I have no right to recall it, when it appears disadvantageous" (Digges, *An answer to a printed book*, p. 44). Ball charged that Parker had set forth an unequivocal defense of the legality of rebellion, which must be regarded as an attack on the fundamentals of government (*A caveat for subjects*, p. 16), while the anonymous but able author of *Animadversions upon those notes which the late Observator hath published* shrewdly pointed out that the revolutionary was really suggesting that the person of the king may be destroyed in order to preserve regality. "My faith," he wrote, "is not strong enough to beleeve these sublime points, and mysteries of state: I shall subscribe this farre, that warre against the kings authority, is warre against the king: but that the king and his person should be in two places, will never . . . . downe with me" (*ibid.*, pp. 11–12).

[72] [Parker], *The cordiall of Mr. David Jenkins*, p. 9.

members, who withdrew from Parliament. Consequently, "that party which remaines constant, and attends duly at the place assigned in the summons for transacting of that businesse which was specified in the summons" retains completely that power and lawful prerogative originally wielded by the entire complex of the constitution.[73] Parliament, it is true, has transcended its normal powers, but it has done so in order to save England and to preserve intact the structure of sovereignty. Thus it levies taxes without the king's consent with plenary authority because such grants proceed normally from its initiative and because in extraordinary times it must do so if the fabric of administration is to be preserved.[74] It has been compelled by historical circumstances to enhance and co-ordinate an authority which rests upon prerogatives and precedents quite as old and respected as those which the king perverted to his own selfish ends.[75] Surely it stands self-evident that "if the kingdomes safety lye upon it, and the king will not concurre in saving the kingdome in an ordinary way, they may have recourse to extraordinary meanes for the saving of it." Parliament could, if it possessed no other sanction, derive its authority in these unhappy times from the general law which permits all men to guard themselves against extraordinary perils by extraordinary means. Parliament has assumed power because the king has provoked a quarrel which is irreconcilable and because he has advanced a theory of government which free men have found to be intolerable. Under these circumstances, "who can doubt, but that princes . . . . are more drawne by the byas of selfe-interests against that which is the good of the communitie, then that court which is not only by the vertue of representation, but even naturally also in some degree the communitie it selfe."[76]

After his careful and elaborate argument that the king had precipitated a crisis in English politics which obliged Parliament to assume the mantle of sovereignty, Parker undertook a thoughtful and persuasive analysis of the structure and extent of parliamentary power. He was the first English thinker to realize fully

[73] *Ibid.*, pp. 15–16.

[74] [Parker], *A political catechism*, p. 8.

[75] [Parker], *Observations*, pp. 5–6.

[76] [Parker], *The cordiall of Mr. David Jenkins*, p. 21.

that the fact and theory of a balanced constitution, posited upon the rock of precedent, had been shattered by an irreconcilable conflict even before recourse had been taken to arms. Thus he advanced the thesis, as early as the disagreement over the Militia Bill, that a crisis had been precipitated which could be resolved only by the assumption of novel and far-reaching powers by Parliament.[77] Since the king and Parliament can no longer find an harmonious basis for regimen, sovereignty must reside somewhere. The Militia Bill, Parker maintained, was essential to the preservation of the state, and hence Parliament must interpose its authority, since it represents the nation at large and aims at no usurpation.[78] It finds itself compelled, owing to the paralysis of the constitution, to intervene with plenary authority as the substitute of the king; to enforce its authority with full exemption from royal interference. This necessity is supported at once by reason and policy, since "the judgement of the major part in Parliament, is the sence of the whole Parliament; and that which is the sence of the whole Parliament, is the judgement of the whole kingdom; and that which is the judgement of the whole king-

[77] The Militia Bill, introduced by Hazlerigg on December 7, 1641, placed the armed forces under the command of a Lord General, to be nominated by Parliament, who would wield plenary military authority. The proposal was a direct and deliberate assault upon an unquestioned—an ultimate—prerogative of the crown. Despite frantic royalist resistance, the bill was twice read during December. The king and Parliament, unable to agree on a formula of compromise, rapidly drifted apart during the early months of the next year. The Houses consequently took the revolutionary step of moving a Militia Ordinance on January 31, 1642, which, despite stout royalist opposition, was passed in February and was ordered put into execution on May 5, 1642 (*L.J.*, V, 46). The quarrel was from this time forward irreconcilable.

Both Ferne and Digges realized that the struggle between the king and Parliament became insoluble during the controversy over the Militia Bill. Ferne quite justly emphasized the fact that the king had yielded on every major issue prior to the introduction of this bill. It was only when Parliament invaded the center of his prerogative that he was obliged to defend the regality (Ferne, *The resolving of conscience*, p. 24 [mispaged 22]). Digges made the same point (*A review of the observations*, p. 14), adding that the king could not yield up his negative without destroying the constitution, breaking "the threefold cord of the state," and dissolving the very frame of English government (*ibid.*, p. 15).

[78] [Henry Parker], *Some few observations upon his majesties late answer to the declaration, or remonstrance of the lords and commons, etc.* (London, 1642), p. 5.

dom, is more vigorous, and sacred, and unquestionable, and further beyond all appeal, then that which is the judgement of the king alone."[79] Parliament stands as the supreme embodiment of the political genius and instincts of the English people. All liberty, all the desires of the nation, are centered in the maintenance of its authority, which is now exposed to the greatest danger from the plots and despotic ambitions of the monarch. Since it stands alone as the guardian of the nation's liberties, it must intervene, when a constitutional impasse has been reached, to set limits beyond which the prerogatives of the crown may not extend. If this be not true, Parker dramatically concluded, "then all nations are equally slaves, and we in England are borne to no more by the laws of England then the asanine peasants of France are there, whose wooden shoes and canvas breeches sufficiently proclaim, what a blessednesse it is to be borne under a meer divine prerogative."[80]

Parker clearly felt that England had arrived at that point of political and institutional maturity which made it possible for Parliament to assume larger, indeed, complete, powers. He found the royalist claims to extensive prerogative insupportable in a modern state and warmly urged the view that the assumption by Parliament of plenary powers was the natural and teleological development of an organic constitution. Nations progress slowly from the brutish sway of an absolute power to the refined liberty characterized by the reign of law and legally imposed limitations on the prerogative.[81] Such mature states have evolved "an art and peaceable order for publique assemblies, whereby the people may assume its owne power to do it selfe right without disturbance to it selfe." In other words, such polities protect the liberties of the state by representative bodies in which ultimate authority is inherent.[82] Therefore, when the hour of crisis comes, decision and responsibility must be vested in those assemblies which truly represent the interests and aspirations of the entire nation. No higher authority can be imagined, "and if we appeal to a lower, that were to invert the course of nature: and to con-

[79] *Ibid.*, p. 9.
[80] *Ibid.*, p. 15.
[81] [Parker], *Observations*, p. 14.
[82] *Ibid.*, pp. 14–15.

found all parliaments for ever; if we call all the kingdom to judge of this, we do the same thing as to proclaim civill warre, and to blow the trumpet of general confusion: And if we allow the king to be the sole, supream competent judge in this case, we resigne all into his hands, we give lifes, liberties, laws, parliaments, all to be held at meer discretion."[83]

Parliament, then, possesses final authority and discretion; when it has spoken even the king must bow to its will. It is, of course, true that in England the substance of sovereignty was formerly vested jointly in the king and Parliament. But England has been called by history to meet the challenge of extraordinary times. The king has withdrawn from Parliament, has raised his spear against the polity, and has embarked upon an arbitrary course which, if successful, "will be made the very engines and scaffolds whereby to erect a government more tyrannicall then ever was knowne in any other kingdome, wee have long groaned for them, but we are likely now to groane under them."[84]

The political issue in England can be accurately and succinctly characterized. A serious and deliberate effort has been made to impose an absolute monarchy on England with the ultimate intention of converting monarchy into tyranny. Parliament lies under the high and legal duty to prevent this perversion of the English constitution, if need be by force of arms.[85] For the two Houses are "the legal judges, when there is danger of tyranny; and they have legal powers to command their judgment to be obeyed, for preventions as well as restraint of tyranny."[86] When Parliament takes this momentous decision, sovereignty has at that moment passed into its hands. Parliament may then command the people, entrust the military to safe captains, raise troops, and levy taxes, whether with or without the king's consent; for the king has already, in these unhappy circumstances, removed himself from the sphere of authority by a kind of self-deposition.[87]

[83] *Ibid.*, pp. 43–44.

[84] *Ibid.*, pp. 21–22.

[85] [Parker], *A political catechism*, p. 10.

[86] *Ibid.*, p. 11.

[87] To this position, Digges rejoined with the allegation that Parker had destroyed the harmony, balance, and structure of the constitution (*A review of the observations*, pp. 7–9). "The erecting of such a superintenary power, would un-sovereign our

Parliament possesses impressive, nay irrefutable, legal authority for the assumption of complete responsibility for governance, since all sovereignty is ultimately derived from it as the representative of the nation. But undergirding this capacity is the more fundamental fact that all monarchy is limited by the public interest and the welfare of the polity. It is this fundamental trust which the crown has betrayed in England. Surely it must be self-evident that "the safetie of the people is to bee valued above any right" of the king. Surely, "it is not just nor possible for any nation so to inslave it selfe, and to resigne its owne interest to the will of one Lord, as that Lord may destroy it without injury, and yet to have no right to preserve it selfe: For since all naturall power is in those which obay, they which contract to obay to their owne ruine . . . . are felonious to themselves, and rebellious to nature."[88] The king, by deserting Parliament and betraying the realm, has alienated his every claim to authority. Under these circumstances the nation has no other alternative than to obey the commands of its representative; the vacuum of authority must be filled, and that instantly.

Henry Parker, as early as 1642, had discarded without evidence of nostalgia the traditional conception of the constitution and had advanced a political theory which was startlingly similar to that which was to underlie not only the revolutionary constitutional experiments but subsequent constitutional development in England. He maintained that the king had endeavored to erect a tyranny in the nation and had thereby forfeited legality of regimen to a Parliament which possessed ultimate political responsibility. More important to his pragmatic intelligence, however, was the fact that the king, having provoked a civil war, no longer

---

king, and make the superintending power soveragine, and when it were made the exercise of it would be subject to more dangerous extravagances than regall power so, and yet lesse capable of regulation than it" (*ibid.*, pp. 12–13). The author of *Animadversions upon those notes which the late Observator hath published* pointed out that Parker proposed to erect a sovereign power more arbitrary than that against which he complained. He, for his part, would prefer to confide his trust to the precedents of law and to the whole structure of the constitutional past (*ibid.*, pp. 1–2, 4–5).

[88] [Parker], *Observations*, p. 8.

possessed the substance of sovereignty, which must be as complete as it is absolute. The Civil War appeared to Parker to be a struggle between king and Parliament which could have no other issue than the vesting of complete power in one or the other. For many reasons which he made abundantly clear, Parker preferred the triumph of Parliament and meeting the bold challenge of the future. The Civil War, he eloquently maintained, had been precipitated by an irresponsible monarch who during seventeen weary and dangerous years had by steady design eroded the laws, liberties, and institutions of a realm composed of free men.[89]

Parliament, then, has accepted the gage of battle and, in so doing, has so enlarged its powers as to assume the responsibilities of sovereignty; for, in addition to its time-honored functions of interpreting and judging, it has now undertaken the final responsibility of enforcing its judgments. This assumption of power, by the very nature of the case, simply excludes the king from the constitution of England. The nation has nothing to fear from this increment of power, since Parliament is in point of fact the very "state itself." It possesses a core of authority, as ancient as the realm, which, having now been expanded to fill the whole circumference of sovereignty, may be employed for the governance of the nation with a perfection not possible in monarchy.

Parliament, which has snatched the nation from the withering breath of tyranny, will found a government of law that will afford a perfect protection to free men. It is a truism indeed that "no nation can injoy any freedome but by the right and share which it has in the lawes . . . . in their true vigour and meaning, as well as to the creation of them . . . . some power we see is of necessity to be reserved in free nations."[90] Parliament is the rock and the refuge of a people who have lain under the threat of very great danger. So strong is its position, so vast its normal and legal authority, that neither the king nor any other force can prevail against the sovereignty which it has assumed.[91] For it "is nothing else but the whole nation of England by its owne free choice, and by vertue of representation united in a more narrow roome, and

[89] [Parker], *Contra-replicant*, p. 5.

[90] *Ibid.*, p. 7.

[91] [Parker], *Some few observations*, p. 6.

better regulated and qualified for consultation then the collective body without this art and order could be. . . . . By its consent royalty it selfe was first founded, and for its ends royalty it selfe was so qualified and tempered."[92] The original of government, and incidentally of monarchy, rested in such bodies of men, in "such counsells as had in them the force of whole nations by consent and deputation."

Hence England need fear neither novelty nor illegality in the assumption, or more accurately the resumption, of plenary powers by Parliament. It has simply taken back into its own hands a trusteeship which has been dangerously and irresponsibly administered. But England should not delude itself concerning what is happening. Parliament has gathered up the reins of sovereignty, which Parker again defined as the complete capacity to make, declare, interpret, and enforce laws.[93] It is vested with a fundamental concern with the protection of the state and with furthering the best interests and the worthy ideals of the whole community of England. It must be guided, particularly during troubled times, by the reflection that laws aim at justice, whereas policy of state is ever concerned with the safety of the commonwealth. "Law secures one subject from another . . . . but reason of state goes beyond all particular formes and pacts, and looks rather to the being, then well-being of a state. . . . . Reason of state is something more sublime and imperiall then law: it may be rightly said, that the statesman begins where the lawyer ceaseth: for when warre has silenced law . . . . policy is . . . . the only true law."[94]

The structure of sovereignty stands complete and uncircumscribed in Parliament. Its power is absolute, but in the very nature of its composition the realm has final assurance that it is not irresponsible. It may make laws, it may "dispose of the treasure of the kingdome," it may abridge the freedom of the subject, and it might, if it were not responsible, even repeal the Great Charter and grant to the king the despotic power which he sought.[95] Its powers may be defined as the totality of the might of the king-

[92] [Parker], *Contra-replicant*, p. 16.

[93] *Ibid.*, pp. 5–7, 8, 16.

[94] *Ibid.*, pp. 18–19.

[95] *Ibid.*, pp. 29–30.

dom.[96] And above all else it possesses an arbitrary power to raise forces and to wage war in defense of its own sovereignty, though, Parker angrily submitted, "to wast time in proving it necessary in times of extremity . . . . were childish and ridiculous."[97] The very heart of government may be defined as unity of authority armed with undivided power. Parliament must jealously remember that "authoritie is the effectuall meanes of producing and propagating unity and therefore whensoever authoritie is divided, unitie may alwaies, and sometimes must admit of division which destroyes it." No prating of the clerics and no imaginings of those who would conjure up a divine sanction for a particular type of government can obscure the hard fact that governance is molded by historical developments and by the convenience of men who know what they want. The state, not a particular form of government, is vested with plenary capacity for the making of the laws by which mankind is guided and ruled.[98]

The theory of sovereignty which, for better or for worse, has dominated modern political thought and development stood complete for the first time in Parker's writing. Hobbes was to add much of proof and logic, but it seems evident that he drew, if not from Parker, from the same reservoir of experience and historical observation. Parker held that the state was man's creation, that it might be molded within the limits of historical destiny to his needs and aspirations. But it was omnicompetent and omnipotent within the confines of the polity. The form of goverment was garbed in the vestments of mortality, not of divinity; power was susceptible to change of form but not to deterioration or division. In Parker's judgment, and at this point he made his most significant contribution to the revolutionary cause and to constitutional development, the interests of England and the hopes of free and reasonable men would be better served by a representative body than by the monarchy which had simply ceased to function as part of an harmonious totality. The Civil War afforded at once the necessity and the opportunity of revolutionary change—a change which Parker embraced with enthusiasm, in-

[96] Parker, *Severall poysonous and sedicious papers*, p. 8.

[97] [Parker], *Contra-replicant*, p. 30.

[98] [Parker], *Jus regum*, pp. 15, 22.

telligence, and a full realization of consequences. Parker was perhaps the first Englishman fully to understand that revolution has no other meaning in politics than revolution.

Moreover, it is interesting to observe, Parker remained completely consistent in his political theory after the triumph of the parliamentary cause, the execution of the king, and the establishment of the Commonwealth. He defended the revolutionary government with a cool pragmatism which gained an enormous increment of strength from his theory of the state and from his views on the nature of sovereignty. To those royalist pamphleteers who disquieted the English conscience on the troubled question of the execution of an anointed king and to those fainthearted parliamentarians, of whom there were many, who shrank back from the full implications of revolution, Parker rejoined that a war in which sovereignty was at stake had been waged and that the late king had paid the inevitable price of defeat. The doctrine that the king was above the law, he submitted, had been the principal issue tormenting England for years—an issue which war finally and decisively resolved by the victories of the parliamentary armies.[99] Charles was executed because his stubbornness, his chronic indecision, and his plots threatened the stability and strength of a new political order created by the parliamentary victory. Parliament had therefore to be moved in its determination not by precedent or law but by the fundamental consideration of the safety of the state, which is, in point of fact, the end of all law and "paramount to the law it selfe."[100]

Under these circumstances a decisive, Parker would almost suggest a symbolic, action had to be taken. Charles had necessarily to be destroyed because so long as he was alive sovereignty, which must be seated explicitly somewhere, hung uncertainly in the balance. In other words, the form of government was finally changed by that action, but the core and structure of government were neither weakened nor overthrown thereby.[101] Hence there can be no question about the fact or the legality of the govern-

[99] Parker, *Scotlands holy war*, p. 19.

[100] Parker, *An answer to . . . . Mr. David Jenkins*, p. 5.

[101] Parker, *Scotlands holy war*, p. 29.

ment of the Commonwealth, principally because legality stems directly from the fact of sovereignty, is, indeed, its essential attribute. "We . . . . hold this to be a true Parliament," Parker wrote, "and . . . . the true Parliament is ever the supreme authority of England." To lend weight to this axiom England has not only the decision of the sword "but also the strongest reason, and [the] majority of suffrages of all the people throughout the land."[102] Actually all other considerations have but an academic interest beside the supreme one of trial of war.

It should be clear, Parker maintained, that it is a matter of political indifference whether the sovereignty of the Commonwealth is *de jure* or *de facto*. No man can possibly question the fact that it is sovereign nor deny that private men may not rise up against a settled government.[103] This conclusion may be distasteful to sentimentalists and irreconcilables, but it must be accepted by all men who prefer order to anarchy. "Government is now devolved, and as it were, naturally resolved into the hands of the people: and as monarchy cost us a vast effusion of bloud, before it necessitated its own ejection, so it is likely to cost as much now," if any effort be made to re-establish it.[104] The revolutionary government has demonstrated its sovereignty and by that very fact has ceased to be revolutionary. It is armed with great power which it has proved it can and will use effectively in its own defense.[105] Nor will that government permit the fabric of its sovereignty to be weakened by factional divisions, clerical ambitions, royalist plots, or the slightest uncertainty concerning the seat of authority in the English nation. It must be understood that the form of government is wholly subordinate to the fact and necessity of government. "Laws create forms, and laws uphold forms by oaths; but neither forms, nor oaths binde longer then the laws: and we see, there is a subordination even amongst laws themselves, and by the rules of that subordination" forms and laws are determined by the necessity and reality of sovereignty.[106]

This stern conception of sovereignty does not mean, Parker

[102] Parker, *A letter of due censure*, p. 29.
[103] *Ibid.*, p. 31.
[104] Parker, *Scotlands holy war*, p. 62.
[105] *Ibid.*, p. 63.
[106] *Ibid.*, p. 77.

hastened to add, that the tyranny which England struggled to overthrow in the Civil War will be re-created by the new government. Parliament derived its power from and built the foundations of its sovereignty on the thesis that free men must be protected by law and must be governed responsibly. However, this does not mean, he wrote in direct attack upon Lilburne and the extremists, that liberty can be permitted to degenerate into anarchy. Liberty is the due birthright of every Englishman. Liberty, however, has "its bounds and rules; and the liberty of every member must be subordinate to the liberty of the whole body." Liberty, he warmly argued in a passage which Hobbes might have written,[107] belongs "to the whole state, as well as of any particular subject: and that liberty of the whole state must supersede the liberty of every particular subject, whensoever both accord not."[108]

Henry Parker, it may be suggested, framed, during an era of intellectual confusion and grave political dislocations, a persuasive, logical, and entirely consistent philosophy of the state. We have frequently suggested that the greater Hobbes owed very much indeed to the keen analysis, the cold speculations, and the pragmatic sense of his contemporary. It should likewise be pointed out that in one important particular Parker was the more honest, or at least the more consistent. Hobbes, though the question evidently perplexed him in the *Behemoth*, never candidly admitted the fact, which lay implicit in his theory of the state, that

[107] Thomas Hobbes, *The English Works of Thomas Hobbes*, ed. Sir William Molesworth (London, 1839–45), II, 178–81; III, 199–205; IV, 157–58, 215–16. *Vide* especially Hobbes's remarkable passage in the *Philosophical Rudiments concerning government and society:* "There are some, who . . . . imagine monarchy to be more grievous then democracy, because there is less liberty in that, than in this. If by liberty they mean an exemption from that subjection which is due to the laws, that is, the commands of the people; neither in democracy, nor in any other state of government whatsoever, is there any such kind of liberty . . . . for the one as truly consisteth with such a liberty, as the other. For although the word liberty may in large and ample letters be written over the gates of any city whatsoever, yet is it not meant the subject's, but the city's liberty; neither can that word with better right be inscribed on a city which is governed by the people, than that which is ruled by a monarch. But when private men or subjects demand liberty, under the name of liberty they ask not for liberty, but dominion" (*Works*, II, 134–35).

[108] Parker, *Scotlands holy war*, p. 69.

the Cromwellian government was *de jure* simply because it was *de facto*. In an age which lent real as well as nostalgic reverence to tradition, Parker courageously faced this problem in his earliest political writings and gave it magnificent exposition in his later works.

Parker's thought was marked by great originality and by a candor badly needed in the confused discussion of political ideas which marked the years of internecine struggle. He disliked and distrusted monarchy, not it would seem because of philosophical objections to it as a form of government, but because he believed it had outworn its usefulness in England. He stressed the fact that it had undergone steady deterioration since the reign of Elizabeth, and fundamentally he attacked it because the sword of sovereignty had slipped from its irresponsible and ineffective fingers. The function of government, he steadily reiterated, is to govern well and strongly. The crown in England had alienated the dominant elements in the political life of the nation by what appeared to be a desperate attempt to erect a tyranny, but what was more accurately a feeble effort to disguise the essential weakness of the monarchical form. Hence sovereignty had burst into particles during an interval of civil war. The clear and prime issue of the constitutional conflict in England had been to decide the question of which hands would re-form the shattered vessel of sovereign power.

It need scarcely be observed that Parker's thought did considerable violence to the theory of the English constitution, but as the historian reflects upon the political situation during the months that preceded and followed the convention of the Long Parliament he is persuaded that it took the political realities accurately into account. Parker, from the very beginning of the war, constantly maintained that a revolution was in progress which could be ended in no other way than the decisive victory of one side or the other. Since he was a parliamentary partisan, he worked and hoped for the victory of Parliament, but he differed sharply from his colleagues in and out of the House in the realization that victory could not be vitiated by compromise. He therefore called upon Parliament to assume the prerogatives of sovereignty, to settle a new government based upon responsibility to the nation at large, the subordination of religious zeal to secular ends, the efficient administration of law and order, and the conscious adaptation of the constitution to the requirements of a new age. This capacity lay within the hands of Parliament, he eloquently proclaimed, not only because it was the original and ultimate source of power and legality in England but because sovereignty flowed to it in a molten stream as the inevitable consequence of victory.

2. HENRY ROBINSON

Although both men display the same temper of mind, Henry Robinson was far less significant as a political thinker than Henry Parker. It would perhaps be fair to say that Robinson was not a political theorist at all in the strict meaning of the term. His ideas about politics were sharply hewn, but they were at bottom derived from his notions of practicality and convenience. Robinson devoted his mature life to the great causes of religious liberty and economic and social reform. These were his dominant passions, and he was quite content to accept any political order which would afford adequate guaranties that these great gains might be attained and preserved for mankind. The forms of governments and the structure of constitutions should consequently be elastic in order to accommodate the aspirations of mankind and the rapid progress which he staunchly believed humanity was about to make toward religious, social, and economic justice. Robinson therefore displayed a keen interest in political reforms, but only a slight interest in or knowledge of political theory.

Above all else, he insisted, men must approach the problems of politics moderately, reasonably, and pragmatically. Abhorring all war, he especially deplored the violence and fanaticism which marked political discussion and political action during the years of the Civil War. Those prudent men who "endeavour to qualifie or decline the precipice of extreames," ought not to be denounced as lacking in convictions, he wrote during the early days of the civil conflict. All those on the king's side are not papists, and certainly all those supporting Parliament are not sectaries or incendiaries. Robinson, in this troubled period, saw grave dangers in the complete triumph of either party, since both the warring groups were extremist and hence not likely to safeguard liberty and tolerance in the flush of triumph. "Surely both parties," he wrote, "should be desirous of composing such a difference, which in so high a nature and degree, is totally destructive unto both. But alas! The jealousies are such, that neither dare well offer, or entertain a treaty, lest the other should make advantage of it."[109] England can in the end gain peace and secure the restoration of order only when men of moderate persuasion and of common sense have assumed the responsibility for founding a government tolerant in its policy, comprehensive in the liberty which it affords, and moderate in its regimen.

Robinson remained cautious in his political judgments during the critical years of the Civil War when it seemed probable that the triumph of Parliament would be synonymous with the victory of an intolerant Presbyterianism. Since he was primarily interested throughout his life in the establishment of a complete religious freedom, he tended to estimate political institutions in terms of this ideal. When, however, it became apparent that the leadership of the Presbyterian faction had been discredited and that religious toleration must be the cornerstone of the triumphant revolutionary government, Robinson directed his full and warm support to that regime. He was deeply persuaded that England could best be served and ruled by an aristocratic government, unmarred by the blemishes of royal or popular irresponsibility, which would be characterized by a completely secular spirit, by a moderate and responsible temper, and which would be sensitive to the currents of historical change. Like Parker, he was no democrat, believing that government in England must be based squarely on those groups within the polity which possessed wealth, the traditions of leadership, and the tangible evidences of personal and community responsibility.

Henry Robinson's principal political writings, save for incidental references in several of his religious works, appeared during the years 1647–1653. As we have previously observed, Robinson was occupied during the critical years of the Civil War with writing a remarkable series of pamphlets in which he lent sys-

[109] [Robinson], *Liberty of conscience*, Pref.

tematic defense to a noble theory of religious freedom. Royalism and Presbyterianism having been defeated, he turned in 1647 to the political and economic problems which he believed the revolutionary government must solve.

The first of his political writings, *Articles and Orders, Made and Agreed upon the 9th Day of July, 1647 . . . . by the Company of Adventurers of the Islands of Eleutheria, Formerly Called Buhama in America, etc.* (London, 1647), may be assigned to Robinson only with reasonable certainty. This remarkable document sketches an ideal constitution for the plantations in the Bahamas. The views here propounded on religious toleration, the separation of church and state, the economic structure of the community, and the essentially aristocratic character of the constitution all strongly suggest that Robinson was the author of this anonymous tract. As significantly, an examination of the syntax, phraseology, and spelling lends confirmatory support to this supposition. Tentatively, at least, therefore, we may attribute this important and somewhat neglected treatise to Henry Robinson.[110]

Two years later (1649) Robinson made his most important contribution to political thought in the *Short Discourse betweene Monarchical and Aristocratical Government.* This short pamphlet brilliantly attacked the principles of monarchical government and sought to demonstrate that an aristocratic constitution was perfectly suited to the requirements of a mature English society.[111] Robinson's later works, *Certain Considerations in Order to a More Speedy, Cheap, and Equall Distribution of Justice Throughout the Nation* (1651) and *Certaine Proposals in Order to a New Modelling of the Lawes and Law-Proceedings* (1653), were principally concerned with his demands for far-reaching economic and political reforms, but both throw considerable light on the able merchant's political philosophy.

110 The attribution was first made by Mr. Fulmer Mood in a careful essay in the *Transactions of the Colonial Society of Massachusetts*, XXXII, 155–73. Mr. Mood has reprinted this scarce tract in *ibid.*, pp. 81–85.

111 This able pamphlet was published anonymously on the press which published several of Robinson's known works. The general point of view and the philosophy here expressed leave little doubt concerning the attribution. The work has been attributed to Robinson by the *D.N.B.*, the McAlpin catalogue, and the University of Chicago catalogue.

Robinson's political thought was marked by shrewd analysis, a blunt pragmatism, and a remarkable ability to move directly to the essentials of an argument. Thus in considering the difficult and elusive problem of the original sources of political authority, Robinson cut through traditional confusion and complexity in order to bring common sense to bear upon the question. It is clear, he wrote, that though government enjoys divine sanction, God's approbation can be claimed for no particular type of government. Those persons, he suggested, about a year after the execution of the king, who decline to accept the sovereignty of Parliament are guilty of rebellion against government, which enjoys the approval of God, while worshiping the traditional form of monarchy, which possesses no other virtue than antiquity. Men have been left completely free to consult their convenience and self-interest in erecting that form of government which most adequately fulfils the needs of a particular time and place. "God, who is a God of order, hath ordained governments, and delights to see his creatures made happy by them, and therefore hath left them to choose what they think may be most fit for that end, and to call it by what name they please."[112] Had God blessed no government save monarchy, no other regimen would possess any authority to the consequent confusion and ruin of humanity. God, it should be understood, estimates the validity of any government by the peace, order, and justice which it secures to its citizenry rather than by its wholly accidental form.

Since the frame of government and the constitution of the state may be regarded strictly as a matter of convenience, we may accept expediency and prudence as the basic principles of politics. Robinson, in expounding this position, was guided by a completely pragmatic view of political theory. No laws, no basic axioms, can be established in politics, since "there are commonly many unknown difficulties to be waded through" and a "multitude" of unpredictable emergencies which afford us no choice but to adapt our political philosophy and our institutions to the requirements of prudence.[113] The form of the government which rules us

[112] [Henry Robinson], *A short discourse between monarchical and aristocratical government, etc.* (London, 1649), p. 9.

[113] *Ibid.*, p. 3.

and administers our affairs is a matter of complete indifference so long as it discharges its responsibility intelligently, justly, and efficiently. Actually, it should be recognized, a despotism may administer the affairs of state so well and so effectively that "a people might enjoy better dayes under it," than within a state which possesses a perfect theoretical frame of government but which is ineffective and careless in attending to the complex business of governance.[114] Those who would govern men must acquire the practical sense of the merchant and must possess talents for hard work and responsibility which, thus far at least, have characterized too few of the rulers of the earth. In England there is at least hope that this ideal may be attained. The nation, Robinson wrote in 1649, has been obliged by history to move quickly and radically in adapting the frame of her government to the requirements of political necessity. The theorist endeavors to discover "design and subtlety" in these developments, but the reasonable man will understand that the nation lay under an inevitable compulsion of change.

Robinson shrewdly observed that the early actions of the Long Parliament foretold the results of the Civil Wars; revealed a dynamic of great power which could have no other possible issue than the destruction of monarchical government in England. It was evident from the very beginning that Englishmen would be content with nothing less than liberty, though at first the stark struggle for power was obscured by the traditional and tender language with which men were accustomed to address the king. Inevitably, when the king was at last defeated, the time had come "to take the advantage of Providence, and [to] make use of that honest power . . . . and go through with that which we did but dally with before."[115] The physical destruction of the king was nothing else than an incident following inevitably, indeed insignificantly, upon his political destruction. His execution was a necessary symbolic act designed to fortify the peace and liberty achieved by the triumph of the parliamentary arms, since "our liberty and his life were grown incompetible, and inconsistent."

Men and nations must accept that which is inevitable in their

[114] Robinson, *Certain proposalls in order to the peoples freedome*, pp. 2–3.

[115] [Robinson], *A short discourse*, p. 6.

destiny; they wander dangerously indeed when they seek to recapture a past that is gone. England has taken a decisive, an irrevocable, step which is sanctioned by the validity of fact. Men must consequently accommodate themselves to what has happened and turn at once to the framing of a new government which shall rest upon broad, deep, and enduring foundations. The nation must seek a common end by a convenient government, carefully adapted to its needs; must forget and forgive the past by an act of oblivion; and must face the future in amity and confidence. England has cast off the shackles of tyranny and injustice; she stands on the threshold of a great and proud future which will be graced and secured by liberty of the subject, freedom of conscience, expansion of commerce, and the reign of law.

It is evident that Robinson was employing his persuasive logic in an effort to relieve the tension and to dispel the fog of uncertainty which followed upon the execution of Charles I. For a short time even the parliamentary leaders were stricken with a paralysis of indecision when in sober afterthought they came to appreciate the full implications, in theory and in fact, of the decisive measures which had at last been taken to end the Civil War. Few English thinkers in 1649 equaled Robinson in his blunt, unflinching, and persuasive analysis of what had happened. He believed that government, like ecclesiastical organization, was a matter of pure convenience to be administered and altered by architects who would build a fitter habitation for liberty. He stood quite alone in his analysis of the teleology of political events which from the convention of the Long Parliament had made the destruction of monarchical power inevitable. The execution of Charles I, he argued, was a trivial incident in the momentous transfer of sovereign power to Parliament.

The transcendent fact, to which every Englishman must adjust his life and loyalties, is that Parliament is sovereign and that the old order has been swept away. No credence can be placed in the consciences of those who would pretend that they are still bound to the monarchy by anterior oaths and covenants. It is at once impudent and unreasonable to pretend that the conscience can be bound to the person of a king who is dead or to a frame of government that has ceased to exist. We all grant that "no oath bindes me when I am dead, neither can any oath binde me to dead persons, or things not in being."[116] Government possesses no sanctions against us save by the simple and demonstrable fact of governing. That government which possesses the power to govern is by definition the legal order within the state to which we owe the full measure of our loyalty and obedience. The Civil War, quite as truly as the Middle Ages, is over in England; history has made a decision of political fact to which all men must adjust their theories.

Actually, Robinson observed, it is fortunate that England has cast off the outworn shell of monarchical government. Whatever past virtues it may have possessed, it has for many years been in process of steady deterioration and was evidently unfitted for a mature polity and a complex economy. The nation is no longer a hostage to the accidents of the succession and can plot its course by bearings taken with certainty and deliberation. Surely no one can entertain any reasonable regrets because of the course which events have taken. When we "reflect on kingly power in this nation, and the sad fruits and effects of it, especially of late . . . . we shall see little reason of being so endeared to it, much less to dote on it. . . . . How nigh were all our liberties to give up the ghost under it?"[117] Princes have characteristically been less zealous and intelligent in the discharge of their high duties than have private men in the conduct of their affairs. Pleasures, wasteful spending, and expensive pageantry have been their consuming interests, whilst their ministers have normally devoted their time to ruinous intrigue.[118] Monarchy is a bankrupt institution, which has no place in a busy, complex, and thickly populated nation.

Moreover, history has amply demonstrated that monarchy and liberty are incompatible, even when, as in England, nations have endeavored to set hedges of restraint about regality. Shall England, after a bitter tuition, seek again to join monarchy and liberty together, Robinson enquired—those incompatibles "which (I had almost said) God and nature have divided. . . . . Have we ventured so hard, for to gain our liberties, and shall not we now take the advantage of procuring them? Or do we think that slav-

[116] *Ibid.*, p. 10. [117] *Ibid.*, p. 11.

[118] Robinson, *Certain proposalls in order to the peoples freedome*, p. 4.

ery is any whit the more amiable, because it hath the name of royalty annexed to it?"[119]

The steady tendency in English politics for many years, Robinson maintained, had been in the direction of securing greater liberty for the subject with a concomitant weakening of the monarchical power. The inevitable culmination of this process was the supplanting of the crown by political instrumentalities directly responsible to the nation and more consonant with the aspirations of a people at last worthy of freedom. The whole issue of politics, focusing in the recent crisis, is at once clear and simple. When a king rules by his own will and caprice, he is nothing else than an irresponsible tyrant. When, on the other hand, he rules by the counsel of Parliament and his advisers, "then its' the council that rules the kingdom, who can do it as well, and with less hazard without him" and the temptations to which a monarch exposes them. As Parliament has matured in responsibility and experience in England, monarchy has become progressively more inconvenient and at last unbearable. The Civil War simply occasioned the final transfer of the full content of sovereignty to a representative and responsible body which had long been competent for the exercise of plenary powers.

These developments should occasion no regret in England, for the nation is well rid of an institution which no longer fits the facts of political life in the community. Indeed, "if we do but cast up our accounts right, we shall find that kings are but meer chargeable ceremonies, or ciphers, of little use but to contract humors, and promote personal designs destructive to the being . . . . of common-wealths." They perform no particularly useful, and certainly no indispensable, functions of government. The institution has gradually ossified until we observe the spectacle of a man "maintained in the greatest state, and glory, meerly to sit still" in order to receive the fawning adoration of the ignorant.[120] England by a kind of surgery has at last freed herself from the restraints, expense, and complications of a form of government which no longer possesses either meaning or function in her political life.

The frame of government which has, happily, replaced mon-

[119] [Robinson], *A short discourse*, p. 12. [120] *Ibid.*, p. 14.

archy in England, Robinson maintained, is an aristocracy. Parliament, he suggested, in the mode of its election, its traditional competence, and in its sense of general responsibility possesses all the commendable features of this form of governance. Aristocracy is in every particular to be preferred above monarchy. It "hath many more curbs, and bridles on it to restrain it from exorbitancy, then can be set on monarchy, and is so less capable of doing mischief to a nation then the other."[121] Quite as importantly, those charged with aristocratic responsibility are not as removed from the nation or as indispensable, in a symbolic sense, as a monarch. Kings, from the very nature of their position, can have no other ultimate ambition than to make their power absolute, whereas an aristocracy reflects the common longings of the nation and enhances the liberties of the entire community in the protection of its own.

Aristocracy, it is fair to say, possesses all the virtues of monarchy and would seem to be free of all its vices, including, it should be remarked, excessive cost. It is, we may believe, "the most even, and just government, that any men have yet come to the knowledge of, it being a middle state between popular anarchy, and prerogative tyranny, whereby men are freed from the necessary exorbitancies of both, and [are] seated securely in a uniform and equal condition free from all extreams."[122] We may say, therefore, that it embodies a moderate point of view which will deliver England from the fanatical extremisms which, as Robinson had observed, animated the opposing sides in the early days of the Civil War.[123] The aristocratic republic is above all else truly representative and sensitively responsive to the needs and grievances of the nation, since it must, as an attribute of its very nature, govern justly within the ambit of law. Furthermore, as the experience of Holland and Venice has amply demonstrated, the aristocratic state may easily and quickly attain stability, wealth, and good repute amongst the nations of the earth. England may be quite sure, "had other nations but the liberty to speak, and the freedom to choose as we have, we should soon hear which way the vote would go."[124]

[121] *Ibid.*, p. 12. [122] *Ibid.*, p. 14. [123] *Vide ante*, pp. 178–79.

[124] [Robinson], *A short discourse*, p. 15.

England, Robinson eloquently and confidently concluded, has at last divested itself of a government which had nothing but the dubious antiquity of tyranny to support it. The crisis of the recent past must not be permitted to obscure the vital fact that the change from monarchy to aristocracy has actually been evolutionary rather than revolutionary. Nor has the change in the seat of sovereignty eroded the basic institutions of the land: the laws, the constitution, and the structure of government remain much the same. But a clean and irrevocable break with the past had of necessity to be made in the destruction of monarchy, with which no compromise was possible and which, in the very nature of the case, could not be altered.[125] A strong and competent government has been founded which will root out tyranny on the one hand and repress the anarchical demands of incendiaries on the other. This government rests securely on all that was sound in the ancient constitution, and it faces the future confident in its own strength and armed with the resolution to invest England with a greater liberty and to guard her with a vigilant governance. It must now lend its hand to the restoration of order and stability within the nation, to the unshackling of the religious conscience, and to the satisfaction of the pressing social and economic requirements of a people already past the threshold of a great and glorious future.

Robinson's political thought is further illuminated by the model constitution which he prepared in 1647 for the plantation in the Bahamas.[126] As we would expect, the *Articles and Orders* for the proposed Independent plantation in the Bahamas established complete religious liberty as a fundamental law.[127] It was pointed

[125] *Ibid.*, p. 18.

[126] *Vide ante*, p. 180, for a discussion of the attribution of this anonymous pamphlet.

[127] The Bahamas had been neglected by seventeenth-century adventurers until 1644, when one George Gardyner visited the islands with a view toward obtaining a grant. A year later the then governor of Bermuda, William Sayle, while in London on official business, petitioned for a grant permitting the colonization of the Bahamas. It is not certain that Parliament granted an official license, but in any case Sayle left Bermuda in 1647 with about seventy Independents for the purpose of founding a settlement (Mood, *Transacts., Col. Soc. of Mass.*, XXXII, 81). The *Articles and Orders* were published in London in the same year with the purpose in mind of attracting capital and settlers.

out that rigorous courses in religion had ever had the effect of fomenting divisions, raising up factions, and weakening the internal order of the state. A destructive intolerance has prevailed in Christendom despite the fact that Christian men cannot possibly hold precisely the same views or give the same account of their talents. Consequently, the new colony had resolved to permit no distinctions, no reproaches, in matters of faith and worship. It had been explicitly determined that the magistrate should confine himself strictly to civil matters and should take no "notice of any man for his difference in judgement in matter of religion."[128]

The proprietors of the colony were to be limited to one hundred, each of whom should contribute the sum of £100. Three hundred acres of land would be assigned to each of them, while a further grant of two thousand acres each was to be made at a later date, presumably after the settlement had been made. Moreover, the proprietors were to receive thirty-five acres of land for each colonist settled at their expense, while twenty-five acres were to be allotted to each colonist after five years of residence in the islands. All minerals, timber, and salt reservoirs, not on lands already allocated, were to be exploited for the common advantage by agents of the proprietors and the community. Careful provision was made for the relations of the colonists with the native Indians. Since some of these had already been sold into the "Caribe Islands," they were to be redeemed and returned. In the future, the colonists should, "in their converse" with the natives, offer them no wrong or incivility, but should "deal with them with all justice and sweetness, so far as may stand with their own safety, thereby to work in them a good opinion of love, unto the wayes and knowledg of God."[129]

The government of the colony was to be vested in a senate of one hundred members, consisting of the original proprietors. This body was to be self-perpetuating, vacancies being filled as the original proprietors died or sold their interest. Directly the settlement had been completed, however, a governor and a coun-

[128] [Robinson], *Articles and Orders*, *Transacts.*, *Col. Soc. of Mass.*, XXXII, 82.

[129] *Ibid.*, p. 84.

cil of twelve were to be elected by all the freemen of the plantation, and thereafter this civil government was to be charged with full responsibility for the administration of the constitution of the colony.[130]

This rather rough constitutional sketch, evidently composed without much knowledge either of the Bahamas or of the prospective emigrants, does at least disclose the basic principles underlying Robinson's political philosophy. Government was to him a frame of administration which should be adapted to time and place and which should be intelligently accommodated to the needs of the community. Distrusting radicalism and respecting property, he was disposed to entrust ultimate political power to an aristocratic group which had a tradition of public service and which possessed the resources of the polity. Government should take carefully into account the economic resources of the state, and its form and policy must ever be molded by the requirements and opportunities of commerce and industry. Above all else, he taught, civil governments in the modern world must legally disavow any responsibility for the conscience and salvation of their citizens. The participation of the magistrate in the affairs of the church has had no other issue than persecution, strife, and disunity. The state must therefore found itself squarely on the rock of religious toleration and, even more importantly, must extend to every man and to every sect an unrestrained freedom of worship.

Henry Robinson's contribution to political theory, when compared with that of Parker, was slight and unsystematic. The merchant was far more interested in concrete abuses and in specific reforms than in the basic problems of politics. A pious, generous, and warmhearted man, he was stirred to wrath by those political and social grievances which he felt must be remedied before England could enjoy the glorious future which he loved to envisage for her. We have seen that he demanded that the parliamentary victory should be made the occasion for the completion of the reformation in religion, for the eradication of intolerance and persecution, and for the extension of a perfect liberty to all men of good will and prudent conduct. Similarly, he taught that

[130] *Ibid.*, p. 85.

the new state which was to be erected upon the ruins of monarchy must be animated by the resolution to effect badly needed social and political reforms. The dry dust of medievalism, he repeatedly urged, must be swept clean from the fair structure of church and state. The wrongs and injuries of the past, rooted deep in tradition, must be eradicated if free men were to enjoy the full measure of their victory and inheritance.

The worst of the evils which afflicted mankind, Robinson firmly believed, was war. Though he failed to address himself to the problem systematically, he appeared to believe that an aristocratic republic, cautious in policy and responsible in its composition, would avoid the senseless wars of aggrandizement and the criminal wars of dynastic ambition which had characterized monarchies throughout history. War has been the worst of the scourges under which humanity has lain. One must admit the possibility of a just war, which Robinson seems to define as the defense of a state against unprovoked attack, or the expectation or diversion of an "eminent invasion,"[131] yet when the dispassionate man examines the facts in any "legal war" he is impressed by the blame which must always be assessed against both sides.[132]

In Europe, he pointed out, wars have been at once more numerous and more savage since the establishment of Christianity. In recent times, particularly, whatever the real occasion for war may have been, religion has been the dynamic cause, to such an extent, indeed, that "no man might adventure to call in question the lawfulnesse thereof, or seem backward in supplying without palpable scandall and suspition of luke-warmnesse in religion."[133] No war, certainly, has ever been waged for a truly religious reason, yet Europe has been reduced to a shambles by wars fought in the name of faith. At bottom this is the result of the tragic identification of the magistrate with the intolerant ambitions of clerical castes which have ever sought to create an exclusive ecclesiastical structure by the destruction of dissent. Moreover, this bloody intolerance has been extended, since the Reformation

[131] *Ibid.*, pp. 84–85.

[132] [Robinson], *Liberty of conscience*, pp. 1–2.

[133] *Ibid.*, p. 2.

shattered the fabric of Catholicism, to the waging of external wars in the name of the "true faith." The only possible hope for saving the structure of society and the vitality of Christian faith must therefore be found in an absolute tolerance within nations and between them. When this has once been obtained, the prime cause for wars of peculiar savagery will at last have been eliminated.

Robinson's general contribution to political theory was provocative and original, if somewhat unsystematic. However, to one particular problem—that of law reform—he was to lend systematic and persistent attention. He devoted two important pamphlets principally to this question, the one published in 1651 and the other in 1653. In the preface to his *Certain Considerations* (1651) he warned Parliament that it must devote itself zealously and persistently to the high task of strengthening and preserving the liberties which the English nation had won. He had, he pointed out, "been known to cast in my little mite, concerning many, if not most matters of publick debate, not so much out of confidence of my own strength, as sincerity of heart, and for provoking others of better abilities to improve them."[134] But of all the remaining problems and political injustices, he could lend his pen to no more important cause than the reform of the law, the taming of the lawyers, and the cleansing and improvement of the courts. The entire system of law, which must be regarded as the framework of the state, must be remodeled and refurbished if the polity designed to replace monarchy is to survive.

Robinson's tracts on the question of law reform are perhaps the most impressive of a considerable body of writings on the subject which appeared during the period of the Commonwealth and the Protectorate.[135] Agitation for the reform of the law, for the simplification of court procedure, the relief of debtors, and the pro-

[134] Henry Robinson, *Certain considerations in order to a more speedy, cheap, and equall distribution of justice throughout the nation, etc.* (London, 1651), Pref.

[135] Among these writings might be mentioned W. Cole, *A rod for the lawyers* (1650); G. Fox, *The law of God* (1658); *The representative of divers well-affected persons with regard to the present laws and government* (1649); *Certain queries for the publike good* (1647); *An appeal from chancery to the Lord General* (1653); S. Chidley, *A cry against a crying sin* (1654?).

tection of litigants from excessive fees and unreasonable delays, which had been latent for at least a century, burst in 1649 into a powerful and widespread demand that the entire body of the law and the structure of the judicial system should be simplified and improved. It should be pointed out that these demands proceeded not only from the radicals but acquired a particular vehemence in the writings of rich merchants like Robinson and amongst the responsible gentry in the House of Commons. Perhaps lawyers in England had never been quite as unpopular, unless it were under the suspicious eyes of Elizabeth, as they were during the decade beginning in 1650. This general feeling was shared by Cromwell, who sought from time to time to stimulate the work of the parliamentary committee for regulating law which was appointed in 1651. In 1652 a committee headed by Whitelocke made a preliminary report which was implemented by acts remedying a few specific abuses. Parliament, in the next year, undertook the more ambitious task of considering a possible codification and simplification of the whole of English law and procedure, only to discover that the difficulties were innumerable, the task Herculean, and the opposition as evasive as it was implacable.[136] But it was spurred on, at least to a consideration of the problems involved, by the persistent and angry demands of thinkers like Robinson, who persuasively pointed out that the foundations of the new government could never be made secure until the structure of law had been accommodated to the realities of the age.

On no other subject did Robinson display quite as much explosive and righteous wrath as in his indictment of the legal profession. England, he submitted, has gained much by the abolition of monarchy, the weeding-out of episcopacy, and the foundation of at least a limited religious freedom. But the task of Parliament in securing the liberation of the people will not be complete until the lawyers have been chastened. It will be generally agreed that "the lawyers, the men of law, the whole tribe, from the judges to the prison-door-keepers . . . . have not onely been

[136] Mr. Goldwin Smith has dealt briefly but thoughtfully with the agitation for reform of the law during this period in his essay, "The Reform of the Laws of England," *University of Toronto Quarterly*, X, 469–81.

mischievous and destructive as canker-wormes . . . . unto these nations, but have ever been those mercuriall spirits . . . . civil tormentors and executioners, to carry on and practise whatsoever our persecuting oppressing governours . . . . have been executed for."[137] Robinson wondered, indeed, whether the profession enjoyed an ethical or legal basis at all, since the lawyers accept more cases than they can possibly care for, charge outrageous fees, conspire to prolong suits, and involve "the whole kingdome in their sophisticall quirkes, tricks and quillets, as that a man can neither buy nor sell, speake nor doe any thing, but he must be lyable to fall into their talons, without ever being able to redeeme himselfe."[138]

The lawyers, Robinson alleged in an unusual burst of reckless estimate, absorbed at least one-fifth of the national income by the devious technique of shifting cases back and forth, delaying trials, and, when a case at last proceeded to adjudication, robbing their clients by piratical fees.[139] Even more serious, in his view, was the fact that they had deliberately created a myth that the law was "the most abstruce and difficult [study], and consequently to require the greatest art and study to be exact and profound therein of any in the world."[140] This is palpably dishonest, for any man can make a valid legal judgment if the law and the offense are clear. The dark and subtle mysteries of the law melt away directly honesty and common sense are applied to any case. Actually, the skill and reputed learning of the profession rest upon an artificial jargon and an illiterate mumble into which the lawyer retreats in order to protect himself with unintelligibility.[141] They have written their mysteries out in what is little more than a "heathen language" and have kept men in captivity by a kind of magic.[142]

It is evident, Robinson insisted, that no reform of the laws and courts can come from the lawyers; that is quite as impossible as

[137] Robinson, *Certaine proposals . . . . to a new modelling of the lawes*, pp. 1–2.

[138] [Robinson], *The falsehood of Mr. William Pryn's Truth Triumphing*, p. 22.

[139] Robinson, *Certaine proposals . . . . to a new modelling of the lawes*, p. 2.

[140] *Ibid.*, Pref. (5).

[141] *Ibid.*, Pref. (6).

[142] [Robinson], *The falsehood of Mr. William Pryn's Truth Triumphing*, p. 22.

the vain hope that reform of the church could proceed from the clergy. This task, like so many others, waits upon the lay intelligence and the sovereign power of Parliament. Robinson therefore desired to submit to the legislature a detailed and systematic criticism of the existing body of law and of judicial procedure with specific recommendations for reform which would secure to all Englishmen greater liberty, more certain justice, and substantial financial relief.

Parliament must first address itself to "the multiplicity of courts of justice" which occasion more confusion than a babel of tongues. The whole judicial system, which has developed without plan, should be reorganized. The surviving special jurisdictions should be eliminated, and procedure should be simplified.[143] Moreover, Parliament should lend its keenest attention to the strange multiplicity of laws which no layman can possibly remember, understand, or respect. It might be better, in fact, to have no written laws at all but to attempt the enforcement of the principles of the Golden Rule, which are engraved in the heart of every human being.[144] Robinson feared that "such a court as we meane by a common law court, must necessarily be so literall, so bestial, as that it must not yeeld a haire upon any occasion," with the unhappy result that revenge and rigidity rather than mercy characterize procedure and determine decisions. England is governed by laws and courts which disgrace her position amongst the nations and which make a mockery of her free institutions. It is a sad commentary that in the Catholic countries abroad, where faith and learning have been kept in chains, justice has for many years been cheaper and more equitable than in England. The whole of the law is nothing else than the vestigial remain of an ancient oppression; law, conservative in its very nature and protected by a skilful vested interest, will be the last area that will yield to freedom and modernity. The laws, therefore, must be entirely recast, simplified, and rationalized if they are to reflect and preserve the liberties and institutions of a free people.[145]

[143] Robinson, *Certain considerations*, Pref.

[144] Robinson, *Certaine proposals . . . . to a new modelling of the lawes*, Pref. (3).

[145] Robinson, *Certain considerations*, Pref.

Robinson maintained that statute law must be subjected to a particularly careful scrutiny by Parliament. It should ever be recalled, he argued with historical carelessness, that it was for many years the favorite device of the crown in its efforts to shackle England with the tyranny of the prerogative. The whole complicated structure of the statutes must be carefully examined to the end that the laws of England may be brought into conformity with the freedom won by the hard trial of arms. The nation must stand as a vigilant master over the law, ever aware that the tentacles of tradition and sophisticated interpretation may once more enslave the commonwealth.[146] Special consideration should be given, as well, to the chancery courts, which have gradually become extra-legal instruments, and, as long as a litigant remains solvent, may be effectively employed for the delay and frustration of justice.[147] The chancery and common-law courts should be "dashed together" as the first step toward establishing an entirely new judicial system framed in such wise that simplicity, reason, and equity shall constantly redress the wrong done by the harsh letter of the law.[148] As a provisional solution, indeed, Robinson proposed the drastic measure of abolishing all of the existing law courts and of lodging judicial capacity in the justices until a new structure of courts could be established.

Parliament, in approaching the difficult and delicate problem of law reform, must of necessity be guided by certain fundamental principles. It will surely be admitted that a free state cannot long exist when its laws and courts reflect an ancient tyranny. As evidently, knowledge of the law is no less necessary to all men who hope to enjoy life and liberty than "the knowledge of those religious, eternall, fundamental principles of faith and love, without which it is impossible to attaine the joyes of heaven."[149] Finally, and most importantly, Parliament must be vigilant against the complaints and recommendations of the lawyers. So like the priests are they, that they desire to perpetuate a system of caste and to pervert truth and justice to their own selfish advan-

146 Robinson, *Certaine proposals . . . . to a new modelling of the lawes*, p. 4.

147 Robinson, *Certain proposalls in order to the peoples freedome*, pp. 1–2.

148 Robinson, *Certain considerations*, pp. 3–4.

149 Robinson, *Certaine proposals . . . . to a new modelling of the lawes*, p. 2.

tage. All efforts thus far have failed to secure a reformation of the laws and law courts because of the subtle skill with which the lawyers have prevented the adjustment of law to the political and social realities of English life. It is because of them that "these poor nations still continued to be mis-governed by a hotch-potch of linsey-wolsey lawes, so numerous, as not to be learned or comprehended, some so differing as that they contradict and give the lye to one another, so irrationall and absurd, to spare worse words, as that they character us to be one of the most barbarous people in the world."[150] The law, the lawyers, and the courts must be reduced by the sheer weight of sovereignty; must be forced to serve the interests of the state; must be made the bulwark, not the enemy, of free institutions.

Robinson's proposals for reform were pithy, concrete, and intelligent. Several of them subsequently found a place in the statute book, while others are still matters of discussion and consideration in England and the United States. His recommendations, taken as a whole, however, display too little understanding of the inevitably conservative nature of the law and of the procedure which must underlie it. Nor is there reason to believe that the system of courts which he proposed would serve much better the ends of justice, promptness, and economy which the reformer hoped to realize. Robinson failed to understand that judicial procedure in free countries must ever be slow if judicial error is to be avoided or that few cases are devoid of that reasonable doubt which habitually obscures the face of justice. Robinson, like most laymen, was unable to appreciate the fact that the judicial process could not possibly be reduced to the simplicity of a commercial transaction.

Robinson suggested, as the first measure of reform, that the procedure under which a prisoner was compelled to enter a plea of guilty or of not guilty should be abandoned. It has meant in practice that men have often been obliged to condemn themselves, which is contrary to natural law, or, more often, that they have incurred the serious guilt of perjury when on trial for relatively trivial crimes. The ends of justice would be better served and

[150] *Ibid.*, p. 3.

human rights more adequately safeguarded if the state simply proceeded against the prisoner with the witnesses and evidence which it had been able to assemble.

Furthermore, all reasonable men know that the ancient system of trying cases by a jury of twelve men, especially on minor charges in the lesser jurisdictions, is at once expensive and unsatisfactory.[151] There are not "a competent number of understanding and fit men to be had in the lesser divisions of a county" for such cases, and men who do possess the competence are generally able to evade service. The whole theory of jury trial actually rests upon the myth that twelve men can arrive at an honestly unanimous verdict. Ordinarily "one or two active and nimble-pated men over-sway all the rest," with the result that a verdict is brought in which has been reached under a kind of compulsion, or attained under the pressure of sheer fatigue. "It is well neer impossible for twelve men, all circumstances considered, much more in a doubtfull case, to be of one opinion; and though the case were never so cleare, yet one peremptory man of a strong constitution, whether his judgement be right or wrong," can usually bend the jury to his opinion.[152]

[151] This statement was vigorously attacked in a brilliant pamphlet by William Walwyn, entitled *Juries justified: or, a word of correction to Mr. Henry Robinson, etc.* (London, 1651). Walwyn, a close friend of Robinson's (*ibid.*, p. 13), was likewise a prosperous London merchant and a member of the Merchant Adventurers' Company. His views on the problem of toleration and on general questions of church and state were strikingly similar to those entertained by Robinson.

But on this question he professed that he must differ sharply with Robinson. His friend, he said, entertained too low a view of the competence of simple men in the hundreds and parishes of England and quite forgot that local freedom had since the Conquest been the great bulwark of national freedom. Robinson, he regretted to say, exhibited a "proneness to invention, a humour for the most part got by travel, but proving very unhappy to this nation" (*ibid.*, p. 2). He had tried without avail to persuade Robinson not to publish this portion of the *Certain considerations*, which he must regard as a threat to English liberties. It must be asserted, Walwyn maintained, that trial by jury is the very wellspring of English freedom. The instinct of justice is more firmly rooted, he acidly commented, amongst the freeholders than amongst "our sharp-sighted, smooth tongued travellers" (*Juries justified*, p. 4). Robinson, despite the fact that so many profitable favors had been bestowed upon him, sought here to bring into question the English conscience and sense of justice. In this "solid stuff" of the nation, justice and freedom in England rest secure (*ibid.*, p. 12).

[152] Robinson, *Certain considerations*, p. 3.

For the ancient jury system in the minor jurisdictions, Robinson proposed the appointment by Parliament of judges in every city, corporation, and traditional local division, before whom all matters of civil and criminal controversy would first be brought. All minor disputes such as questions of trespass, assault, and actions for debt, when the sum involved was less than 40*s.*, should be tried at once before the nearest justice, who should render his decision within two days.[153] Moreover, the whole antiquated law of debt should immediately be reformed to provide that any person unable to pay his debts after six months' imprisonment should, upon the assignment of all his property save "his own," his wife's and children's wearing apparel, bedding, and instruments particular to his calling, be legally discharged of his obligations.[154] All cases must in the first instance be brought before the local judge in the jurisdiction in which the defendant resided. The judge should deal with the litigants informally at the outset, attempting with the help of the local minister to settle the case out of court. If this could not be done, the litigants should proceed immediately to free trial, and a judicial decision should be pronounced by the local judge, who should be competent to determine civil suits when the sum or penalty involved did not exceed 50*s.*[155]

The local judges, appointed by and responsible to Parliament, would, Robinson believed, be able to secure a compromise in a majority of cases and certainly to settle most of the minor cases which came up for trial. More serious cases would be sent up to the county court, which should likewise entertain appeals from

[153] Robinson, *Certaine proposals . . . . to a new modelling of the lawes*, p. 8.

[154] *Ibid.*, pp. 20–21. During the revolutionary era more progress was made in the reform of the law of debt than in any other branch of the law. Robinson's proposal evidently sought further to lighten the act of 1649 (Firth and Rait, *Acts and Ordinances*, II, 240), which discharged all debtors in prison who could swear that they had not more than £5 of real or personal goods and not more than the same amount in clothing, bedding, and tools. A parliamentary committee was appointed further to consider the problem in July, 1653, with the result that an act was passed in October, 1653, which instructed the judges to examine the facts in every case of imprisonment and which permitted the discharge of debtors under certain stipulated conditions (*ibid.*, II, 753–64).

[155] Robinson, *Certain considerations*, p. 4.

the lower jurisdictions.[156] If the judgment of the lower court should be sustained by the shire judge, the penalty should automatically be increased by one-sixth, while if the original judgment should be reversed, the local judge should be held financially responsible for the costs of the appeal.[157]

The judges of the county courts, who were particularly essential to Robinson's scheme, must be men of learning, wisdom, and broad experience. They should be well paid, should be subject to extremely heavy penalties for accepting bribes and gratuities, and should hold their courts every day save Sundays and public holidays.[158] Moreover, the shire judges, like their colleagues in the local jurisdiction, should be chosen by Parliament rather than by popular vote, lest the people "make choise of such as may be swayed with alliance, of one kind or another."[159] The judge should stand aloof from the popular passions and should be moved by no persuasion save that of justice. In order to prevent them from striking their roots too deeply in any particular community, they should be transferred periodically to a new jurisdiction. Their position in the community must be beyond any possibility of reproach and their loyalty should extend only to Parliament and the laws of England.

The shire judge, carefully selected and generously paid, should be empowered to hear and try all cases. He should perhaps be relieved of the pressure of minor litigation by a last effort, when cases were brought up from the lower courts, to settle them by the intervention of two justices of the peace, familiar with the issues involved, who should attempt to arrive at a settlement satisfactory to the litigants. When a case is finally admitted to the court of the shire judge, all evidence and depositions should be filed with him in advance of the trial in order to make possible the introduction of new evidence and the preparation of cross-examination before the case is formally opened. This having been done,

[156] Robinson, *Certaine proposals . . . . to a new modelling of the lawes*, p. 8; *Certain considerations*, p. 7.

[157] Robinson, *Certain considerations*, p. 8.

[158] Robinson, *Certaine proposals . . . . to a new modelling of the lawes*, pp. 8–12, 2–6.

[159] Robinson, *Certain considerations*, p. 11.

all cases can be tried promptly and decisions handed down without excessive delay.[160] Every effort should be made to simplify procedure and to make the processes of law clear, orderly, and economical.

The judgment of the shire court should be regarded as final and binding unless an appeal be made within eight days to Parliament, the supreme court of the realm. The judge should be made liable to heavy penalties in the event of his decision being reversed upon appeal, but such reversals will be rare since the only ground for an appeal would be the deliberate perversion of justice by the shire court. The judge must be protected against frivolous appeals, and Parliament reserved for the correction of grievous miscarriages of justice, by the provision that the unsuccessful plaintiff will be liable to precisely those heavy penalties which the judge would incur in the event of his decision being reversed.[161]

Finally, Robinson suggested that the chancery jurisdiction should be abolished and that all courts should be endowed with equal powers in law and equity. The distinction between the common-law courts and chancery has for many years been a menace to the liberty of the subject, has occasioned unreasonable delays in the settlement of suits, and has been exploited by greedy lawyers for their private gain. It is true that the common-law courts have been notoriously slow and expensive, but once a case has proceeded to chancery it has stayed there until the funds of the weaker litigant have been exhausted. It would almost seem as if justice itself had been sacrificed between these two grinding and crushing stones of jurisdiction. "How easie a matter were it then," Robinson exclaimed, "to prevent such waste of time and moneyes in following two courts so diametrically opposite? Had you not better that either of them should dispatch you, and put you out of paine speedily, then to be ground in pieces between them both so long together?"[162]

[160] Robinson, *Certaine proposals . . . . to a new modelling of the lawes*, pp. 12–13.

[161] Robinson, *Certain considerations*, pp. 9–10; *Certaine proposals . . . . to a new modelling of the lawes*, pp. 12–14.

[162] Robinson, *Certaine proposals . . . . to a new modelling of the lawes*, p. 7.

It may be suggested, in summary, that Henry Robinson made fresh, thoughtful, and forthright contributions to the discussion of political issues in England. While his thought in this sphere was unsystematic, it was honest in its appraisal of the problems which harassed the nation and vigorous in its prescription for their solution. Robinson was in the forefront of those who discarded traditional and conventional theories regarding politics; he sought at every point to think of government in terms of the needs and aspirations of his age. He regarded the frame of government as a matter of convenience and expedience, denouncing with effective rhetoric those who sought to find in conscience reasons for declining to lend their loyalty to the revolutionary regime. It is doubtful whether any thinker of the age subjected the institution of monarchy, as it had developed in England, to such withering and telling criticism. Moreover, he rendered invaluable assistance to the infant Commonwealth by declining to be drawn into the hysterical controversy precipitated by the execution of Charles I, and by advancing the bold argument that this definitive action was in point of fact an insignificant incident stemming inevitably from the course of events since the opening of the Long Parliament.

But Robinson's political views were neither radical nor democratic. It was his considered judgment that sovereignty in England had for many years been gathering into the hands of an aristocracy which perfectly represented the nation in Parliament. The landed and commercial classes, which he thought constituted the aristocracy, were at once responsible in their habits, skilled in the complex business of government, and sensitively attuned to the needs of the nation. The future belonged to these classes, which possessed the wealth and intelligence of the nation. The Civil War was for Robinson nothing else than a decisive indication that England had attained a political maturity which permitted, nay necessitated, the extension and strengthening of free institutions.

The aristocratic republic envisaged in his political writings was to be dedicated to the maintenance of order, the preservation of liberty, the protection of property, and the safeguarding of the individual man's freedom to carry on his lawful pursuits without undue hindrance. This state was to be purely secular in its instincts and policy. It should sharply and clearly dissociate itself from the ecclesiastical affairs of the nation save for the institution and maintenance of a complete religious liberty for all sects which did not endanger sovereignty. It must reform and simplify the law, cleanse and modernize the judicial system, and make of law a great supporting buttress for free men living within the protection of free institutions. Robinson's was a noble vision of a free nation which would extend to the men of which it was composed a larger freedom, a richer life, and a finer dignity than mankind had hitherto enjoyed.

VI

SOCIAL AND ECONOMIC THOUGHT

1. INTRODUCTION

THE revolutionary decades in England were characterized by a ferment of discussion of social and economic problems which had hitherto been scantily treated or ignored. The era was germinal: the entire structure of modern social and economic thought was to be foreshadowed in at least rough outlines. Much of this discussion, as revealed in the hastily written pamphlets and memoranda of the revolutionary years, was extraordinarily fruitful, provocative, and, as time was to show, prophetic. These thinkers, of whom Robinson is perhaps the most important, were resolved that the attainment of political and religious freedom should be accompanied by the reform of social abuses and by the enlargement of economic opportunities for individual and nation alike. They were, on the whole, relatively conservative in politics, while their social and economic thought proceeded from the assumption that wealth, whether landed or mercantile, must undertake responsibilities which were essentially aristocratic. This group of theorists made notable and lasting contributions to that body of thought which lies at the foundation of the liberal polity.

On the whole, however, much of the economic and social literature of the period is undistinguished and unimpressive. Much of it ranges from the impracticable dreams of the visionary to the disordered gropings of the demented. In general, it may be suggested that the thought of the incendiary political groups—the Fifth Monarchy Men, the Levellers, the Diggers, and the more violent republicans—was quite as divorced from the economic realities of the age as it was from the political necessities of the period. Moreover, the economic and social thinking of the more radical sectaries, animated as it was by the vision of the Kingdom of God on earth, was in most instances so detached from the trend of English development as to be without great significance for the period. There has been a tendency in recent years for historians to place particular emphasis on a body of materials which during the age that produced them was regarded as eccentric or unbalanced. Such sources have novelty to recommend them, they may actually suggest the course which later historical development has taken, but they remain, none the less, inadequate and untrustworthy guides to the historian who is seeking to analyze the morphology of thought in an earlier era.

The economic and social writings of Robinson and Parker, on the other hand, lay in the main stream of thinking during the revolutionary period. Both men were more radical than the government of the Protectorate, though they were intimately associated with it as advisers and civil servants. Both men exhibited in their thought a striking degree of independence from the various "pressure groups" which sought so vigorously to divert the revolutionary movement to special and non-national ends. Robinson, particularly, was a respected counselor of the government in social and economic matters, though he ever stood just a little in advance of contemporary development. He was chief of a group of original, responsible, and intelligent men who constituted the vanguard of the revolution, who explored ahead, opening up new vistas toward which men of a liberal and tolerant persuasion ever since have been pressing.

It should be borne in mind, in attempting to estimate the importance of the social and economic ideas of Parker and Robinson, that their proposals, and particularly those of Robinson, reflect the thought and aspirations of only a small and enlightened wing of a rich, powerful, and selfish merchant aristocracy. The two men stood closer, actually, to the government of the Commonwealth and Protectorate than to the class to which they belonged. We should remember that though the commercial aristocracy of London was almost solidly allied with Parliament at the outset of the Civil War, though it lent valuable assistance to parliamentary arms by its counsel and its loans, the unity and enthusiasm of the group very soon disintegrated. This development was occasioned in part because the long years of war seriously unsettled trade and because the levies of Parliament soon made the earlier impositions of the crown insignificant by comparison. More important, however, was the fact that from the beginning the merchants of London formed the one group lending solid support to the Presbyterian ambition to establish a tightly knit, exclusive, and disciplined Calvinistic Church in England. The war was brought to a successful conclusion and a new government was founded by men who had specifically repudiated this ideal; by men who were persuaded in conscience and reason that a tolerant and comprehensive religious structure could alone secure peace, order, and stability in England. As this policy began to be implemented by the Protectorate, many of the merchants passed into positive, if unorganized, opposition to the trend which the revolution had taken.

Moreover, the merchant classes were alienated because they were not often consulted in the formulation of policy and because they were, on the whole, excluded from the seats of power. It should be pointed out that Cromwell's government was less influenced by the City than was the government of his royal successor. In matters of fiscal and commercial policy Cromwell and the Council very frequently consulted with Robinson and with Martin Noell, both of whom were enlightened merchants, or with the great goldsmith, Thomas Vyner, but the decisions taken were invariably guided by political or strategic considerations. Indeed, Cromwell's policy was rarely influenced and was on no occasion deflected by specifically economic objectives. The Council of State was almost entirely composed of landed gentlemen, while Parliament, throughout the period, was dominated by the landed aristocracy and by the remarkable group of Erastian lawyers whose contributions had been of momentous significance during the crucial days of civil war.[1]

[1] Mr. M. P. Ashley has dealt carefully with this question in his excellent *Financial and Commercial Policy under the Cromwellian Protectorate* (Oxford, 1934). He estimates that there were only twenty-seven merchants in the Long Parliament, two, aside from London merchants, in the Nominated Parliament, and not more than seventeen in any one of the parliaments of the Protectorate (*ibid.*, pp. 5–7).

The Cromwellian government, partly because of the genius of its head and partly because of the dangers to which it stood exposed abroad, was above all things else political in its conception and implementation of policy. It might be suggested, indeed, that Cromwell's hand bore more heavily upon the merchant class, in such matters as taxation and concern for the profits and prerogatives of the great companies, than had the "tyrannous sceptre" of the first and second of the Stuarts. Cromwell's regime was prudent in politics, conservative in its approach to social reform, extremely cautious in its commitments to economic experimentation, and, on the whole, suspicious of the aspirations of the merchant class which had invested so heavily and rashly in the stock of revolution. Men like Robinson and Parker, however, who had contributed so vastly to the philosophy which undergirded the political and spiritual revolution, who had courageously and steadfastly taught that the new constitution must embrace the idealism and welfare of the entire nation, who had from 1641 onward moved in the center of thought and action, were at once more trusted and more respected by those who wielded revolutionary power in England.

2. HENRY PARKER

Henry Parker's social and economic thought, when compared with that of Robinson, is at once slight, unsystematic, and undistinguished. His most important work, *Of a Free Trade* (1648), was a vigorous and intelligent defense of the Merchant Adventurers' Company, then under heavy attack in and out of Parliament, and was written in Hamburg, where he was residing as a servant of the company.[2] His other pamphlet, *The Vintners Answer*, was likewise written as a defense of a company under particularly vigorous attack and, the text would suggest, may well have been composed under commission. Parker's economic thought, in brief, does not exhibit that originality, grasp, and vision so characteristic of his more important contributions in politics and religion.

[2] The pamphlet, which was dedicated to John Kendrick, alderman of London and governor of the company, and to the members of "the said famous company," was signed at Hamburg, December 30, 1647.

The attacks on the commercial monopolies, widespread since the beginning of the century, acquired violence and velocity as the Civil War came to an end. Inspired by the irrepressible Lilburne, the radical Kiffen, and the more thoughtful Johnson, the dislike for all trading monopolies became focused in 1648 on the Merchant Adventurers, the oldest and most powerful of the companies. There is a considerable body of this pamphlet literature, supplemented by innumerable petitions from the clothiers and small tradesmen to Parliament, which sought to persuade the government that all restraints on the cloth trade should be removed. The privileged traditional monopoly of the company was declared to be a survival of royal prerogative, to operate in restraint of trade, to snuff out small enterprises, to contribute to the decay of the woolen industry, and to threaten the political liberty so recently won in England.

Parker's first defense of the commercial monopolies appeared in 1642 when the vintners were under attack in Parliament for having consented in 1637 to the levying of an imposition of 40*s*. a tun on the importation of wine. The parliamentary investigation disclosed that a proprietor named Kilvert, who was a confidant of Weston, a member of the Council, had conspired with Abell, a London alderman and master of the Vintners' Company, to secure a patent.[3] In November, 1640, the vintners, alarmed by the hostility engendered by the increase in the price of wines and by the suspicion voiced in Parliament, petitioned to the Committee for Grievances against Abell and his assistants.[4] In May, 1641, Parliament resolved that the imposition was illegal, and that, though Abell and Kilvert were particularly culpable, the company had at least connived at securing an illegal and profitable patent.[5]

Parker came to the defense of the harassed vintners with the somewhat unimpressive plea that the company had yielded to intolerable royal pressure and that it had been deceived and mulcted by its responsible head. He pointed out that Weston, as early

[3] *A dialogue or accidental discourse betwixt Mr. Alderman Abell, and Richard Kilvert, the two maine projectors for wine, etc.* (London, 1641).

[4] *C.J.*, II, 37.

[5] *Ibid.*, II, 156–57.

as 1633, had sought to persuade the company to accept an imposition and that £6,000 had been paid to the crown in order to protect their existing privileges.[6] A few years later, in 1637, the company had been informed by Abell and Kilvert that if it would accept the imposition on imported wines, it would enjoy the special favor of the Court, whereas a second refusal would lead to its ruin. In other words, Parker maintained, the company yielded only under systematic compulsion; its records had been tampered with by Abell; and the individual members had not profited from the increased price of wines.[7]

Parker's argument was at once halfhearted and unconvincing. Although it was evident that considerable pressure had been brought to bear by the Court, it is likewise clear that the company expressed no distrust of Abell until it was haled before the parliamentary committee. Moreover, the evidence would indicate that it did profit, at least as a corporate entity, from the increased price of wine. We have also observed that Parker's conclusion that the company did not share in the responsibility of its duly constituted officers was not in accordance with the formal findings of Parliament.

Parker's careful defense of the Merchant Adventurers' Company against its vociferous critics, in and out of Parliament, was far more important than the hastily written and unpersuasive apologia for the vintners. In the later work Parker not only undertook to reply to the specific allegations which the radical pamphleteers were bringing against the company but likewise expounded the benefits which "disciplined trade" brought to the commonwealth and eloquently extolled the social and political virtues of the commercial aristocracy.

The Merchant Adventurers had unquestionably enjoyed privileges, Parker agreed, but this did not necessarily condemn the company, unless it could be proved that these privileges had been abused or that they had become at some precise date suddenly harmful to the economy of the nation. He maintained that

[6] [Henry Parker], *The Vintners answer to some scandalous phamphlets, etc.* (London, 1642), pp. 3–4.

[7] *Ibid.*, pp. 5 ff.

in recent years the company had been under heaviest attack by the clothiers,[8] who had sought to maintain that the conduct of the export business by the Adventurers had been ruinous to the woolen industry. Parker, however, acidly observed that the clothiers, however expert they might be in the manufacture of cloth, knew nothing whatever about the complex problems of selling it abroad and quite forgot that manufacturing and merchandising were wholly separate functions. It must be agreed that "the breeding of the clothier does [not] so much inable him to sell cloth, especially in great quantities, and that to forrein nations, as the merchants. . . . . Forasmuch as there is not onely an art and mysterie in the sale of cloth . . . . but also an art more abstruse, eminent, and exquisite then that is which consists in the mechanicall way of making and dressing the same."[9]

It is to be frankly admitted that the English woolen trade has languished, but the privileges of the Adventurers have in no sense contributed to this unfortunate development. The antiquated and expensive methods of the clothiers, the devastating effects abroad of the Thirty Years' War, and the political uncertainty at home have been the fundamental causes for the decay of trade. The woolen industry has been further injured by the rapid development of weaving on the Continent, especially in Silesia, so that whereas twenty English vessels were heretofore required for the Hamburg trade alone, six now suffice. England therefore faces difficult problems in securing the revival of her most important industry and export, but they certainly cannot be resolved by destroying the delicate and efficient instrument which has been carefully devised to administer export trade. The privileges and constitution of the company must be preserved, Parker

[8] The clothiers were depressed and restless during most of the revolutionary period, principally because of the political and economic dislocations of the era (Margaret James, *Social Problems and Policy during the Puritan Revolution, 1640–1660* [London, 1930], pp. 166–70). For examples of their complaints against the Merchant Adventurers, who were naturally principally blamed for the distress of the cloth industry, *vide C.J.*, III, 486; *L.J.*, IV, 237; *The humble petition of many thousands of clothiers* (1647).

[9] Henry Parker, *Of a free trade. A discourse seriously recommending to our nation the wonderfull benefits of trade, specially of a right governed, and ordered trade, etc.* (London, 1648), p. 30.

warmly maintained, if the woolen trade is ever to be regained. This is true because the company has gradually evolved techniques of distribution which cannot be replaced and because it contributes essential services to commerce and to English culture generally.

Thus the company has been principally responsible for maintaining and gradually improving the quality of English cloth prepared for the export trade. It has always been vigilant in observing improvements abroad and in accommodating the industry to changed needs and tastes. But in this important function it has always encountered stubborn opposition from the clothiers, who, particularly of late, have rebelled against the qualitative standards which the company has sought to lay down. So far has deterioration in quality proceeded that the company will be wholly unable to maintain the requisite standards unless the state "reach forth their helping hands yet further."[10] The clamor against the company's privileges has been raised principally by unscrupulous manufacturers who would ruin the industry by the further lowering of qualitative standards.

More importantly, the privileges and constitution of the company must be preserved because it alone is equipped to deal with the complex problems involved in foreign trade. The sensitive mechanism of commerce would be irreparably damaged should the company be permitted to disintegrate. The Merchant Adventurers have a vast fund of knowledge about foreign lands and possess an intimate understanding of markets essential to the conduct of commerce. Since they have for many years contributed to the prosperity of foreign cities, they are in a position to gain concessions which would be denied to any private trader. Indeed, since the trade of the world has been carefully apportioned among the several companies, a disastrous dislocation would result if all restrictions on export were to be removed.[11]

The freedom which the clothiers and interlopers demanded, Parker gravely warned, was actually nothing else than economic chaos. The regulated trade of the company, on the contrary, has been most carefully designed to secure an even flow of goods, to

[10] *Ibid.*, pp. 15–16.

[11] *Ibid.*, pp. 12–14.

study and gauge the markets, to exploit to the full corporate control over the sources of supply, and to drive out unscrupulous competition.[12] The plea for free trade rests upon the naïve assumption that the demand for goods is insatiable and the potential value of commerce unlimited.[13] The simple fact is that the lifting of restrictions would immediately so enlarge the volume of exports that trade itself would be destroyed with disastrous consequences to the economy of the nation. This is not to argue that the company has or should have privileges of a monopoly in the true meaning of the term. The Merchant Adventurers sell abroad, especially in woolens, in direct and vigorous competition with other foreign exporters. Since the total volume of the English export trade is actually insufficient to support all the merchants engaged, it has been necessary to impose careful restrictions on the number of apprentices admitted by the company. Then, too, the charge of monopoly is belied by the fact that any Londoner can gain membership in the company upon the payment of £100, which presumably is a true index of the value of the privileges accruing to the exporter. It should be evident that the Merchant Adventurers have no desire whatsoever to limit trade, since the members profit only by the expansion of the volume of commerce.[14] Such restrictions as have been imposed were necessary simply because supply must be kept in at least rough correlation with foreign demand.

Nor should the critics of the company forget that it has made profoundly important contributions of a less tangible nature to England. The trading companies have for many years made adequate provision for their sick, their aged, and their widows and orphans. They have not infrequently served in a diplomatic capacity abroad, supplying England with valuable information, and have entertained foreign princes with a lavish hospitality.[15] They have carefully devised an apprenticeship system which develops highly specialized skills and which ensures the perpetuation of the delicately complex structure of commerce. So thorough and commendable is the training provided by the company

[12] *Ibid.*, pp. 17–19.

[13] *Ibid.*, pp. 19–20.

[14] *Ibid.*, p. 22.

[15] *Ibid.*, p. 10.

that Parker warmly professed he wished "our young gallants which learn in France to weare ribbons, and in Spain and Italy to be perfidious, and do worse things," could be obliged to receive as careful and useful an education.[16] These are amongst the values which irresponsible persons, imbued with a greedy lust, seek to destroy when they propose the ruin of one of the most ancient and honorable of England's corporate societies.

Finally, Parker submitted, the Merchant Adventurers had made a contribution of very great significance by advancing the cause of religious toleration. They have insisted that they must be permitted freedom of religion in all countries, and in many have been able to gain freedom of worship as well. They have abundantly demonstrated that men of differing faiths can live and work harmoniously together and have shown that religious liberty contributes directly to the advancement of trade. The Merchant Adventurers have been foremost amongst those who have sought to establish the principle of international tolerance and they have set a wedge in the hard and encrusted shell of European intolerance. No thinking man can believe that this priceless gain could for long be maintained were the company to be dissolved and foreign trade thrown open to men devoid of any sense of commercial, national, or ethical responsibility.[17] For if that should occur, "our trade will become instantly both straggling, and confused," just as an army degenerates into a rabble when discipline is removed.[18]

Parker was by no means content simply with the defense of the privileges and contributions of the Merchant Adventurers. More significant and revealing was his eloquent apologia for the new commercial aristocracy and his earnest plea that commerce must lie at the foundation of the modern state. The merchant class, which had come into conscious and important existence in England during the sixteenth century, had been harassed by the fact that it possessed no clear status in a society which still retained so many essentially medieval characteristics. It has been suggested that the quest for status had not a little to do with the fact that Calvinism, with the assurance which it lent to commercial

[16] *Ibid.*, p. 15. [17] *Ibid.*, pp. 8–9. [18] *Ibid.*, p. 11.

aspirations and its emphasis upon the spiritual aristocracy of the elect, appealed so widely and profoundly to merchant groups throughout northern Europe. Furthermore, the social and political, quite as much as the economic, discontent of the London merchants was contributory to the movement which enlisted practically all the mercantile aristocracy in that complex revolt against the antique order which we call the English Civil War. As the Civil War came to a successful conclusion, the merchant class, if its pamphleteers may be regarded as typical of the group, was buoyed up by a lively hope that a new political and social structure was in process of creation which would take into adequate account the aspirations of an intelligent, wealthy, and powerful, but psychologically insecure, social stratum. The articulate aspirations of the merchant aristocracy, which were so rudely dashed by the landed gentry who dominated the Commonwealth and Protectorate, found eloquent and skilful exposition in the writings of Henry Parker and Henry Robinson.

Parker, descended from an ancient landed family, had been thrown by the accident of junior birth and the harsh reality of making a living into intimate contact and complete sympathy with the class of which Robinson was a perfect exemplar. Trade, he maintained, was the lifeblood of the modern state. Consequently, the future of the nation may be said to depend upon the merchant, who commands greater sums of liquid capital than "other men commonly though[t] better landed, and estated can raise upon suddaine, publick exegencies." Moreover, men have finally come to realize that commerce is quite as important as are natural resources in ensuring national prosperity. It might well be called the key which unlocks the resources of the state. Cities like Antwerp and Amsterdam, blessed by nature with no better resources than Bristol or Newcastle, have raised themselves to eminence and great wealth simply by the full exploitation of the vast potentialities inherent in commerce. For it "is visible in the Hollander that the mines of Peru are as serviceable to him, as to the poore Indian, that diggs in them: that the furs of Russia are equally parted betwixt him and the Muscovite: that the plaines of Cots-Would, and Lemster do as well graze his sheepe, as they do the Englishman."[19] Society owes a vast debt indeed to the merchant, who by his skill and devotion has so greatly enhanced and enriched the life of nations.

The rise of the merchant class and the extension of commerce, Parker believed, betokened a happier and more prosperous future for mankind. As we have previously observed, the English theorist was firmly persuaded that the Dutch rebellion and the English revolution were symptomatic of the end of an old order which had for many years lain athwart the path of progress. In the new political and social order which England was even then fabricating, commerce, Parker suggested, and the steady advice of the merchant must have their due place. England will recall that wars and conquerors have filled the world with carnage and have consumed the very substance of society.[20] Commerce, on the other hand, "beautifies, inriches, impowers little states, and so alters their naturall dimensions, that they seem to swell, as it were, into spacious empires."[21] Heroes may record their battles and kings their conquests, "but in the meantime that gentle unbloody prince which by his severall dispersed carricks visits each climate of the world onely to plunder the earths caverns of her metalls, or the rocks of their diamonds, or the deepe it self of its pearles" remains the common benefactor of all mankind.[22] That nation which abandons the marauding lust of war, which disavows the ambitious pride of princes, and which builds solid foundations for the empire of commerce will be at once great and mighty in the age to come.

Parker was quick to add that the aspirations of the merchant class and the true interests of commerce were best served by a republic. We have seen that well before 1648, when *Of a Free Trade* was published, he had vigorously attacked monarchical institutions and had laid a firm basis in political theory for the republican experimentation which was to follow the conclusion of the Civil War. Not the least of the reasons which should persuade England to abandon the outworn structure of monarchical government, he submitted, was the fact that it was ill prepared to

[19] *Ibid.*, p. 2.

[20] *Ibid.*, pp. 32–34.

[21] *Ibid.*, p. 34.

[22] *Ibid.*, pp. 34–35.

administer a future in which the policy and requirements of the merchant must loom large.

Republican states, on the other hand, have been shrewd and quick in exploiting the possibilities afforded by commerce. "The reason hereof may be, because in popular states the merchant usually has more share in administration of publick affaires: whereas in monarchies, those that have the charge of the rudder, have commonly little insight into trade, and as little regard of traders."[23] It is well known, Parker wrote in another connection, that Holland quickly lifted herself from poverty to greatness by the devotion of a republican government to an intelligent commercial policy. Hamburg with fewer potential resources than those frequently inherited by private persons in England has built an incredibly rich civilization upon its trade and fisheries. England, on the contrary, though rich in resources, strategically located, and "as much courted by the circumambient sea" as any part of the universe has lagged behind simply because her government has possessed neither the wit nor the energy to support the legitimate ambitions of her merchants. The Civil War, Parker implied, would unlock the immense economic resources with which God had endowed England, just as it would liberate men's consciences, perfect her institutions, and safeguard the freedom and dignity of all Englishmen. It was a brave new world indeed which the prescient and courageous Parker envisaged.

3. HENRY ROBINSON

Henry Robinson was perhaps the most original and important of the considerable group of thinkers who sought to extend into the social and economic life of the nation the great gains which had been made in politics and religion. Robinson's social and economic thought is impressive, not only because of its amazing sweep and scope but because it was so extraordinarily persuasive. He envisaged a society in which government would assume large and intelligent responsibilities for a planned economic life, designed at once to augment the wealth and power of the nation and to enlarge the opportunities of the individual citizen. This state

[23] *Ibid.*, pp. 3–4.

would take into full account, as the recent monarchical government had failed to do, the fact that a new economy and a new society had been created by the Commercial Revolution. It would call to its counsels the commercial aristocracy which must be the prime instrument for exploiting the boundless potentialities facing mankind. It would discover this aristocracy of the counting-houses to be at once more conscientious in its conception of its responsibilities and more intelligent in discharging them than the ancient landed gentry.

Robinson was an early and an enthusiastic harbinger of the great cultural era which is perhaps only now drawing toward a close. Trade was to him the solvent that would loosen the ossified structure of the past that had stultified and constrained the forces which were enlarging the opportunities of mankind; free enterprise, staunchly supported by intelligent political policy, was to him a rushing stream which would water and enrich plains that still lay barren under the declining glow of the medieval sun. The merchant's confidence in the integrity and intelligence of the mercantile aristocracy, his conviction that men were, or could become, wholly rational in planning the architecture of the social and economic edifice of the future, his deep persuasion that the rapid enlargement of commerce would bring nothing save benefits to the nation, perhaps convict Robinson of naïveté in his conception of the processes of social and institutional revolution. Yet it must be said that in all of Robinson's numerous economic writings we discover a keen and penetrating insight, a careful and frequently brilliant understanding of the basic problems and needs of the national economy, a fearless and attractive honesty in diagnosis, and a shrewd practicality in the specific proposals which he advanced for his design of the new world that lay ahead. Finally, it should be remarked that Robinson was perhaps the only man in his age fully to understand that the liberal society of the future was to be compounded of three essential elements, inextricably fused by the pressure of historical events. In estimating Robinson's importance in the history of thought, it is sufficient to say that he made great and original contributions to the definition and vindication of all three. No seventeenth-century man understood as did he the nature of, and the necessity for, a complete religious liberty, few men lent such notable defense to the thesis that free men in a mature society must govern themselves within the frame of free political institutions, and no contemporary perceived so clearly or elaborated so carefully the design of a free economy within which the standard of living might be universally raised and opportunity generally extended.

It should be recalled that Henry Robinson was more than an academic social and economic theorist during the period when his principal writings were published. We have noticed that he was an active merchant trading in the companies in which the fortunes of his family had been gained and for so long maintained. For rather more than a decade he was vitally and occasionally belligerently interested in the post office, which he probably administered for a short time and for the improvement of which he had many stimulating suggestions.[24] During the period of the Commonwealth and Protectorate he served the revolutionary government as a civil servant charged with numerous and important responsibilities. Considered an expert on trade and finance, he was a member of the commission appointed to dispose of the royal properties, was frequently called upon to advise the government on questions of coinage and foreign exchange, was consulted regarding the scheme for the foundation of a national bank, which he persistently urged, and was for some time a member of a powerful committee vested with the general oversight of the customs.[25] His was a busy and fruitful career, charged with a considerable administrative responsibility, which did not, however, as so often happens, retard the steady flow of his thinking and writing or restrain the nervous quest of his restless genius.

Robinson, in the preface to his *Briefe Considerations* (1649), summarized brilliantly and cogently the scope and content of his social and economic thought, while eloquently proclaiming the high necessity for extending to its economy the gains that had been won in the polity of the nation. He was, indeed, not a little vain in his estimate of the importance to England of the contributions which he was making in this area of thought. He submitted

[24] *Vide ante*, pp. 55–62.

[25] *Vide ante*, pp. 62–65.

that his earlier *Englands Safety, in Trades Encrease* (1641) had been, despite haste in composition and printing, "of greater concernment, than is imagined," and had dealt with a problem of great import that "hath not publiquely been propounded unto any nation, since the discovery of the West Indies."

England, Robinson insisted, having won by trial of civil war the political and religious liberty toward which she had for so long striven, must complete her task by lending immediate attention to the innumerable social and economic problems which likewise cry out for solution. "I presume," he wrote, that "we have not only cleared it up, but gained that liberty, never hereafter to be indangered." But liberty remains an empty catchword until it has been extended to the full sphere of man's activity and yearnings. Great advances have been made, but it is not enough for England to rest content with a partial grasp on freedom. The time is ripe to secure "both to the present and future generation, with all things conducing to the plenty and happinesse thereof; to root up and reforme the rotten constitution of our lawes and customes; to anathemize the endlesse vexatious proceedings thereof, with their unmerciful expensivenes; to invite the importation of bullion; regulate the marchandizing exchange; . . . . prevent the exportation of the little remainder of our moneyes"; and to posit free institutions upon the firm rock of a flowering commerce.[26]

Robinson stoutly maintained that the liberal state, in the true sense of the term, could be neither framed nor preserved unless the commercial aristocracy assumed with the landed gentry an equal dignity in the governance of the nation and an equal responsibility for the preservation of its institutions. In an interesting and revealing essay he warmly vindicated the status of the merchant aristocracy, exhibiting, as had Parker, the vestiges of uncertainty and insecurity which still troubled an articulate, wealthy, and intelligent class in its political and social relations with the traditional aristocracy.[27]

Actually, he submitted, merchants have no occasion whatsoever to feel inferior to the gentry, since they are even more capa-

[26] Robinson, *Briefe considerations*, Pref.

[27] *Vide ante*, pp. 212–15.

ble and valuable servants of the state. Merchants could easily possess "breeding, abilities, and advantages . . . . above all others" were they intelligently to exploit their opportunities. It is true that the merchants should shun "the superficiall complement and ceremonies of gentilitie, more attending their businesse at exchange than court," but they must jealously insist upon proper recognition of their status. Some critics have maintained that the merchant, since he is preoccupied with his personal fortunes, should not be as highly respected as the traditional gentleman. It is quite sufficient, Robinson asserted, to point out to these critics that one merchant should "be valued as hundreds of ordinarie men, because many hundreds of men are employed and maintained by one merchant."[28]

If the true status and importance of the merchant were fully recognized, Robinson believed, a firm basis for responsible government could be laid by the fusion of the interests and capabilities of the landed and mercantile aristocracies.[29] The tyranny and irresponsibility, the poverty and suffering which have characterized governments in the past, can be remedied only when those who "take upon them to be masters of the world," acquire some knowledge of how commerce may be expanded with the consequent enrichment and contentment of the people and the enlargement of governmental revenues.[30] The merchants, for their part, could learn much about breeding and manners from the landed aristocracy; they could contribute much to it by advising its members on the management of their estates and the husbanding of their wealth. The two groups, in England at least, clearly have complementary resources, while history has imposed upon them a common responsibility.

The merchant class need envisage this association in functions hitherto the prerogative of the traditional aristocracy with no misgivings and with no inhibitions. The merchant lies under no stigma because he has attended conscientiously to his private

[28] Henry Robinson, *Englands safety, in trades encrease. Most humbly presented to the high court of parliament* (London, 1641), p. 47.

[29] We extend Robinson's remarks slightly by inference here.

[30] Robinson, *Certain proposalls in order to the peoples freedome*, pp. 2–3.

business. He should reflect that no man ever soils "his hands with doing his owne businesse; and everie one, whether he will or no, is a merchant for what he buyes or sels, be it lands, houses, or whatsoever else, and more gentile it is to sell cloth, silk, sattins, jewels . . . . as meere merchants doe, than cattell, hay, hides, wooll, butter, cheese, as countrey gentlemen, and others of best note and worth" have always done.[31] Moreover, it should not be forgotten that most merchants are actually derived from gentle stock. They are normally descended from the younger branches of gentle families, though "wanting means to blazen it in due equipage and colors to the world." Being absorbed in more important undertakings, they have often forgotten the facts of their own ancestry.[32] They too might soon build great, and if need be landed, fortunes, if they fixed as their goal the formation of vast family estates. Actually, however, Robinson reflected with his acutely sensitive social conscience, it is much better for a merchant to retire directly he has won a competence in order that opportunity shall be always free and that wealth may not be canalized in a few families.[33]

This remarkable vindication of the social status of the mercantile aristocracy is of fundamental significance in Robinson's thought because he was deeply persuaded that the basis for government in England must be enlarged and strengthened by the fusion of the landed and commercial classes. No democrat, he was convinced that a new aristocracy, possessed of the resources of England, enlightened in its ideals and policies, and responsible to the nation at large, must assume the task of government. Moreover, this government must take into full account the resources and opportunities which the Commercial Revolution had made available to the modern state, must frame its policy and define its ends in terms of the potentialities of the future rather than in slavish conformity with the habitual conduct of the past. Hence it was of prime importance that Englishmen should grasp ade-

[31] Robinson, *Englands safety, in trades encrease*, p. 48.

[32] It will be recalled that Robinson was here sketching quite exactly the history of his own family.

[33] Robinson, *Englands safety, in trades encrease*, pp. 48–49.

quately the conception of the commercial state, since God and history had decreed that the nation must discover its future greatness in far-flung and imperial trade.

Robinson sought to sketch with broad strokes his conception of the commercial state of the future and to summon Parliament to undertake responsibility for the implementation of his design. The London merchant clearly believed that a new and larger base must be found for the English polity and economy if the nation was to assume its true role in the modern world. In all his consideration it is evident that Robinson, like so many of his contemporaries, was profoundly impressed by the rapid and solid progress which the Netherlands had made toward power and prosperity during the first half of the century. He was, moreover, deeply persuaded that the deterioration of Spanish power had been caused by the failure of an inept government to accommodate the policy of the nation to the requirements and potentialities of a complex modern world.

Parliament, Robinson steadily maintained, must exhibit quite as much intelligence and imagination in reordering the economic life of England as it has shown in reforming the political and religious life of the land. It should remember that political greatness has ever rested squarely on the commercial prosperity and economic well-being of the nation. England can gain no lasting security in the modern world without an abundant and untrammeled trade. It must likewise be taken as axiomatic that "the greatest trade of the world hath a capacity of undermining and eating out the lesser trades of the world." Furthermore, trade can neither be maintained nor expanded unless it be protected by the might of sea power. The coming struggle for power in Europe will be sharp and decisive: "whosoever can make and continue the greatest strength at sea, will enjoy the greatest dominion of the world."[34] Political dominion, then, will belong to that nation which possesses an unchallenged sea power, which lends adequate protection to the slender fibers of commerce reaching out throughout the world.

Nor is this all. Political power tends to increase of its own

[34] Robinson, *Certaine proposals . . . . to a new modelling of the lawes*, Pref. (13).

strength and would lead finally to universal dominion were it not for the inevitable tendency of governments to make mistakes or to fail in the understanding of a nation's true policy. The Dutch, Robinson believed, might well have established a dominion over the world had it not been for the fact that their trade and sea power were gravely weakened at the outset by the failure to unite all the United Provinces in one commonwealth.[35] None the less, the success of the Netherlands has been spectacular and continued. England would do well indeed to study carefully that success and to frame her commercial policy along comparable lines. Dutch commerce is distributed amongst numerous cities, none of which is too large for its efficient and economical prosecution. The Dutch have fully exploited the sea upon which modern commerce must be borne. They have learned to build ships cheaply but well, to man them with small but skilled crews, and to offer their efficient services to the nations of the world at lower charges than any other people.[36]

Spain, on the other hand, though blessed with incomparably greater resources, has been ruined because her government failed to accommodate an essentially medieval polity to the necessities of the new world created by the Commerical Revolution. She has been too proud to bend before the requirements of policy and has been cursed by the "gentility" of her governing classes. Gentility in Spain has come to mean "a condition not to be necessitated to worke, as that they will not labour in any calling an houre longer then to keepe themselves from starving."[37] The Spanish empire was endowed with every asset required for dominion save the capacity for prosecuting commerce. The Spanish have wasted their substance and have squandered their power simply because their pride was so overwhelming that they refused to bestir themselves to meet the requirements of a new age.

England must heed the fate of Spain, and that quickly. For the Dutch have made notable progress in exploiting their discovery of the "grand engine and state-mistery of encreasing trade

[35] *Ibid.*, Pref. (13–14).

[36] Robinson, *Certain proposalls in order to the peoples freedome*, p. 8.

[37] Robinson, *Certaine proposals . . . . to a new modelling of the lawes*, Pref. (14).

and navigation for acquiring dominion, and conserving it by good government." They are gaining in power more rapidly than any other nation in the world, and unless Britain rallies her strength under the leadership of "great trade statesmen," it may be too late ever to overtake her rival across the Channel. It is to this task that Parliament must now dedicate itself with an intelligent consideration of the essentials of the policy which must safeguard the commercial state.[38]

Above all, Parliament must heed the counsel of the nation and must lend attentive consideration to every proposal made in the interests of the nation as a whole. All persons in the realm should be encouraged to address petitions and criticisms to Parliament and the Council. Freedom of address and criticism is important not only because it provides an adequate safety-valve for emotions but because governments must learn to assess and implement the aspirations of a people. It may be said, in truth, that the refusal of the magistrate to pay careful attention to the complaints and suggestions of the commonalty "is a symptom of the most desperate lethargy . . . . and consequently of sudden innovations and misery to the nation."[39]

Basic to Robinson's conception of the commercial state was his deep conviction that no nation could enjoy peace at home, prosperity in trade, and political power unless it accepted the principle of unqualified religious liberty as part of the fundamental law of the land. We have dealt at length with Robinson's contribution to the development of the theory of religious toleration. His devotion to religious freedom, it must be emphasized, was based on moral and philosophical grounds. But he was likewise sensitively aware of the fact that any nation which would find greatness and prosperity in commerce must be compelled on grounds of policy and necessity alone to guarantee a perfect religious freedom to all men.

Persecution, and the internal and foreign wars which flow from it, is peculiarly dangerous to the complex and delicate structure of the modern world. It inevitably injects a morbid vi-

[38] *Ibid.*, Pref. (14–15).

[39] Robinson, *Certain proposalls in order to the peoples freedome*, p. 5.

rus into any polity based primarily upon foreign trade. Economic ruin has been courted in numerous European states by driving substantial citizens and skilled artisans into exile because they differed in faith from the dominant religious group. Religious wars have swept across Europe again and again, having been fanned into incandescence by bigoted zealots careless at once of the peace, well-being, and prosperity of their native lands. The modern state must intervene in order to impose the decency, strength, and stability required for the good life. "If wee may not suffer hereticks to live amongst us," Robinson pointed out, "then is the Parliament to blame for suffering German, French, Spanish, and Portugal papists or Dutch Brownists and Anabaptists to live here amongst us, though as marchants . . . . since their marchandizing gives them greater advantage of working people to their opinions."[40] England, like Holland, must permit all men to think and to worship as they please so long as their religious life does not threaten the security of the state or rupture the bonds of civil order. No greater contribution could possibly be made to the conditions which must underlie commercial prosperity and greatness.

Furthermore, Robinson eloquently insisted, England must found her policy squarely on the conviction that political prestige and power in the future will accrue to that nation which exercises dominion over the high seas. England's political thinking and her economic planning must ever be guided by this basic principle. Every effort must be taken to secure an unquestioned mastery of the seas, since that nation which "can attaine to and continue the greatest trade, and number of shipping, will get and keepe the soveraignty of the seas, and consequently, the greatest dominion of the world."[41] England has been blessed with incomparable resources and with sound traditions of sea power, but, unfortunately, lethargy in government combined with political disturbances have gravely weakened her maritime strength at a time when other nations are making very rapid advances in navigation and shipping. Hence every energy should be em-

[40] [Robinson], *A short answer to A. S.*, p. 2.

[41] Robinson, *Briefe considerations*, p. 1.

ployed to surpass the rivals that have sprung up and to regain unquestioned dominion over the waters of the earth.

In particular, England must deal quickly and decisively with the Dutch, who, without great resources of naval stores, have pressed England hard in fishing, in commerce, and in the vastly important East India trade. Holland, raised up from subjection by English "assistance and wel wishes," has discovered that prosperity and political power depend not so much upon the extent of territory, as upon an international commerce resting solidly upon sea power. The Dutch have shown rare capacity for trade and have built a merchant marine far surpassing the crippled English fleets. The future greatness of England therefore demands that she dedicate her policy and all her strength to wresting control of the seas from her rivals. With a truly imperial arrogance, Robinson demanded that his country require that "other states and princes rest contented to keep only such a number of men of warre as may not make us with just cause suspect their strength and force." England must win and then defend her imperial supremacy.

The Dutch, when confronted with this great decision, will at once complain that a diminished sea power will expose them to the vengeance of Spain. But England, Robinson piously remonstrated, will employ her immense power for the protection of weaker states: in this instance she would combine with Holland to curb the insolence of Spain. Holland, then, should be made a satellite, moving in the orbit of English policy, while the sea power of the other nations of Europe must be very strictly controlled. England must by an heroic effort regain her inheritance of the sea. Robinson called upon his country to "consider the ods wee had of other states in sea-forces but halfe an age agoe," and to reflect with all due gravity on the powerful fleets her rivals now have "in the ocean and Mediteranean Sea." This challenge must be faced immediately or the essence of power will have been forever alienated: "unlesse wee show ourselves sole soveraigne of the sea, and with our trident scepter give lawes (whilst we may) to all nations there, wee must receive them from others, when wee cannot helpe it."[42]

[42] Robinson, *Englands safety, in trades encrease*, p. 2.

Only sea power, Robinson contended, could provide the foundations upon which a flourishing trade and a sound economy could be built. Parliament must act quickly and wisely to restore English maritime dominion, since the commercial power of the nation has been gravely weakened, recently by civil disturbances and earlier by governmental ineptitude. Only a decade ago, Robinson lamented in 1649, England's trade was famous "amongst all knowne nations" and her ships were "dreadfull to whomsoever became our enemies."[43] But her naval power had deteriorated and, so Robinson inaccurately estimated, her foreign commerce had shrunk to a scant quarter of the normal volume of trade. The result has been that England stands gravely weakened at a time when foreign states are making rapid advances in their commercial economy. Foreign fleets now fish in English waters, hostile laws militate against the export of English goods, and capable merchants and artisans have emigrated to Holland "in swarmes," to the consequent weakening of the fabric of national life.[44]

The maritime weakness of England, Robinson believed, could be remedied only by the careful framing of a state founded on the stout pillars of commerce. More immediately, however, a fundamental correction might be made by the careful stimulation of fisheries. The fishing industry was regarded by Robinson as basic for a nation which must seek power and greatness in foreign trade.[45] It is "predominant over all others, as having in it selfe, a capacity of drawing all other trades after it, not only serving as a nurserie for breeding marriners, and compleatly victualling us for three dayes a weeke," but in providing the most profitable commodity for export.[46] England should therefore turn at once to the vigorous exploitation of the fisheries, since, if her policy is properly ordered, no other nation can possibly compete with her in this lucrative trade. Foreign vessels should be excluded from English waters by a government which must lend every possible protection to a trade in which the nation should achieve a virtual monopoly.

[43] Robinson, *Briefe considerations*, p. 2.

[44] Robinson, *Englands safety, in trades encrease*, pp. 2–3.

[45] *Ibid.*, p. 49.

[46] Robinson, *Briefe considerations*, p. 8.

In all of his numerous economic tracts Robinson persistently and vehemently stressed the prime importance of fisheries to the English economy. Indeed, so preoccupied was he with the importance of maritime power that he urged that every Englishman should be taught to swim. It would be much better if instead of "putting malefactors to their clergie, they may learne to save their lives by swimming."[47] Moreover, instruction in swimming should constitute a part of the curriculum in every school. The English race must, if it is to achieve its true destiny, feel equally at home on the sea and land. Fisheries will serve as the cradle for this great sea power, providing at once the principal commodity of commerce and the substance of naval might. England's task is to win an undisputed sovereignty of the seas, a sovereignty which can be won and preserved only by "the fishing of herrings, king of . . . . fish."[48]

Parliament should lend every possible assistance to this industry, out of which sea power will quickly, almost miraculously, arise. For example, the vehemently anticlerical Robinson insisted, the eating of flesh should be sternly prohibited by law during Lent and during two or three days each week.[49] This law would greatly stimulate the demand for fish and, incidentally, would tend to discourage the gluttony of a nation too devoted to meat. England has the boats, she can train the seamen, and she has an unrivaled geographical location; she requires nothing else than a policy designed to exploit her priceless assets. The Dutch must therefore be driven from the fishing grounds; England must lend every assistance to the restoration of her sea power by prohibiting the use of timber for any other purpose than shipbuilding, and she must lend steady support to those brave men who stand ready to wrest control of the seas from all arrogant interlopers upon English waters.

Robinson's conception of the modern commercial state was sharply etched. The commercial aristocracy, which had already contributed much to England under the weight of so many disadvantages, must be awarded full social and political status. The

[47] Robinson, *Certain proposalls in order to the peoples freedome*, pp. 24–25.

[48] Robinson, *Englands safety, in trades encrease*, p. 16.

[49] Robinson, *Briefe considerations*, pp. 8–9; *Englands safety, in trades encrease*, p. 16.

governance of a commercial state could, so Robinson vigorously maintained, be preserved only when the merchant was admitted to a responsibility which had long been the exclusive prerogative of the landed gentry. A new aristocracy must be formed which will broaden the base of government and which will frame the policy of the state along lines consonant with the destiny of the nation. Government can no longer neglect trade, since its substance and power will hereafter be derived principally from commerce. England, which has so recently reformed its political and religious life by stripping away the barnacles of outworn traditions and outmoded institutions, must likewise reform, vitalize, and broaden its economic and social structure. The nation must trade or it will sink into insignificance and poverty. And if England would trade, if she would assume her rightful place amongst the nations of the earth, she must bend every effort toward regaining mastery of the seas.

Robinson discussed with prophetic clarity the outlines of English development during the next two centuries. His conception of policy was sound, and his analysis of the social revolution that was taking place in the realm was shrewd. But he was by no means content with framing in general terms a conception of the modern commercial state. He sought as well to lend substance to that conception by careful and precise recommendations of policy from which might be fabricated the architecture of his design. Many of these proposals were to be carefully considered by the revolutionary government and most of them, it will be observed, were to be adopted by future generations. The restless genius of Robinson's speculations was given balance and strength by the extraordinary precision and practicality of the proposals with which he persistently sought to implement his theory. These proposals we must now consider.

Robinson first addressed himself to the difficult question of the tariff policy which should be formulated by the commercial state. In this consideration Robinson made a major contribution to the theory of international trade and displayed a remarkably clear and penetrating understanding of a subject about which his age had so many misconceptions. Being theoretically persuaded that free trade was most beneficial to a maritime and commercial state, he carefully organized his ideas around the proposition that an intelligent government will seek rather to enlarge the volume of trade than to regard commerce as a convenient source of customs revenues. The state must bear firmly in mind the fact that its prosperity is ultimately determined by the extent of the nation's commerce. Consequently, its every diplomatic effort should be disciplined toward securing at home and abroad the reduction or elimination of all customs barriers in order to enlarge the basis of trade and to increase the velocity of the flow of commodities.[50]

This sane conception of tariff policy had not been accepted, Robinson taught, because of the prevailing notion that a nation must carefully guard against admitting an excess of imports lest an adverse balance of trade result which will be followed by the exportation of bullion and the ruin of the national economy. This by no means follows and it is a particularly dangerous illusion to be entertained by England. For one thing, it fails to take into account the large balances received by England for carrying foreign goods in English bottoms, a lucrative source of bullion which will automatically increase when commerce itself expands. Moreover, since England has no bullion mines, she must depend upon commerce for the augmentation of her monetary stocks.[51] But bullion is not properly the end of trade, nor can the desire for it be permitted to influence the national policy with respect to commerce. When one nation imposes unreasonable or discriminatory levies upon trade, other nations must protect themselves by retaliatory measures which can only lead to the diminution of the volume of commerce. National wealth, therefore, can be measured in no other terms than commodities and can be increased by no other means than enlarging the flow of commerce.

Robinson probed even more deeply into the mercantilist theories which found wide acceptance in his generation. Since trade is highly complex and extremely volatile, it cannot be expanded if a too narrowly nationalistic view is taken of its enlarge-

[50] Robinson, *Englands safety, in trades encrease*, pp. 10–11.

[51] *Ibid.*, p. 50.

ment. Furthermore, that nation is most strongly armed which is interested in the increase of the total volume of foreign trade. A determined nation, which understands the principles involved, can in truth very nearly force other nations to accept the benefits of free trade, if it so desires. "Can France drinke all the wine she makes," Robinson enquired, "or heare willingly a bill of banishment against her babies and such like toyes for exporting no little summes of golde and silver yearely?"[52] Actually, the advantages of free trade are so self-evident when it is once undertaken that any nation can easily be persuaded that a treaty to accomplish this end will be to its benefit.

England, blessed with incomparable advantages, can easily and quickly raise herself to pre-eminent power directly her government realizes that national wealth can be measured only in terms of the volume of trade. "I beleeve," Robinson professed, that "it will bee thought more beneficiall for a commonwealth to vent store of their native commodities, at such lower, but moderate rates, as both manufactors and merchants may live thereby, though with lesse profit, than to sell a lesse quantitie at greater rates, the profit of the greater parcell in the whole exceeding that of the lesser, especially so many men more being set a work untill we have other employment for them."[53] The merchant, upon whose activity and prosperity the modern state depends, traffics, it must be remembered, in goods and not in bullion. International trade consists in the exchange of commodity for commodity and not, unless trade is to wither, in the exchange of commodities for bullion. We cannot, in other words, "expect that all should come home in bullion: for that (presupposing the possibilitie) would utterly impoverish other countries, and cause those princes, to prohibit the exportation of it, and the verie scarcitie it selfe, through our exporting it, would make it in a short time so hard to come by, and our commodities for the same cause so much beaten downe in price, as the trade without doubt would bee quite abandoned at last; for it is our benefit that monies bee plentifull also in such countries where we carrie our commodities to sell."[54]

[52] *Ibid.*, p. 11. [53] *Ibid.*, pp. 55–56. [54] *Ibid.*, p. 57.

There are perhaps a very few commodities essential for defense, such as ammunition, timber, and naval stores, which should be excepted from the general policy of free trade. But even these commodities will be produced elsewhere if England does not supply them. Save in those rare instances, and England is not a case in point, when a nation enjoys an absolute monopoly over the source of supply, it lays restrictions on trade at its own peril. This may be conclusively demonstrated by a consideration of two commodities regarded as essential for defense. England might easily have enjoyed a lucrative trade in ordnance had not unwise restrictions and excessive export duties led the Germans, Danes, and Swedes to undertake manufacture on their own account with the result that they soon captured the whole of the export market while arming themselves at the same time. Similarly, outrageous export levies on tin, which raised the price at Leghorn from sixteen to twenty-six ducats, led to the opening of marginal mines on the Barbary coast with the consequence that the price on the Continent was speedily restored to its former level.

Robinson was almost alone amongst the English economic theorists of his generation in his advocacy of free trade.[55] His remarkable exposition of theory is, indeed, more reminiscent of nineteenth- than seventeenth-century discussion. His thinking was completely consistent, his argument well sustained, and his grasp of theory mature. Robinson detected and pointed out the principal fallacies in the mercantilist argument and sought to

[55] *Vide* Jacob Viner, *Studies in the Theory of International Trade* (New York, 1937), pp. 91–103, for the best discussion of early free-trade literature. Heckscher has commented briefly on Robinson's contribution to the theory of international trade. He suggests that the important Swedish theorist, Johan Risingh, who wrote a decade later, was considerably influenced by Robinson's thought (E. F. Heckscher, *Mercantilism* [London, 1935], II, 295).

Professor Buck, in his interesting discussion of the thinkers who dissented from the prevailing mercantilist doctrines in this important particular, confines himself to "some exceptional men of the late seventeenth century" (P. W. Buck, *The Politics of Mercantilism* [New York, 1942]). Actually, the free-trade views advocated by Roger Coke (1671), Nicholas Barbon (1690), Dudley North (1691), and others in the post-Restoration period had been systematically expounded by Robinson a full generation earlier.

persuade England that she would gain prosperity and power only by freeing her own trade from restrictions and by employing diplomatic and occasionally naval persuasion in the extension of a policy of free trade to the world at large.

Customs duties, Robinson would suggest, should be most carefully regulated by the state which desires to increase the volume of foreign commerce. In theory Robinson would have favored a general policy of free trade, but he realized that such a program was not immediately obtainable in England. None the less, an intelligent government will know that, since most foreign trade is really barter, England cannot expect to sell her goods abroad without taking foreign commodities in direct exchange.[56] Hence he recommended that the government should exercise very great caution when it levied tariff charges against imports. Raw materials and semifabricated goods, such as cotton, wool, yarns, and gold and silver thread, should not bear more than nominal duties, since they increase the demand for labor within the nation and are often re-exported after fabrication has been completed.[57] Obviously, essential commodities, such as naval stores, silk, flax, and goats' hair, which are not produced in England in sufficient quantities, should likewise be admitted without restrictions or impositions.[58] Finished goods, such as velvets, satins, and luxury articles, may be more heavily assessed without serious injury to the economy, though it must ever be borne in mind that excessive charges will lead to the withering of trade and to retaliatory measures abroad. All foodstuffs, Robinson suggests, with a purpose in mind prophetic of the Manchester School, should be admitted duty free in order to keep food prices and wages at a reasonable level. Wine may pay a heavy levy, not only because it is not an essential commodity but because its excessive consumption should in any case be discouraged as part of governmental policy. Jewels, however, should be reasonably taxed, since they are easily smuggled in unless men are searched, which would be a violation of the English conception of liberty, and since they are actually an addition, though a non-liquid one, to the national wealth.

[56] Robinson, *Englands safety, in trades encrease*, pp. 8–9.

[57] *Ibid.*, p. 9.

[58] Robinson, *Briefe considerations*, pp. 5–6.

These specific recommendations certainly represent considerably less than Robinson would have desired to gain, but, had they been applied, would have constituted an important advance in the direction of free trade. He was aware that customs receipts would fall off sharply for a time, but he was firmly persuaded that the lowering of tariff impositions would quickly result in an expansion of the volume of trade. This would be to the great benefit of the commonwealth, since "a little custome upon a great trade is equivalent to a great custome on a little trade, and the people employed and multiply'd to boote which are both the strength and riches of a kingdome."[59]

Moreover, Robinson recommended that a sweeping reorganization should be effected in the customs service. Since his proposals would considerably lessen the temptation for smuggling, he saw no reason why importers could not declare dutiable goods, rendering their accounts and payments quarterly.[60] All the paralyzing confusion and expense of customs examinations would be avoided if merchants were simply obliged to keep accurate books which would be open to public examination. This measure would likewise have a beneficent effect upon the conduct of business. Trade can never really prosper and capital cannot be secured in adequate quantity until merchants have become responsible in their financial conduct and habits. So careless are most merchants, Robinson alleged, that when "a man put in a summe of money in stocke with a merchant, shop-keeper, or grasier, or other dealer, it is twenty to one but such adventurer shall not only loose his money, but never have good account how it came to be consumed and wasted."[61] This unfortunate condition can automatically be corrected if every importer be required to declare his own goods on the basis of scrupulously maintained records.

Robinson was likewise an early, indeed perhaps the first, exponent of the *entrepôt* trade.[62] Writing in 1641, he advocated the

[59] Robinson, *Englands safety, in trades encrease*, p. 9.

[60] Robinson, *Certaine proposals .... to a new modelling of the lawes*, Pref. (10–11).

[61] *Ibid.*, Pref. (12).

[62] A considerable body of literature appeared during this period, especially under the Protectorate, in support of the *entrepôt* trade. These writers urged that customs

elimination of duties on all commodities imported for re-export as a means to secure the revival of the merchant marine.[63] He pointed out that England was blessed with very great resources which could easily be exploited in order to make her the commercial depot for the whole of western Europe. Her ports are numerous and are open during the whole year; she enjoys favorable winds and, above all, is endowed with a matchless location for prosecuting the carrying trade. In particular, she is in a position to exploit the cotton requirements of the Low Countries and of France, since Spain controls the Strait of Gibraltar and the chronic piracy in the Mediterranean makes supplies extremely uncertain.[64] Hence England should establish several free ports into which goods designed for re-export could be admitted without tariff charge to the great benefit of shipping and the bullion supplies of the nation.[65]

We have previously observed that Robinson, who had dealt with monetary problems in his earliest economic tract (1641), was regarded as a fiscal expert by the Commonwealth and Protectorate governments.[66] He was repeatedly consulted by the Council in 1650 when the government was gravely disturbed by the precarious condition of the public credit and by the flight of funds. Robinson's monetary theory, like that of most of his con-

---

duties on articles intended for re-export should be abolished, that foreign merchants should be permitted to settle in England, and that merchant courts should be set up in order to facilitate this trade. Among these thinkers Sir Ralph Maddison (*Great Britains remembrancer, looking in and out, etc.* [London, 1640?, *1655*]) and Robinson (*Englands safety, in trades encrease* [London, 1641]) were the first to espouse the proposal. Thomas Violet (*The advancement of merchandize: or, certain propositions for the improvement of the trade of this commonwealth, etc.* [London, 1651]) lent the doctrine mature support, as did an anonymous author in his important and too much neglected tract, *Free ports, the nature and necessitie of them stated.*

[63] Robinson, *Englands safety, in trades encrease*, pp. 20–21.

[64] *Ibid.*, p. 21. This was, of course, written during the closing years of the Thirty Years' War.

[65] Robinson, *Briefe considerations*, p. 6; *Certain proposalls in order to the peoples freedome*, pp. 11–12. England was never to have free ports, though there were experiments in that direction during the period of the Restoration (14 Carol. II, cs. 11, 25, 27).

[66] *Vide ante*, pp. 62–65.

temporaries, was actually extremely hazy. Two principles appear to dominate his thinking in this particular: the first, that the fiscal difficulties of the revolutionary government could be quickly cured by the expansion of foreign trade, and, secondly, that order and stability might best be secured by the erection of a national bank.

Robinson, in a careful memorandum laid before the Council in 1650, pointed out that bills of exchange had gradually developed as a means for settling balances and that they were designed to prevent the export of bullion and the risk and expense involved in specie settlement.[67] "Politic and expert" merchants therefore use bills of exchange, "which being subscribed by men of credit" possess all the characteristics of money and which are in a true sense money. The use of this normal medium of exchange has broken down because of unsettled conditions in England and because certain merchants have sought their own selfish advantage rather than the national good. Hence, as he had earlier suggested, the monetary problems of the government and of its citizens should be first attacked by setting up an agency which would register and guarantee bills of exchange.[68] Furthermore, a money market should be established which would enable merchants to borrow on short-term paper which, properly endorsed, will itself serve as a medium of exchange.

The drain of bullion to foreign centers cannot be checked, however, until trade has revived under the stimulation of intelligent governmental policy and until a national bank has been established. In the meantime, however, the government should undertake certain emergency measures designed to protect English bullion and credit. English money, he argued, was undervalued and hence tended to flow abroad. Consequently, a par should be established, tables of fair exchange should be published, and a public exchange might well be instituted which alone would possess the legal right to export bullion. All exports and imports of bullion would then flow through one regulated channel and a far more accurate account could be kept of the bullion stocks of

[67] *S.P. Dom., Commonwealth and Protectorate*, ix, 64.

[68] Robinson, *Certain proposalls in order to the peoples freedome*, p. 16.

the nation. The melting-down of coin should be strictly prohibited, the fabrication of decorative articles from precious metals must be forbidden, the export of money to Ireland and the colonies curtailed, and the amounts of currency carried out on shipboard strictly controlled until the forces of recovery might have sufficient time to become fully operative.[69]

These measures, designed to stop the drain on bullion and to restore the credit of the nation, were, however, to be regarded as nothing more than emergency expedients. For more than twenty years Robinson was a staunch advocate of a national bank which would, he maintained, serve innumerable useful functions. Such an institution, if properly managed, could be expected to control the flow of precious metal, to restore the public credit, to enlarge the supply of capital available for commercial undertakings, and to serve as the prime financial instrument for the implementation of the many economic proposals which Robinson's fertile mind envisaged.

Robinson's proposal for a central bank, legally empowered to issue paper money as well as private bills with the validity of currency, first systematically presented by him in 1641, may be regarded as the earliest mature suggestion of its kind in English economic literature.[70] We have noticed that his plans were seriously

[69] Robinson, "Observations on Exchanges," *S.P. Dom.*, *Commonwealth and Protectorate*, ix, 64.

[70] Robinson's proposal for the organization of a national bank, first made in 1641, was certainly the first to be published. R. D. Richards, in his valuable study, *The Early History of Banking in England* (London, 1929), has discussed a fragmentary scheme dating from the Jacobean era and another submitted in the early Caroline period (pp. 93–94).

In 1646 Robinson's suggestion won support in Benbrigge's *Usura accommodata*, which recommended the establishment of a bank for the relief of the poor and another to supply the requirements of commerce. Four years later Potter proposed that banks should be established in the various towns of England with authority to accept deposits, to issue negotiable currency, and to advance loans on proper security (*The key to wealth* [London, 1650]). More thoughtful was the elaborate proposal of Lambe, in 1658, for the erection of a bank in London under the supervision and control of a board of governors to be chosen by the leading trading companies (Samuel Lambe, *Seasonable observations, etc.* [London, 1658]). There were other banking proposals as well, but none dealt with the problem as maturely or as persuasively as did Robinson's.

discussed by the Council in 1650 and that the Restoration government was so favorably impressed by his persuasive logic that preliminary steps were undertaken in 1665 to empower Robinson to organize a bank.[71] Moreover, his persistent discussion of the economic merits of the proposed bank seems to have aroused considerable interest among a number of pamphleteers, most of whom were merchants, who supported and enlarged Robinson's scheme. It may be suggested, indeed, that the project for a national bank remained a matter for active discussion until plans were laid for its foundation rather more than fifty years after Robinson's first recommendations had been published.

The bank, Robinson proposed, should be founded by an act of Parliament, with the very strict legal provision that "neither principall nor profit shall bee stirred or employed, save for their account, according to [the] expresse order and direction" of that body.[72] The directors of the bank should be drawn, mainly at all events, from the merchants of London, who will be the largest depositors and who are most conversant with Continental banking practices. Robinson, writing in 1641, was most disturbed by the possibility that the bank might suffer from the arbitrary seizure of funds by the crown, but seemed to feel that parliamentary protection might serve as an adequate guaranty for the integrity of its accounts.[73] He was comforted, as well, by the reflection that the Medici, though irresponsible despots, had never tampered with the funds of the Florentine banks. Every effort must be taken to ensure the strength and fluidity of the bank in order to attract large amounts of specie which have always been kept in private homes for safekeeping. The bank, which would soon become the "grand cash-keeper of this whole kingdome," would vastly enlarge the credit available for the prosecution of the numerous projects which Robinson had in mind for the stimulation of trade. Correspondents, who would be maintained in all the principal commercial centers abroad, would guarantee bills of exchange and thereby prevent an unnecessary drain on the bul-

[71] *Vide ante*, pp. 63–66.

[72] Robinson, *Englands safety, in trades encrease*, p. 36.

[73] *Ibid.*, p. 35.

lion stocks of the nation.[74] If the bank were founded under parliamentary auspices and if it were carefully administered in order to guarantee the safety of deposits, there was every reason to believe, so Robinson concluded, that 5 per cent interest could be paid on deposits, that the capital funds of the nation would be considerably augmented, and that credit would be more easily available for worthy adventurers.[75]

One of the great benefits which would follow upon the establishment of a national bank, Robinson maintained, would be a sharp decline in the interest rate for capital sums required for commercial uses. He refers repeatedly to the fact that England would find it quite impossible to overcome Dutch competition in the markets of the world until the prevailing interest rate in England could be reduced to terms comparable to those prevailing in the more sophisticated money market of the Netherlands. Robinson felt that there was still some naïve confusion of usury with interest amongst his countrymen which might actually be contributory to the excessive charges laid upon merchants for the use of capital. Interest charges, he submitted, are essential for the pursuit and expansion of trade. The taking of interest differs not at all, either ethically or economically, from the "lending" of a house, which is house rental, the lending of a horse, which is hire, or the lending of an apprentice, which is wages. When a merchant borrows funds he does so, not because he is in dire want, but because he "sees certaintie of profit" and is therefore in a position to make the transaction profitable for himself and for the lender.[76]

Actually, a kind of usury does prevail in England, since merchants are obliged to pay from 8 to 10 per cent for funds borrowed upon wholly adequate collateral. It is quite impossible for London merchants to compete with the Hollanders until they too can obtain loans, secured by sound collateral, at 4 or 5 per cent. This great benefit cannot be attained, however, in the way Parliament

[74] *S.P. Dom., Commonwealth and Protectorate*, ix, 64.

[75] Robinson, *Englands safety, in trades encrease*, pp. 35–36; *S.P. Dom., Commonwealth and Protectorate*, ix, 64.

[76] Robinson, *Englands safety, in trades encrease*, p. 41.

has attempted, by a prescriptive reduction of the legal interest rate.[77] Such a measure simply results in the flight of capital abroad to the consequent ruin of trade. It is much better to be able to borrow needed capital at 12 per cent than not to have it available at all. The cure is rather to be found by establishing safe depositories for capital and by the careful reorganization of the entire economy of a state which can attain greatness only on the sound basis of commerce. It has been argued that as the interest rate gradually falls under these conditions, investors will tend to purchase land with their available funds. This may very well happen, Robinson agreed, but the corrective is to be found in the fact that land prices will immediately rise with the result that funds will flow back into the more profitable channels of trade. Moreover, the effect upon agriculture would be stimulating and it might actually induce farmers, of whom Robinson entertained a very low opinion, "to become more industrious setting their wits and hands a worke for improving of the soile, wherein questionlesse they come short of other nations."[78] Furthermore, England would be protected against a sharp rise in the price of foodstuffs by Robinson's corollary proposal that agricultural commodities should be admitted without customs charges.

The numerous suggestions he had advanced for the revival of foreign trade must be supplemented, Robinson pointed out, by the vigorous support of governmental policy. In particular, intelligent and aggressive measures should be undertaken to secure and enlarge the English colonial holdings in the New World, to protect and expand trade in the East, to clear the Mediterranean of pirates, and to establish the finest and largest merchant marine in the world. The government, in which the merchant aristocracy will of necessity be more adequately represented, must work hand in hand with the merchants if the illimitable potentialities which lie before the new commercial England are to be fully exploited.

[77] Robinson, *Certain proposalls in order to the peoples freedome*, p. 10. Professor Buck would seem to misinterpret Robinson on this point when he suggests that Malynes and Robinson "have no doubts at all of the usefulness of limiting the interest rate to six per cent or less by government fiat" (Buck, *Politics of Mercantilism*, p. 40).

[78] Robinson, *Englands safety, in trades encrease*, p. 7.

England, Robinson submitted, was peculiarly fitted for colonial expansion and must take the lead in founding strong plantations abroad, if she was to survive in the struggle for power. England is but "a little spot of ground" which must establish the basis of its future abroad before rival nations have taken possession of the rich resources of the earth.[79] It was especially important, he believed, that strong plantations be established in Newfoundland, which would place firmly within English control the great fishing banks, which would afford an unlimited source of wealth for the nation.[80] Robinson was likewise greatly interested in the projected plantation of the Bahamas, where he had been led to believe rich mineral deposits and sound timber were ready for exploitation.[81] Other regions should likewise be colonized that would secure to England adequate reserves of naval stores. Ideally, men of good family, possessed of ample means, should be encouraged to emigrate to these overseas dominions. But until such persons can be attracted by the opportunities available abroad, the government should transport all beggars and delinquents, in order to relieve the nation of the charge for their care and, even more importantly, to establish in each colony an adequate labor supply for the future development of the several plantations.[82]

Quite as important, Robinson submitted, was the high necessity for wresting the lucrative East India trade from the unscrupulous Dutch, even though a war should be required to regain England's rights. The East Indian policy should be firmly postulated on a plan designed to make England the European purveyor to the Indies, to make them economic satellites dependent upon the economy and merchant marine of Britain. If this could be effected, Robinson brutally if honestly argued, the East Indies would be bound to England by a complete economic dependence, would be content "to be fed with a bit and a knock, and alwayes be forced to stand in awe" lest England should "picke a quarrell,

[79] Robinson, *Certain proposalls in order to the peoples freedome*, p. 11.

[80] Robinson, *Englands safety, in trades encrease*, p. 13.

[81] *Vide ante*, pp. 187–89.

[82] Robinson, *Englands safety, in trades encrease*, p. 13.

and set the dice on them, or starve them out-right, before they could be relieved from other hands."[83]

The only possible instrument which can restore English prestige and economic power in the East, Robinson wrote with the enthusiasm of a member, is the East India Company. It is true that the company has not fully exploited its potentialities, but it has not been well supported at home and has been obliged to face grave obstacles abroad.[84] The government has not lent full assistance to the company, which has for years been locked in pitched combat with the Dutch, who have no other aim than to drive the English from the East. The East India trade can never be regained or maintained until the Dutch are compelled to restore the plantations which they have seized and until the steel of governmental policy supports the commendable aspirations of the company.[85] Robinson repeatedly indicated that he believed the East India trade must be regarded as fundamental in the future economy of the nation. England, he warned, had permanently lost her monopoly in the European cloth trade. This trade, so essential to the nation's prosperity, can be revived only if Indian markets replace those that have been lost to European competition. Therefore a steady endeavor should be undertaken to reduce the price and to enhance the quality and variety of English cloth. Time and resources should not be wasted in an effort to revive the moribund Continental market when a vast and untapped market awaits English traders in the Orient.[86] To the numerous critics of the East India Company, Robinson would reply that common sense taught that this trade could not possibly be carried on by individual merchants destitute of capital and devoid of effective organization. "A corporation it must be" for this trade, "and a powerful one too . . . . able to plant colonies by degrees and make head in the Indies."[87] Ships must be built for the trade, factories erected up and down the coasts, and a mili-

[83] Robinson, *Briefe considerations*, p. 6.

[84] Robinson, *Englands safety, in trades encrease*, pp. 21–22.

[85] Robinson, *Briefe considerations*, p. 7.

[86] Robinson, *Englands safety, in trades encrease*, p. 24.

[87] *Ibid.*, pp. 24–25.

tary establishment provided able to defend English merchants and their property from the Dutch and other rivals.

The vast foreign trade which Robinson believed lay within England's grasp would be guarded by the dominant sea power which he so persistently urged must be the cornerstone of English strength.[88] The fisheries would provide a training school for sailors and would instruct Englishmen once more in the art of building clean, stout, deep-sea vessels cheaply and quickly. But much more must be done by a government truly cognizant of its responsibilities and genuinely interested in tapping the sources of financial strength and political power. The harbors should be heavily fortified and marine depots set up at the principal ports at which vessels might be cheaply victualed and outfitted. The navy should be based on these ports in order to provide adequate protection for the stream of shipping issuing forth to all the waters of the earth. Shipyards would likewise be required in all of the principal ports of the commonwealth. Sailors should be settled around the chief ports in order to expedite the prompt departure of the loaded vessels, while the normal complement of the merchant marine should be maintained by regular salaries which would make available well-trained crews at any time.[89] Not only would this reform ensure a supply of skilled seamen, but it would finally bring to an end the barbarous practice of pressing crews.[90]

Foreign trade, as Robinson had so urgently insisted in his discussion of fisheries and of East India policy, must be supported by a firm diplomatic and naval policy on the part of the government. In one of his earliest works, the London merchant had dealt at length with a specific problem which illustrates his conception of the role which economic policy should play in politics. Robinson, who had traded in the Levant on his own account, wrote a forceful treatise in 1642 in which he demanded that the government should frame a careful and intelligent policy designed to extirpate the Barbary pirates. Doubtless remembering

[88] *Vide ante*, pp. 224–28.

[89] A sensible proposal, not yet fully realized in most maritime countries.

[90] Robinson, *Certain proposalls in order to the peoples freedome*, pp. 13–14.

Mansell's unsuccessful attack on Algiers two decades earlier, Robinson pointed out that neither a patrolling fleet nor a blockading action could bring the pirates to heel, since they were at once elusive and numerous and since the distinction prevailing between pirates and merchants was very hazy indeed along the north African coast.[91]

The better policy, Robinson submitted, would be to bring direct and cumulative pressure to bear on the Sultan, who possessed legal suzerainty over the north African states and who, if placed under compulsion, could force them to abandon their marauding activities. Such an action would naturally endanger the trade with Turkey, which, however, because of losses to the pirates, had been steadily dwindling. England's exports to Turkey, mostly of cloth, Robinson estimated, did not amount to more than £20,000 annually, while its imports from Turkey of cotton, cotton yarns, galls, and grograms could be replaced from other centers. During the past decade, Robinson believed, merchants had not earned more than 5 per cent on capital employed in the Turkey trade and this petty profit failed to take into account how "prejudiciall it is to this commonwealth to lose so many ships, the strength and safety of the kingdome, so much money and merchandize, the wealth and riches of the kingdome, and so many men all marriners, able to winne and keepe a kingdome."[92]

This trade, therefore, is actually a liability under prevailing conditions in the Mediterranean. The government, after warning merchants to withdraw stocks of goods in Turkey, which probably amount to £300,000 in value, should make strong diplomatic demands upon the Sultan for the release of English

[91] The depredations of the Barbary pirates had been chronic throughout the century. The London merchants, after particularly vicious raids on English commerce, had in 1617 enlisted the support of Southampton in a design for a great punitive naval expedition against Algiers. The Spanish, with whom James was then treating, raised the strongest objections, however, and the plan was abandoned. Three years later the merchants won the support of Digby, who, despite the protestations of the Spanish government, was able to outfit a naval force which under Mansell laid unsuccessful siege to the port of Algiers in 1621.

[92] Henry Robinson, *Libertas, or reliefe to the English captives in Algier, etc.* (London, 1642), p. 6.

captives and for the immediate cessation of piracy.[93] If this procedure is not successful, a strong naval force of forty vessels should be dispatched with orders to blockade Constantinople, severing all lines of trade and communication until the Turks yield.[94] Constantinople is much too strong to be carried by assault, but it can be forced into submission by blockade and reprisals can be effected by raids on the exposed coastal towns in the Sultan's dominions.[95] This policy, if ruthlessly sustained, can compel the Sultan to suppress piracy, and England need have no fear that it will lead to the loss of Turkish trade. Commerce, Robinson astutely insisted, follows the channels of economic convenience and is not for long hindered by political prejudice.

Since Robinson was principally interested in foreign trade, his most persuasive recommendations were concerned with the formulation of an economic policy which would provide England with firm foundations for commercial greatness. It is evident in his discussion of tariff policy and monetary reforms that he was thinking in terms of the merchant preoccupied with the problem of competing successfully abroad with the more sophisticated economy which the Dutch had evolved during his lifetime. Even so, Robinson fully realized that England could not possibly attain economic strength in the competitive markets of the seventeenth-century world unless her domestic economy were likewise reformed and rationalized. Inland trade, he submitted, must therefore be regarded as the cornerstone, not only of domestic prosperity but of the export trade as well.[96] England can no longer depend principally upon the ancient woolen trade, but must lend intelligent attention to new commodities and to new processes which will revitalize and profoundly alter her domestic economy.

England has lagged far behind her Continental rivals in accommodating her industrial techniques to those new processes and products which have placed her at a great disadvantage. So exclusive has been her devotion to the manufacture of woolen cloth, for example, that she is wholly inefficient in the fabrication of

[93] *Ibid.*, p. 12.

[94] *Ibid.*, pp. 8–9.

[95] *Ibid.*, p. 10.

[96] Robinson, *Briefe considerations*, p. 3.

cloth from materials like cotton, grogram, hemp, silk, and flax. The nation can best overcome its handicap, can most easily secure the modernization of its industrial plant, by offering foreign workmen and capital every reasonable inducement to settle in England.[97] These skilled artisans should be given equal privileges and should be taxed on terms of equality with native manufacturers. Nor should it be feared that they will injure English industry, since their competition will harm only "such natives as are negligent, lesse industrious, or that use false arts in their wayes and trades."[98] Since sloth and inefficiency should be driven out of industry in any case, new and remunerative undertakings will have a tonic effect upon the whole of the national economy.

Robinson, as we have observed, was by no means sure that England could ever recover her ancient position in the Continental markets for woolens, and was consequently inclined to favor a policy which would accommodate the industry to the opportunities offered by the Indian trade. None the less, every encouragement should be given to the industry by the government, which must insist, however, that it reform and modernize its techniques. Foremost amongst these reforms was the necessity for exercising a rigid control over quality and measure.[99] Moreover, Dutch and German competition could not possibly be surpassed until ways and means were discovered to effect a considerable reduction in the price of English cloth. This price disadvantage was probably caused, Robinson shrewdly argued, by the fact that expensive and inefficient methods had been developed and crystallized during earlier centuries. In particular, his orderly mind was outraged by the fact that wool was transported to London for sale, then back to the provinces for manufacture, and then as finished cloth was returned to London for sale to the exporters.[100] This costly and time-consuming practice could easily be corrected if the trade were decentralized around self-sufficient

[97] Robinson, *Certain proposalls in order to the peoples freedome*, p. 22; *Englands safety, in trades encrease*, p. 19.

[98] Robinson, *Certain proposalls in order to the peoples freedome*, p. 12.

[99] Robinson, *Englands safety, in trades encrease*, pp. 17–18.

[100] Robinson, *Briefe considerations*, pp. 3–4.

cloth centers which could lay the finished goods down on the exporters' wharves without excessive handling and transport charges. Moreover, all taxes should for the time being be removed from the cloth industry, including other fabrics than wool, in order to assist in the revival of the languishing trade and to help in the cure of the problem of unemployment.[101] Finally, since the recent civil disturbances have combined with the sheep rot seriously to reduce the number of sheep in England,[102] the slaughtering of sheep for meat should be strictly prohibited and the export of wool expressly forbidden until the native flocks have been restored.[103] In the same connection, Robinson held it imperative that England should contrive, and he offered to demonstrate that it could be done, to secure a monopoly on Irish, Scottish, and Spanish wool until her own stores had been replenished.

But England can no longer depend entirely for her commercial prosperity on the woolen trade or, indeed, on the revival of the fishing industry, which Robinson regarded as her most important single commercial asset. Parliamentary commissions should be set up at once with power to superintend all trade, to punish all abuses in quality and measure, and, most importantly, to lend encouragement to new industries which will restore England's commercial position. In particular, attention should be paid to the manufacture of a woolen cloth much lighter in weight than the traditional English fabrics, and he would recommend that an attempt be made to compete with the "accomplish't apparelling" fabrics in whose manufacture the French were pre-eminent.[104] Moreover, the manufacture of linens, especially heavy sailcloth, of silks, and the new dyeing processes recently developed in Holland and Venice, should be systematically undertaken.[105] Strong efforts should be made to encourage the growing of hemp, and

[101] *Ibid.*, p. 4.

[102] Robinson estimated by as much as 75 per cent.

[103] Robinson, *Certain proposalls in order to the peoples freedome*, p. 11; *Englands safety, in trades encrease*, pp. 4–5. The export of wool, legally forbidden long before 1640, had apparently been resumed during the unsettled era of the Civil War.

[104] Robinson, *Englands safety, in trades encrease*, p. 19.

[105] Robinson, *Certain proposalls in order to the peoples freedome*, p. 22.

the backward cordage industries should be assisted. And, finally, the salt industry should receive very careful attention, particularly the new processes for extracting salt from sea water, in order to provide the fisheries with an essential commodity and bring to an end an unnecessary and wasteful import.[106]

The stimulation of new manufactures and the necessary lowering of costs of production would likewise be greatly advanced, Robinson believed, if intelligent town planning were undertaken by governmental commissions. Numerous towns, especially the important ports, should be assisted by the extension of generous privileges. In general, the financial and commercial monopoly of London should be decentralized, since the capital, so Robinson with most of his generation believed, had attained its maximum size. Furthermore, the industry and commerce of England were so dangerously concentrated in the metropolis that an invasion of the Thames Estuary would result in the complete disruption of the economic life of the nation. More immediately important, however, were the facts that business could not be efficiently conducted in the sprawling mass of London, that rentals and costs were high, and that food had of necessity to be drawn from so wide an area that the costs of transportation often exceeded the initial cost.[107]

New commercial and manufacturing centers ought therefore to be systematically developed on the basis of a plan which would take low costs and maximum efficiency strictly into account. The dispersion of industry amongst "stragling tenements, villages and townes" should be discouraged by seeking to secure its concentration in planned and self-sufficient manufacturing centers.[108] The new shipping, fishing, and manufacturing cities could easily be established with great benefit to the whole commonwealth, if they were encouraged by differential duties, by free house rentals for a number of years and, above all, by making available, presumably as governmental loans, generous sums of capital at an interest rate not to exceed 4 per cent.[109]

[106] Robinson, *Englands safety, in trades encrease*, pp. 19–20.

[107] *Ibid.*, p. 5.

[108] Robinson, *Briefe considerations*, p. 4.

[109] Robinson, *Englands safety, in trades encrease*, pp. 5–6.

The practical Robinson realized that his proposal for a planned economy could scarcely be successful unless the transportation system of the nation were speedily modernized. He angrily complained on numerous occasions that England's transport was so costly, slow, and unsafe that the nation could scarcely compete with states like Holland until goods could be carried cheaply and efficiently in inland trade. Hence all rivers should be made navigable at the first practicable moment, inland towns should be made ports by the cutting of canals, and new centers should be planned with strict reference to costs of transport.[110] In particular, the peculiar advantages of the fen country should be fully exploited by cutting navigable drainage canals and by planting great centers of trade and industry in this perfectly situated area. Highways must be "kept cleane of robers," must be maintained in good condition, and whenever possible should be surfaced in order to quicken and cheapen communications. Finally, trade would be greatly assisted if fast, cheap, and reliable posts were established for the entire country in order to facilitate communications and the conduct of business. Robinson constantly stressed the high importance of this improvement in his long altercation regarding the proprietorship of the posts and professed to stand ready to reduce postal rates by one-half, if the administration of the service were entrusted to him.

Robinson likewise maintained that trade would be notably advanced were all merchants organized into corporate bodies that could be held responsible legally and morally for the conduct of business. His reply to the numerous and vociferous attacks on the trading companies was the bold proposal that these corporations should actually be increased in number and vested with control of all export business, that their supervision over the quality of exports should be enlarged, and their privileges considerably extended. We have previously commented at some length on his argument that the East India trade could be revived only if the company were given wide and substantial powers.[111] All merchants trading with any given region should be organized into cor-

[110] Robinson, *Certain proposalls in order to the peoples freedome*, p. 9; *Briefe considerations*, p. 4; *Englands safety, in trades encrease*, p. 42.

[111] *Vide ante*, pp. 240–42.

porations along similar lines with power to regulate trade and prices in order to eliminate ruinous competition and the glutting of markets. These corporate bodies would then be in a much better bargaining position and would speedily develop an adequate understanding of the complex and delicate problem of export trade. Unquestionably, if all corporate controls were removed, there would be a temporary increase in the volume of trade, but the ultimate effect would be disastrous to the entire economy of the nation.[112] The merchant class must assume a corporate responsibility in the life of the nation, which can best be discharged within the frame of an organized mercantile society rather than in the primitive barbarism of anarchical private trading.

At the same time, Robinson strongly recommended the establishment of merchant courts empowered to deal quickly, cheaply, and sensibly with all kinds of disputes arising between merchants. The decision of these courts, which would be able to assess damages and impose fines, would be final save in cases of palpable injustice.[113] Since commercial disputes are usually highly technical, the court should be composed of merchants who have enjoyed at least a grammar-school education, who have lived abroad, and who are intimately conversant with commercial practices in the various European countries. It would perhaps be desirable if the president of the court were a "skilfull civilian," though his role should be subordinate to that of his merchant colleagues lest he "too much sway, and with his more volubil tongue overtalke the marchants and run away with the cause according to his singular opinion."[114] Above all else, the court should be so arranged that it can give quick decisions. Since most commodities are perishable, profits have always vanished when merchants have become embroiled in lengthy litigation. The work of the court would likewise be greatly assisted, and its docket lightened, if a registry were established where all contracts, mortgages, judgments, and other encumbrances were entered as a matter of permanent record.

Robinson's design for the commercial state likewise included

[112] Robinson, *Englands safety, in trades encrease*, pp. 45–46.

[113] *Ibid.*, p. 25. [114] *Ibid.*, p. 26.

numerous proposals for the social reformation of the commonwealth. In general, it should be said that his several schemes for social improvement display neither the originality nor the maturity of his economic thought, but they do bear witness to the range of his interests and the persistence of his effort to extend the gains of the revolutionary movement to the social structure of the nation.

In 1650 Robinson announced that he had opened an office of addresses, in Threadneedle Street, "over against the Castle Tavern, close to the Old Exchange," which stood ready to render many public services. The poor were to be accommodated without charge, whereas all other persons were to be served at the rate of sixpence for each enquiry or entry in the office, which was to be open daily, save for Sunday, from eight to twelve in the morning and from two to six in the afternoon.[115] We have found no evidence to suggest that Robinson's ambitious undertaking survived for long, but it is important to notice that his establishment attempted to serve a need to which attention had been called, in part at least, by such earlier writers as Raleigh, Bacon, and Samuel Hartlib.[116]

[115] Henry Robinson, *The office of adresses and encounters: where all people of each rancke and quality may receive direction and advice for the most cheap and speedy way of attaining whatsoever they can lawfully desire, etc.* (London, 1650), pp. 5–6.

[116] Hartlib, who was rather closely associated with Robinson in several undertakings, had explored the possibility of an office of addresses in his *A further discovery of the office of publick addresses for accommodations*, published in 1648, and reprinted in *The Harleian Miscellany* (London, 1808–11). He felt that great savings could be effected, confusion lessened, and trade advanced, if a public office could be opened which would have complete files on all subjects on which general information was inadequate. Its most important function would be to serve as an employment exchange. The special needs of the poor would be most carefully administered (*Harl. Misc.*, VI, 164–66). A complete file of vendible commodities would be maintained (*ibid.*, VI, 166–67). Commercial opportunities would be listed and commercial intelligence would be available upon the payment of a nominal fee. Legal information would be procured, difficult and delicate commissions would be executed, and, in general, all problems too complex for the resources of ordinary men would be undertaken by the office of addresses. In 1657, seven years after Robinson's announcement, Hartlib stated in his *Office of public advice* that he had set up offices in London and Westminster which stood ready to provide employment, to dispense information regarding land, houses, commodities, and merchandise, and to undertake difficult commissions. Hartlib's experiment, like that of Robinson, must have been short-lived.

An office of addresses, Robinson maintained with the warmth of a reformer, would vastly advance the affairs of all classes. "Oh the stupidity of this nation," he exclaimed, "if not of man-kind, that boasts it selfe to be constituted an absolute tyrant over the whole creation," while failing to frame a social organization competent for the fulfilment of its most elementary needs. Thus multitudes of honest laborers have been reduced to beggary "because they doe not timely meet with any one to set and continue them at worke; And yet at the very same time, we likewise meete with multitudes of others, both merchants and shop-keepers of all callings, that cannot furnish their customers so cheape and speedily as were to be desired, because either they cannot presently get work-folk, or else not at such cheap rates as to make a benefit thereof."[117] This serious defect in the social and economic organism could easily be corrected if some mechanism were devised which could bring employer and laborer together. This agency, moreover, would eliminate an element of serious waste in the economy and, if it functioned efficiently, would assist in lowering wages by providing steady employment. The need for such an organization is particularly serious in England, since commerce and industry have come to be concentrated in London, which is too large and complex for efficient commercial intercourse.[118] The proposed office in Threadneedle Street would, therefore, undertake to supply a cement badly needed by a loosely organized economic society.

Furthermore, Robinson soberly indicated, his exchange would dedicate itself to the assistance of the poor and, in so far as possible, to the eradication of poverty. It would seek to provide a mechanism wherewith the poor might "relieve themselves by their own labour and industry, without losse of time, or expence of money," and would endeavor to protect them against the "beating down the price of poore mens labour" by opening up new sources of employment and by furnishing free information regarding opportunities for labor. If this could be done, the poor would be relieved of a frightful disadvantage which has made the

[117] Robinson, *The office of adresses*, pp. 1–2.

[118] It will have been observed that Robinson recurs again and again to this view.

poor man's search for honest employment "rather a begging, than a bargaining," which "rich men take advantage of, to the daily more and more undervaluing poore mens paines, and labours."[119]

The exchange which Robinson had founded stood prepared, so he announced, to perform an extraordinary variety of services. Most important, of course, was its registry of employment for all lawful occupations. But it was likewise equipped to buy, sell, or mortgage real property in any part of England; to traffic in merchandise; to lend money upon adequate security; to dispatch funds to domestic and foreign points; and to arrange for the transport of commodities. Moreover, the office stood ready to buy or sell bonds, to discount debts, and to buy or sell public obligations, leases, annuities, household goods, and wearing apparel. Lost and found articles would be handled for an appropriate reward. Traveling accommodations and suitable traveling companions could be secured, a registry of the arrival and departure of ships would be maintained, public auctions would be arranged upon application, and the legal and financial affairs of persons residing outside London would be managed for an appropriate fee. And finally, the enthusiastic Robinson announced, "such as desire to dispose of themselves, or friends, in marriage, may here likewise be informed, what encounters there are to be had, both of persons and portions."[120]

This rather ingenuous proposal, which represents a first groping toward a rational solution of certain social needs even now not adequately supplied, was but part of Robinson's vast design for an ordered modern state in which the economy would be rationalized and in which a larger measure of social justice would prevail. These aims were further expounded in his interesting proposals for the financial relief of the poor. There were no reputable agencies available, he complained, at which the poor might obtain distress loans at reasonable rates upon the security of their personal property. This grievous need, a scandal in a civilized society, might well be cured, with the most salutary results, if the government would set up a network of pawnshops

[119] Robinson, *The office of adresses*, p. 4. [120] *Ibid.*, p. 5.

over the nation empowered to lend money for short terms on pawns or other assets. The poor should be lent small amounts, upon the deposit of a satisfactory pawn, without any interest charge whatsoever for a period of six months in order to relieve temporary distress and to carry them through short seasons of unemployment.[121] Loans should be arranged for longer intervals at an interest rate not to exceed 10 per cent per annum when satisfactory security was available. Such a service would stimulate industry and trade, but, more importantly, it would protect the poor from ruinous extortion. "Believe me," Robinson earnestly wrote, "there are thousands in this city whose faces are thus grinded, yet live, whose succour would bee of so much greater consequence to the whole masse of inland commerce, being stirring people, whom need hath made industrious, and taught to turne their peny as you heare, or else could never live under such extortion, which notwithstanding at last must grinde them quite to powder before their time, for scarce being able in their youth by reason of these blood-suckers, heavie burthens to save so much for themselves as will keep life and soule together."[122]

This reform, when fused with the larger economic improvements which he had suggested, would, Robinson was persuaded, protect the industrious poor from indigence and provide an opportunity for them to rise in station. The practical Robinson realized, however, that under the most favorable circumstances England would be obliged to deal with the problem of the indigent and the unemployable. He proposed that such persons, together with petty criminals, be transported to the colonies where the labor supply was inadequate and where greater opportunities for the rehabilitation of the poor might be afforded.[123] That failing, such persons should be provided for in public workhouses which should be erected throughout the nation.[124] The poor should be employed in these centers in the manufacture of useful and vendible articles of commerce at wage rates slightly lower

[121] Robinson, *Certain proposalls in order to the peoples freedome*, pp. 22–23.

[122] Robinson, *Englands safety, in trades encrease*, p. 44.

[123] *Vide ante*, p. 240.

[124] Robinson, *Englands safety, in trades encrease*, p. 43.

than those paid by private enterprise in the trade in question.[125] By this means production would be increased, the poor might become self-supporting, and their rehabilitation would be assured. Begging and slothfulness, however, should under no circumstances be tolerated. Beggars should be set to work under supervision for no more than their food and clothing. The lame, the infirm, and homeless children, on the other hand, should be given every opportunity to earn their living and to learn a useful trade in the public work centers. The need for the solution of the problem of indigence was so great, Robinson professed, that were he sure that his life would be spared much longer, he would devote all his energies to the task of rehabilitating the unfit.[126]

It should be the steady aim of an enlightened government to eradicate poverty and afford to families of limited opportunity and means every possible assistance. Robinson was in no sense an advocate of democracy, but he clearly thought that the social strata should be fluid and that the aristocracy in which he would vest control of the political and economic polity must be fed constantly from below. In so far as possible, therefore, opportunity should be equal for all men, and men of talent should be steadily assisted in their effort to better their condition. Hence Robinson favored the foundation of a state school system throughout England under the direction of carefully chosen instructors. These schools should be free for all children, boys and girls alike, and the children of the poor should be taught at least to read and write. Abler children, however, should receive free tuition "untill they be fit for the universities, or any other kinde of clerkship."[127] The reforming Robinson could not resist as well, it should be noted, offering certain suggestions for the improvement of what would in our age be called "educational efficiency." He was convinced that most of the time was wasted when children were kept at school for eight hours as was ordinarily the custom. He therefore proposed that better instruction could be provided and far more children accommodated if the students should attend school in shifts. Since two or three hours

[125] Robinson, *Certain proposalls in order to the peoples freedome*, p. 23.

[126] *Ibid.*, pp. 23–24.

[127] *Ibid.*, p. 24.

probably represent as much time as a child can apply himself assiduously, he should then be sent home "to conn his lesson, or practice by himselfe, untill he be aweary . . . . and have the remainder of the day to serve his poore parent in, which will become as a recreation to himselfe."[128]

Moreover, the government should lend intelligent attention to the medical needs of the poor, which have always been scandalously neglected. Robinson proposed that competent physicians, paid by the state, should be appointed in every section of England in order to serve all persons requiring medical care. Furthermore, normal medical care should be supplemented by public hospitals, to be erected in every principal center, "to which it may be free for all poore people to repaire for taking physicke, as well to prevent sicknesse before it comes."[129]

Robinson dealt only briefly and inadequately with the agricultural problems of his day, despite the fact that a revolution in agricultural methods was already under way which was altering the social and economic structure of the nation. In part this neglect is to be explained by the fact that Henry Robinson, quite unlike his great-grandfather, was an urban man with little knowledge of rural life and problems; in part, because this member of the commercial aristocracy seems to have regarded the farmer, whether squire or tenant, with an almost contemptuous disdain. Robinson frequently complained of the backwardness and stubbornness of country men. We have observed that he fervently taught that the future greatness of England depended upon trade rather than upon the soil and that he was disposed to abolish all forms of tariff protection for the products of agriculture.

The average farmer, Robinson vehemently asserted, is slothful and stupid, too dull in wit even to exploit the possibilities of profit which lie in his soil. Many farmers are too lazy to plant a single fruit tree or bush, rather preferring to gorge themselves on

[128] *Ibid.*, p. 25. These brief remarks on educational reform seem somewhat immature when placed in the context of the remarkable discussion of educational theory which marks the revolutionary decade. *Vide* James, *Social Problems and Policy during the Puritan Revolution, 1640–1660*, pp. 314–26, for an excellent discussion of this matter.

[129] Robinson, *Certain proposalls in order to the peoples freedome*, p. 26.

"flesh, cheese, and pudding," as if determined to enhance their native stupidity.[130] Little can be done for these men who are too careless to help themselves. The food supply and the prosperity of the nation could be considerably increased, however, if certain badly needed reforms were carried out.

The fens should be drained, not only to furnish a great commercial and industrial area, but to make available an incredibly rich agricultural region. More importantly, however, all the commons in England should be immediately enclosed. Robinson espoused this unpopular proposal because he was persuaded that no considerable progress could be made in agricultural methods until the common field system had been entirely replaced by private holdings.[131] The abolition of the commons, he wrote, would at once "produce a great encrease of all things that the land brings forth, provided it be done with so large alotments unto all people that have any interest or present benefit thereby, as they may be gainers by such enclosures, if they will be industrious."[132]

The agricultural economy could likewise be improved, Robinson submitted, by freeing land from the heavy weight of "Leviticall tithes."[133] Robinson, like all the sectarian and lay thinkers of the age, was principally opposed to tithes because he was per-

[130] Robinson, *Englands safety, in trades encrease*, p. 45.

[131] Robinson's contribution to the vigorous and intelligent discussion of agricultural problems which characterized this period is of little significance. Hartlib, Plattes, Lee, and Blith were especially important in demanding better agricultural methods, including enclosures, and in making intelligent suggestions for the relief of rural distress. One of the most remarkable of the many pamphlets dealing with these problems was the anonymous *Wast land's improvement, or certain proposals made and tendred to the consideration of the honorable committee appointed by Parliament for the advance of trade, and general profits of the Commonwealth, etc.* (London, 1653), which proposed that all undeveloped lands be immediately enclosed and taken over by the state. These lands should be let under long leases to industrious tenants. Production would thereby be greatly increased, the typical injustices accompanying enclosures would be avoided, and the whole nation would benefit from the reform. Stylistic and textual evidence at one time disposed this writer to attribute this pamphlet to Robinson, but the ascription seems improbable in view of the fact that the London merchant displayed no particular interest in or knowledge of agricultural problems in his numerous known works.

[132] Robinson, *Certain proposalls in order to the peoples freedome*, p. 19.

[133] Robinson, *Certaine proposals . . . . to a new modelling of the lawes*, Pref. (15).

suaded that they inevitably tended to create a clerical caste with all the unfortunate characteristics of a vested interest, but he evidently disliked them almost as much on purely economic grounds. No scriptural warrant can be found for tithes, which have ever devitalized religion and which have placed the ministers of Christ in dependence upon "hackney wages."[134] The minister of the gospel should be well, indeed liberally, provided for by a community or state stipend which will free him from all distractions in order that he may "more fully employ all thoughts and studies on" his ministry.[135] So deeply rooted was the tithe system, however, that Robinson recognized the fact that it could not immediately be extirpated. Until this desirable end could be attained, therefore, he proposed that all tithes should be made payable to the state, which would thereupon assume responsibility for the salaries of all clergymen, whether within or without the Established Church.[136] Finally, steps should at once be taken to lighten the burden upon agriculture and to stimulate production by lowering the tithe rate upon plowed land and by sharply increasing the levy upon unproductive property.

Robinson, it may be said in summary, had made bold yet sensible contributions to the economic and social thought of his century. Writing as a member of the new commercial aristocracy, he warmly defended its status and privileges while summoning it to the assumption of those heavy responsibilities which had for rather more than a century been imposed upon the landed gentry. Robinson desired to deepen and broaden the foundations of a new England which he saw rising out of the chaos of civil war. This England would attain power and dominance by the arm of a mighty sea power, at once required and sustained by a vigorous and expanding foreign trade. The future, he believed, belonged to the teeming docks, the sprawling warehouses, and the dusty counting-rooms which fed the maw of commerce.

Robinson sought as well to frame the architecture of the new state in an elaborate series of proposals which reveal the order, the coherence, and the remarkable grasp of his fertile mind. He

[134] [Robinson], *John the Baptist*, p. 4. [135] *Ibid.*, p. 7.

[136] Robinson, *Certain proposalls in order to the peoples freedome*, p. 7.

demanded that government should, as a prime function of its responsibility, assist in ordering and altering the social and economic structure of the commonwealth in accordance with the requirements of a new age. No other economic theorist of his generation dealt as fully or as adequately with the tangled problem of tariff and monetary policy. His shrewd support of *entrepôt* trade, his insistent demands for a national bank, his reasoned arguments for the necessity of a lowered interest rate for commercial loans, his brilliant exposition of colonial policy, and his suggestions for the improvement of the merchant marine attest the maturity and range of his thought.

Nor was Robinson exclusively concerned with the immediate problems of foreign trade. He likewise sketched with rapid and brilliant strokes the design of a new domestic economy. His suggestions for the improvement of the languishing woolen industry and his proposals for the stimulation of new manufactures reveal a shrewd and vigorous intellect. The economy of the nation, he insisted, must be rationalized and purged of the wasteful and tangled habits of the past. New ports and new industrial areas must be planned and planted at home with that same boldness which should characterize colonial plantations abroad. Transport must be improved, communications bettered, foreign capital protected, and the worthy aspirations of the merchant fostered. At the same time, Robinson revealed a social conscience of a quality and sensitivity rare in any age. He loathed poverty not only because it was an economic drain but because it was a blight upon the body of the community. Want must therefore be conquered, not by tender palliatives, but by enlarging the circumference of opportunity until it included all fit and industrious men within its spacious ambit. The poor must be guarded and assisted by an intelligent mechanism for ensuring employment, by protection against extortion, and by better educational and medical facilities in order that they too might enjoy a full franchise in the vast potentialities which Robinson believed belonged to the England of the future. The attainment of the good life in this world, Henry Robinson believed, for the first time lay securely within the hands of mankind.

BIBLIOGRAPHY

I. SOURCE MATERIALS

ABBOTT, W. C. *The Writings and Speeches of Oliver Cromwell, etc.* Cambridge [Mass.], 1937——.

Acts of Court of the Mercers' Company, 1453–1527. Ed. LAETITIA LYELL and F. D. WATNEY. Cambridge, 1936.

Acts of the Privy Council of England. New Series, 1542–1604. Ed. J. R. DASENT. 32 vols. London, 1890–1907.

Acts of the Privy Council of England, 1613——. London, 1921——.

Allegations for Marriage Licenses Issued by the Bishop of London, 1520–1610. "Publications of the Harleian Society," Vol. XXV. London, 1887.

ALTHUSIUS, JOHANNES. *Politica methodice digesta, etc.* Herborn, 1603; *1614.*

Animadversions upon those notes which the late Observator hath published, etc. London, 1642.

An answer or necessary animadversions, upon some late impostumate observations, etc. London?, 1642.

BALL, WILLIAM. *A caveat for subjects, moderating the observator, etc.* London, 1642.

BASTWICK, JOHN. *Independency not Gods ordinance, etc.* London, 1645.

———. *The second part of the book call'd Independency not Gods ordinance, etc.* London, 1645.

BRAMHALL, JOHN. *The serpent salve, or, a remedie for the biting of an aspe: wherein, the Observators grounds are discussed and plainly discovered to be unsound, etc.* [Published anonymously.] London, 1643; *Works*, Oxford, 1842–45 [Vol. III].

A Calendar of the Marriage Licence Allegations in the Registry of the Bishop of London, Vol. I: *1597 to 1648.* Ed. R. M. Glencross. "The Index Library, Issued by the British Record Society, Ltd.," Vol. LXII. London, 1937.

Calendar of Patent Rolls . . . . Edward VI, 1547–1553. Ed. R. H. BRODIE. 5 vols. London, 1924–26.

Calendar of the Patent Rolls Preserved in the Public Record Office. [Mary, 1553–1558.] 4 vols. London, 1937–39.

Calendar of the Proceedings of the Committee for Advance of Money, 1642–1656, etc. Ed. M. A. E. GREEN. 3 vols. London, 1888.

Calendar of the Proceedings of the Committee for Compounding . . . . 1643–1660. Ed. M. A. E. GREEN. 5 vols. London, 1889–92.

CALENDARS OF STATE PAPERS. *Letters and Papers, Foreign and Domestic, of the Reign of Henry VIII, 1509–1547.* Ed. J. S. BREWER *et al.* London, 1862——.

———. *Calendar of State Papers, Domestic Series, of the Reigns of Edward VI, Mary, Elizabeth* [1547–1603]. Ed. ROBERT LEMON and M. A. E. GREEN. 12 vols. London, 1856–72.

CALENDARS OF STATE PAPERS. *Calendar of State Papers, Domestic Series, of the Reign of James I.* Ed. MARY GREEN. 4 vols. London, 1857–59.

———. *Calendar of State Papers, Domestic Series, of the Reign of Charles I, etc.* Ed. J. BRUCE *et al.* 23 vols. London, 1858–97.

———. *Calendar of State Papers, Domestic Series, 1649–1660, etc.* Ed. M. A. E. GREEN. 13 vols. London, 1875–86.

———. *Calendar of State Papers, Domestic Series, of the Reign of Charles II, 1660*——. Ed. M. A. E. GREEN *et al.* London, 1860——.

COKAYNE, GEORGE EDWARD. *Complete Baronetage.* 6 vols. Exeter, 1900–1909.

A dialogue or accidental discourse betwixt Mr. Alderman Abell, and Richard Kilvert, the two maine projectors for wine, etc. London, 1641.

DIGGES, SIR DUDLEY. *An answer to a printed book, intituled, Observations upon some of his majesties late answers and expresses.* [Expanded, 1643, into *The unlawfulness of subjects taking up arms, etc.*] [Published anonymously.] Oxford, 1642.

———. *A review of the observations upon some of his majesties late answers and expresses.* [Published anonymously.] Oxford, 1643.

DONNE, JOHN. *Fifty sermons, etc.* London, 1649.

———. *The Poems of John Donne, etc.* 2 vols. Oxford, 1912.

EDWARDS, THOMAS. *The first and second part of Gangraena, etc.* London, 1646.

———. *Gangraena: or a catalogue and discovery of many of the errours, heresies, etc.* London, 1646.

An examination of the observations upon his majesties answers. Wherein the absurdities of the observators positions, and inferences are discovered, etc. London, 1643.

FERNE, HENRY. *The resolving of conscience, upon this question, Whether upon such a supposition or case, as is now usually made (the king will not discharge his trust, but is bent or seduced to subvert religion, laws, and liberties) subjects may take arms and resist? And whether that case be now?* Printed at Cambridge, and reprinted at London, 1642.

FIRTH, C. H., and RAIT, R. S. *Acts and Ordinances of the Interregnum, 1642–1660.* 3 vols. London, 1911.

G., E. *Wast land's improvement, or certain proposals made and tendred to the consideration of the honorable committee appointed by Parliament for the advance of trade, and general profits of the commonwealth, etc.* London, 1653.

GILLESPIE, GEORGE. *A late dialogue betwixt a civilian and a divine, concerning the present condition of the Church of England, etc.* [Published anonymously.] London, 1644.

———. *Wholsome severity reconciled with Christian liberty, etc.* [Published anonymously.] London, 1645.

GOODWIN, J.; NYE, R.; *et. al.* *A reply of two of the brethren to A. S.* [Adam Steuart] *Wherein you have observations on his considerations, annotations, &c. upon the Apologeticall Narration, etc.* [Published anonymously.] London, 1644.

HALLER, WILLIAM. *Tracts on Liberty in the Puritan Revolution, 1638–1647.* 3 vols. New York, 1934.

The Harleian Miscellany; or, a Collection of Scarce, Curious, and Entertaining Pamphlets and Tracts, etc. 12 vols. London, 1808–11.

HARTLIB, SAMUEL. *A further discovery of the office of publick address for accommodations.* London, 1648; *Harl. Misc.*, VI, 158–74.

HISTORICAL MANUSCRIPTS COMMISSION REPORTS. *Calendar of the Manuscripts of .... the Marquess of Salisbury .... Preserved at Hatfield House, Hertfordshire.* London, 1883——.

———. *The Manuscripts of .... the Duke of Portland, Preserved at Welbeck Abbey.* London, 1891——.

———. *Report on the Manuscripts of the Earl of Ancaster, etc.* London, 1907.

HOBBES, THOMAS. *The English Works of Thomas Hobbes.* Ed. SIR WILLIAM MOLESWORTH. 11 vols. London, 1839–45.

HYDE, EDWARD, EARL OF CLARENDON. *The History of the Rebellion and Civil Wars in England Begun in the Year 1641.* Ed. W. DUNN MACRAY. 6 vols. Oxford, 1888.

Journals of the House of Commons, 1547–1714. 17 vols. [*s.l.*], [*s.a.*].

Journals of the House of Lords, 1509——. [*s.l.*], [*s.a.*].

MADDISON, SIR RALPH. *Great Britains remembrancer, looking in and out. Tending to the increase of the monies of the commonwealth, etc.* London, 1655.

MORTON, THOMAS. *Christus Dei, the Lords annoynted. Or, a theologicall discourse, wherein is proved that the regall or monarchicall power .... is not of humane, but of divine right, etc.* [Published anonymously.] London, 1642; *1643.*

OVERTON, RICHARD. *The araignement of Mr. Persecution: presented to the consideration of the House of Commons, and to all the common people of England, etc.* [Published anonymously.] London, 1645.

———. *Martin's eccho: or a remonstrance, etc.* [Published anonymously.] London, 1645.

———. *A sacred decretall, or hue and cry. From his superlative holinesse, Sir Simon Synod, for the apprehension of Reverend Young Martin Mar-Priest, etc.* [Published anonymously.] London, 1645?

PARKER, HENRY. *The altar dispute, or a discourse concerning the severall innovations of the altar, etc.* London, 1641.

———. *An answer to the poysonous sedicious paper of Mr. David Jenkins.* London, 1647.

———. *The case of shipmony briefly discoursed, according to the grounds of law, policie, and conscience.* [Published anonymously.] London, 1640.

———. *The cheif affairs of Ireland truly communicated, etc.* [Published anonymously.] London, 1651.

———. *The contra-replicant, his complaint to his majestie, etc.* [Published anonymously.] London, 1642.

———. *The cordiall of Mr. David Jenkins: or his reply to H. P. barrester of Lincolnes-Inne, answered.* London, 1647.

———. *The danger to England observed, upon its deserting the high court of parliament.* [Published anonymously.] London, 1642.

PARKER, HENRY. *A discourse concerning Puritans, etc.* [Published anonymously.] London, 1641.

———. *Of a free trade. A discourse seriously recommending to our nation the wonderfull benefits of trade, specially of a right governed, and ordered trade, etc.* London, 1648.

———. *Jus populi. Or, a discourse wherein clear satisfaction is given, as well concerning the right of subiects, as the right of princes.* [Published anonymously.] London, 1644.

———. *Jus regum. Or, a vindication of the regall power: against all spirituall authority exercised under any form of ecclesiasticall government, etc.* [Published anonymously.] London, 1645.

———. *A letter of due censure, and redargution to Lieut. Coll: John Lilburne: touching his triall at Guild-Hall-London in Octob: last. 1649, etc.* London, 1650.

———. *The manifold miseries of civill warre and discord in a kingdome, etc.* London, 1642.

———. *The oath of pacification: or a forme of religious accommodation: humbly proposed both to King and Parliament. Thereby, to set an end to the present miseries and broyles of this discomposed, almost ship-wrackt state.* [Published anonymously.] London, 1643.

———. *Observations upon some of his majesties late answers and expresses.* [Published anonymously.] London, 1642.

———. *The observator defended, etc.* [Published anonymously.] London?, 1642?.

———. *A petition or declaration, humbly desired to be presented to the view of his most excellent majestie . . . . shewing the great danger and inconveniences that will happen both to the king and kingdome, if either his majestie or his people desert his grand and most faithfull Councell, the high court of Parliament.* [Published anonymously.] London, 1642.

———. *A political catechism. Or, certain questions concerning the government of this land, answered in his majesties own words . . . . with some brief observations thereupon.* [Published anonymously.] London, 1643.

———. *The question concerning the divine right of episcopacie truly stated.* London, 1641.

———. *Scotlands holy war. A discourse truly, and plainly remonstrating, how the Scots out of a corrupt pretended zeal to the Covenant have made the same scandalous, and odious to all good men, etc.* London, 1651.

———. *Severall poysonous and sedicious papers of Mr. David Jenkins answered, etc.* London, 1647.

———. *Some few observations upon his majesties late answer to the declaration, or remonstrance of the lords and commons, etc.* [Published anonymously.] London, 1642.

———. *The Trojan Horse of the Presbyteriall government unbowelled. Wherein is contained,* I. *The power of the Presbyterian government.* II. *The persons in whom this power is placed.* III. *The exercise of the Presbyterian power in Scotland, and the Lawes there imposed on the peoples necks.* [Published anonymously.] [*s.l.*], 1646.

PARKER, HENRY. *The true grounds of ecclesiasticall regiment set forth in a breife dissertation. Maintaining the kings spirituall supremacie against the pretended independencie of the prelates, &c. Together, with some passages touching the ecclesiasticall power of parliaments, the use of synods, and the power of excommunication.* [Published anonymously.] London, 1641.

———. *The vintners answer to some scandalous phamphlets published, (as is supposed) by Richard Kilvert; and abetted in some points, by his brother Roger, and alderman Abel, etc.* [Published anonymously.] London, 1642.

PARKER, HENRY; SADLER, JOHN; and MAY, THOMAS. *The king's cabinet opened: or, certain packets of secret letters and papers, written with the kings own hand, and taken in his cabinet at Nasby-Field, June 14, 1645, etc.* [Published anonymously.] London, 1645.

PRYNNE, WILLIAM. *Diotrophes catechised, etc.* [Published anonymously.] London, 1646.

———. *A fresh discovery of some prodigious new wandring-blasing-stars, etc.* London, 1645.

———. *A full reply to certaine briefe observations and anti-queries on Master Prynnes twelve questions about church-government, etc.* London, 1644.

———. *The lyar confounded, or a briefe refutation of John Lilburnes miserably-mistated-case, mistaken-law, etc.* London, 1645.

———. *Truth triumphing over falsehood, antiquity over novelty, etc.* London, 1645.

The Records of the Honorable Society of Lincoln's Inn: Admissions, 1420–1893, and Chapel Registers. 2 vols. London, 1896.

The Records of the Honorable Society of Lincoln's Inn. The Black Books. 4 vols. London, 1897–1902.

The Registers of St. Helen's, Bishopsgate, London. "Publications of the Harleian Society," Vol. XXXI. London, 1904.

ROBINSON, HENRY. *An answer to Mr. John Dury his letter which he writ from the Hague, to Mr. Thomas Goodwin. Mr. Philip Nye. Mr. Samuel Hartlie. Concerning the manner of the reformation of the Church, etc.* [Published anonymously.] London, 1644.

———. *An answer to Mr. William Prynn's Twelve Questions concerning Church Government, etc.* [Published anonymously.] London, 1644.

———. *Articles and orders, made and agreed upon the 9th day of July, 1647 . . . . by the company of adventurers for the plantation of the Islands of Eleutheria, formerly called Buhama in America, etc.* [Published anonymously.] London, 1647; reprinted in *Transactions of the Colonial Society of Massachusetts*, XXXII (1936), 81–85.

———. *Briefe considerations, concerning the advancement of trade and navigation, etc.* London, 1649.

———. *Certain briefe observations and antiquaeries: on Master Prin's twelve questions about church-government, etc.* [Published anonymously.] London, 1644.

———. *Certain considerations in order to a more speedy, cheap, and equall distribution of justice throughout the nation, etc.* London, 1651.

ROBINSON, HENRY. *Certain proposalls in order to the peoples freedome and accommodation in some particulars, etc.* London, 1652.

———. *Certaine proposals in order to a new modelling of the lawes and law-proceedings, etc.* London, 1653.

———. *Englands safety, in trades encrease. Most humbly presented to the high court of parliament.* London, 1641.

———. *The falsehood of Mr. William Pryn's Truth Triumphing, in the antiquity of popish princes and parliaments, etc.* [Published anonymously.] London, 1645.

———. *John the Baptist, forerunner of Christ Iesus: Or, a necessity for liberty of conscience, etc.* [Published anonymously.] London, [1644].

———. *Libertas, or reliefe to the English captives in Algier, etc.* London, 1642.

———. *Liberty of conscience; or the sole means to obtaine peace and truth. Not onely reconciling his majesty with his subjects, but all Christian states and princes to one another, etc.* [Published anonymously.] London, 1643.

———. *A moderate answer to Mr. Prins full reply to certaine observations on his first twelve questions . . . . a short description of the Congregationall way discovered. Some arguments for indulgence to tender consciences modestly propounded.* [Published anonymously.] London, 1645.

———. *Observations on Exchanges.* MS [6 pp.]. *S.P. Dom., Commonwealth and Protectorate*, ix, 64.

———. *The office of adresses and encounters: where all people of each rancke and quality may receive direction and advice for the most cheap and speedy way of attaining whatsoever they can lawfully desire, etc.* London, 1650.

———. *A short answer to A. S. alias Adam Stewart's second part of his overgrown Duply to the two brethren, etc.* [Published anonymously.] London, 1645.

———. *A short discourse between monarchical and aristocratical government, etc.* [Published anonymously.] London, 1649.

———. *Some few considerations propounded, as so many scruples by Mr. Henry Robinson in a letter to Mr. Iohn Dury upon his epistolary discourse, etc.* London, 1646.

RUTHERFORD, SAMUEL. *A free disputation against pretended liberty of conscience tending to resolve doubts moved by Mr. John Goodwin, John Baptist, Dr. Jer. Taylor, the Belgick Arminians, Socinians . . . . contending for lawlesse liberty, or licentious toleration of sects and heresies.* London, 1649.

SAINSBURY, ETHEL B. (ed.). *A Calendar of the Court Minutes of the East India Company.* 5 vols. Oxford, 1907——.

SHAW, W. A. *Select Tracts and Documents Illustrative of English Monetary History, 1626–1730.* London, 1896.

SPELMAN, SIR JOHN. *A view of a printed book intituled Observations upon his majesties late answers and expresses.* [Published anonymously.] Oxford, 1642.

VERNEY, FRANCES P. *Memoirs of the Verney Family during the Civil War, etc.* 4 vols. London, 1892.

VIOLET, THOMAS. *The advancement of merchandize: or, certain propositions for the improvement of the trade of this commonwealth . . . . presented to the . . . . Council of State. And also, against the transporting of gold and silver, etc.* London, 1651.

The Visitations of the County of Sussex, etc. Ed. W. B. Bannerman. "Publications of the Harleian Society." London, 1905.

W., B. *Free ports, the nature and necessitie of them stated.* London, 1652.

Walker, Clement. *Anarchia Anglicana: or, the history of Independency. The second part, etc.* [Published anonymously.] London, 1649.

Walwyn, William. *Juries justified: or, a word of correction to Mr. Henry Robinson; for his seven objections against the trial of causes, by juries of twelve men.* London, 1651.

II. SECONDARY MATERIALS

Ashley, M. P. *Financial and Commercial Policy under the Cromwellian Protectorate.* Oxford, 1934.

Beaven, A. B. *The Aldermen of the City of London, etc.* 2 vols. London, 1908–13.

Berry, William. *Pedigrees of the Families in the County of Sussex, etc.* London, 1830.

Brown, Alexander. *The Genesis of the United States.* 2 vols. Boston and New York, 1891.

Buck, P. W. *The Politics of Mercantilism.* New York, 1942.

Clode, C. M. *The Early History of the Guild of Merchant Taylors, etc.* 2 vols. London, 1888.

———. *Memorials of the Guild of Merchant Taylors of the Fraternity of St. John the Baptist, in the City of London.* London, 1875.

Collections for a History of Staffordshire. William Salt Archaeological Society. London, 1880–97; 1898–1909; 1910——.

Comber, John. *Sussex Genealogies.* Cambridge, 1931.

Cox, J. E. *The Annals of St. Helen's, Bishopsgate, London.* London, 1876.

East Anglian; or, Notes and Queries on Subjects Connected with the Counties of Suffolk, Cambridge, Essex, and Norfolk. Lowestoft (N.S.), 1885——.

Firth, C. H. "An Anonymous Tract on 'Liberty of Conscience,'" *English Historical Review*, IX, 715–17.

Foster, Joseph. *Alumni Oxonienses, etc.* 4 vols. Oxford, 1891–92.

Gardiner, S. R. *History of England from the Accession of James I to the Outbreak of the Civil War, 1603–1642.* 10 vols. London, 1895.

———. *History of the Great Civil War, 1642–1649.* 4 vols. London, 1904–5.

Gay, E. F. "The Rise of an English Country Family: Peter and John Temple, to 1603," *Huntington Library Quarterly*, I, 367–90.

———. "The Temples of Stowe and Their Debts: Sir Thomas Temple and Sir Peter Temple, 1603–1653," *Huntington Library Quarterly*, II, 399–438.

Gooch, G. P. *English Democratic Ideas in the Seventeenth Century.* Cambridge, 1927.

Heckscher, E. F. *Mercantilism.* 2 vols. London, 1935.

Hemmeon, J. C. *The History of the British Post Office.* Cambridge [Mass.], 1912.

Horsfield, T. W. *The History, Antiquities, and Topography of the County of Sussex.* 2 vols. Lewes, 1835.

JAMES, MARGARET. *Social Problems and Policy during the Puritan Revolution, 1640–1660.* London, 1930.

JORDAN, W. K. *The Development of Religious Toleration in England from the Accession of James I to the Convention of the Long Parliament.* London, 1936.

———. *The Development of Religious Toleration in England from the Convention of the Long Parliament to the Restoration (1640–1660).* London, 1938.

———. *The Development of Religious Toleration in England: Attainment of the Theory and Accommodations in Thought and Institutions (1640–1660).* London, 1940.

JOYCE, HERBERT. *The History of the Post Office, etc.* London, 1893.

JUDSON, MARGARET A. "Henry Parker and the Theory of Parliamentary Sovereignty," in *Essays in History and Political Theory in Honor of Charles Howard McIlwain*, pp. 138–67. Cambridge [Mass.], 1936.

LANGFORD, J. A.; MACKINTOSH, C. W.; and TILDESLEY, J. C. *Staffordshire and Warwickshire, etc.* 2 vols. London, [*s.a.*].

LONDON COUNTY COUNCIL. *The Parish of St. Helen, Bishopsgate.* "Survey of London," Vol. IX, Part 1. London, 1924.

LOWER, M. A. *A Compendious History of Sussex, etc.* 2 vols. Lewes, 1870.

MOOD, FULMER. "Henry Robinson and the Authorship of the Bahama Articles and Orders," *Transactions of the Colonial Society of Massachusetts*, XXXII, 155–73.

PEASE, T. C. *The Leveller Movement.* Washington, D.C., 1916.

READ, CONYERS. *Mr. Secretary Walsingham and the Policy of Queen Elizabeth.* 3 vols. Oxford, 1925.

RICHARDS, R. D. *The Early History of Banking in England.* London, 1929.

SHAW, STEBBING. *The History and Antiquities of Staffordshire, etc.* 2 vols. London, 1798, 1801.

SMITH, GOLDWIN. "The Reform of the Laws of England," *University of Toronto Quarterly*, X, 469–81.

SUSSEX ARCHAEOLOGICAL SOCIETY. *Collections.* London, 1848——.

Sussex Notes and Queries. Lewes, 1926——.

SUSSEX RECORD SOCIETY. *Publications.* Lewes, 1902——.

THOMAS-STANFORD, CHARLES. *Sussex in the Great Civil War and the Interregnum, 1642–1660.* London, 1910.

VINER, JACOB. *Studies in the Theory of International Trade.* New York, 1937.

WATNEY, SIR JOHN. *History of the Mercers' Company of the City of London.* London, 1914.

INDEX